DRIVIN

SWITZERLAND

Macmillan • USA

CONTENTS

Written by David Allsop

Original photography by S L Day

Edited, designed and produced by AA Publishing.

© The Automobile Association 1995.

Maps © The Automobile Association 1995.

Published by AA Publishing.

Published in the United States by Macmillan Travel
A Prentice Hall Macmillan Company
15 Columbus Circle
New York, NY 10023

Macmillan is a registered trademark of Macmillan, Inc.

ISBN 0-02-860070-3

Color separation: Daylight Colour Art Pte, Singapore

Printed and bound in Italy by Printers SRL, Trento

Title page: *Gstaad in wintertime*

Above: *a sprawling carpet of wild Alpine flowers, Sustenpass*

Opposite: *an autumnal lakeside view of Brienz's 16th-century church*

INTRODUCTION

This book is not only a practical touring guide for the independent traveller, but is also invaluable for those who would like to know more about the country.

It is divided into eight regions, each containing between three and four tours. Switzerland is a small country and therefore there is some inevitable overlapping of routes. Where towns and villages have been described elsewhere in the book, the appropriate tour number is mentioned in brackets in the route directions. The tours start and finish in major towns and cities which we consider to be the best centres for exploration. Each tour has details of the most interesting places to visit en route. Side panels cater for special interests and requirements and cover a range of categories, for those whose interest is in history, wildlife or walking, and those who have children. There are also panels which highlight scenic stretches of road along the routes and which give details of special events, gastronomic specialities, crafts and customs. The numbers link them to the appropriate main text.

The simple route directions are accompanied by an easy-to-use map of the tour and there are addresses of local tourist information centres in some of the towns en route, as well as in the start town.

Simple charts show how far it is from one town to the next in kilometres and miles. These can help you to decide where to take a break and stop overnight, for example. (All distances quoted are approximate.)

Before setting off it is advisable to check with the information centre at the start of the tour for recommendations on where to break your journey and for additional information on what to see and do, and when best to visit.

ENTRY REGULATIONS

A valid passport is required for entry into Switzerland and Liechtenstein. Visitors do not require a visa if they are holders of a valid national passport from any country in Western Europe, North America and Australasia and are intending to stay for no longer than three months for touristic purposes only.

CUSTOMS REGULATIONS

Citizens of other countries may import the following goods into Switzerland free of duty and other taxes: personal effects such as clothing, toilet articles, sports gear, cameras, cine cameras and amateur camcorders with relevant film, video equipment, musical instruments and camping equipment; food provisions up to the amount a single individual normally requires for one day; other goods declared on crossing the border and imported for gift purposes (with the exception of meat and meat preparations which are governed by special regulations, butter and quantities of goods intended to be stored) provided their total value does not exceed Sfr200. Visitors aged under 17 are entitled to half this limit. Alcoholic beverages and tobacco may be imported in the following quantities:

Visitors from European countries
Alcoholic beverages up to 15 per cent volume: 2 litres
Alcoholic beverages over 15 per cent volume: 1 litre
Tobacco goods: 200 cigarettes or 50 cigars or 250g tobacco

Visitors from non-European countries

Alcoholic beverages up to 15 per cent proof: 2 litres
Alcoholic beverages over 15 per cent proof: 1 litre
Tobacco goods: 400 cigarettes or 100 cigars or 500g tobacco

The exemption from alcohol and tobacco duty applies only to persons of at least 17 years of age.

There are no restrictions on the import and export of foreign or Swiss currency.

EMERGENCY TELEPHONE NUMBERS

Police: 117
Fire: 118
Ambulance: 117 (or 144 in some areas)

HEALTH

As a general rule vaccination and inoculation are not required by visitors entering Switzerland from western countries. As there is no state medical health service in the country, travellers are strongly advised to take out insurance cover against personal accident and illness.

CURRENCY

The unit of currency is the Swiss franc. Notes are issued in denominations of 10, 20, 50, 100, 500 and 1,000. Coins are issued in denominations of 5, 10, and 20 centimes, and ½, 1, 2, and 5 Swiss francs.

CREDIT CARDS

Most large stores, restaurants,

hotels and petrol stations accept all major credit cards.

BANKS

Usual banking hours are 8.30am to 4.30pm, Monday to Friday. In small towns and villages times vary, and banks may well close for lunch. All banks are closed at weekends and on national holidays.

POST OFFICES

Post offices in large towns are open from 7.30am to noon and from 2pm to 5pm, closing on Saturday at 11am except in major cities. In small towns and villages times vary.

TELEPHONES

To operate a public telephone insert the relevant coin (or a phonecard called Taxcard which is available for Sfr10 or Sfr20 in post offices and newsagents) after lifting the receiver. The dialling tone is a continuous sound. Use coins to the value of 60 centimes for local calls, and Sfr1 or Sfr5 for national and international calls. The dialling code for the UK is 0044; omit the initial digit 0 of the STD code. Otherwise dial 191 for details of dialling codes when calling abroad. Remember that there is always a surcharge when telephoning from hotels.

There is a 24-hour English-speaking information line which will answer all queries about travelling and staying in Switzerland. Dial 157 50 14 from anywhere in Switzerland – calls cost Sfr1.40 per minute.

TIME

Switzerland and Liechtenstein observe Central European Time – namely, one hour ahead of GMT and six hours ahead of New York.

SWISS TRAVEL SYSTEM

Switzerland has arguably the most efficient and sophisticated public transport system in the world. Even if you are travelling by car you would be well advised to enquire into the various passes and cards which entitle the holder to unlimited travel, or reduced fares. The Swiss Half-Fare Card, for example, enables the holder to purchase tickets at 50 per cent of the full fare for scheduled services of railways (including some mountain railways), post buses, lakeboats and some privately owned funiculars. Further details are available from the SNTO or any Swiss railway or bus station.

Left: a view across the ramparts of the historic medieval town of Murten
Above, right: looking out from a flower-festooned chalet in the lovely Val d'Hérens

Zurich to Check.- Lausanne → Geneve Chamonix Zermatt

The small town of Sierre, Valais

ELECTRICITY

The current is 220 volts AC, with plugs of the two-pin type. It is advisable to take an adaptor for the use of electrical equipment with British manufactured fittings.

NATIONAL HOLIDAYS

New Year's Day, Good Friday, Easter Monday, Ascension Day, Whit Monday, National Day (1 August), Christmas Day, 26 December. Different cantons observe different religious festivals, such as Corpus Christi, etc.

LANGUAGES

The national languages of Switzerland are German 65 per cent (Central and Eastern Switzerland), French 18 per cent (Western Switzerland), Italian 10 per cent (Southern Switzerland), Romansch 1 per cent (Southeastern Switzerland). Many Swiss, especially those connected with travel and service industries, also speak English.

MOTORING

Documents

A valid driving licence and the vehicle's registration details are the only documents needed by visiting motorists. Domestic motor insurance policies generally provide the minimum legal cover for driving in Switzerland, and production of a Green Card is not compulsory. However, Green Card insurance is strongly advised.

Breakdowns

SOS telephones are located at regular intervals along all motorways and mountain-pass roads. The emergency breakdown number is 140. Breakdown and recovery insurance is strongly recommended because of the high cost of roadside assistance (especially on high mountain passes). Most European breakdown organisations are affiliated to the Touring Club Suisse (TCS) which operates a nationwide 24-hour breakdown service. Carry warm clothes at all times if driving at altitude; breakdown vehicles can often take more than a couple of hours to reach a car on a mountain road.

Car rental

A circular giving details of rental charges is available from the SNTO. All the major rental firms are represented in Switzerland, and cars can be rented from all usual transit points. Booking in advance tends to be more cost effective than turning up at a car hire desk.

Motorway tax (Vignette)

An annual road tax of Sfr40, known as the vignette, is levied on all cars and motorcycles using Swiss motorways. An additional fee applies to trailers and caravans. The green sticker is valid between 1 December of the year preceding and 31 January of the one following the year shown. It can be purchased at border crossings, post offices and service stations throughout the country and is valid for multiple re-entry into the country within the duration of the licence period. It is not advisable to drive on autoroutes in Switzerland without one; fines are heavy, and the relatively modest amount involved represents the cheapest form of toll-road driving in Europe.

Driving regulations

Vehicles must keep to the right-hand side of the road and overtake on the left. The wearing of seat belts is compulsory for drivers and all passengers (front and rear seats). Children under 7 must travel in rear seats. Motorcyclists

[handwritten notes:] rain - St. Moritz → Zermatt ?? / Zermatt → Lugano = get car. / 11 nights Italy / 6 nights

GERMANY

Schaffhausen
Kreuzlingen
Bodensee

BASEL Rhein Baden Winterthur ST GALLEN

Aarau ZÜRICH NORTH EAST

Olten Zürichsee APPENZELL

Solothurn Zug SWITZERLAND Vaduz AUSTRIA

THE SWISS CENTRAL Zuger Walensee LIECHTENSTEIN
PLATEAU LUZERN See GLARUS

Bieler See SWITZERLAND SCHWYZ

BERN Vierwald- stätter See Chur Klosters

Glarner Alpen AROSA DAVOS

Fribourg/ THUN Brienzer Vorderrhein GRAUBÜNDEN
Freiburg See Inn/En

Thuner INTERLAKEN Andermatt Alpi Lepontine ST MORITZ Alpi Retiche Bórmio
See 3970 Airolo
BERNESE Eiger
OBERLAND 4158 Jungfrau Alpen Ticino Alpi Retiche

Berner TICINO Chiavenna
Sierre
SION Rhône Brig BELLINZONA Adda

VALAIS AND LOCARNO Lago di Como
SAAS-FEE Domodóssola LUGANO
ARTIGNY ZERMATT Lago ITALY
THE VAUD ALPS Maggiore
Alpi Pennine
4478 Lago di
Matterhorn Lugano

Aosta ITALY

must wear crash helmets. Foreign cars entering Switzerland are required to display their nationality plate at the rear of the car (and caravan). Driving with sidelights only in bad visibility is not permitted and dipped lights are compulsory in road tunnels. On mountain roads vehicles ascending always have priority, except for yellow post buses which have priority at all times. On bends their approach is signalled by a blast of their distinctive triple-note horns. Note that many mountain pass roads are closed from October to June. Conspicuous signs on all main access roads indicate whether they are open (green) or closed (red).

The laws concerning speed limits, lighting and seat belts etc are strictly enforced and police are authorised to demand on-the-spot fines.

Speed limits

On motorways the speed limit is 120kph. Other roads, unless signposted otherwise, have a maximum speed of 80kph. In built-up areas and on secondary roads (even when not signposted) the limit is 50kph.

The River Inn winding through the lush Engadine valley on its way to join the Danube

GENÈVE (GENEVA) & THE JURA

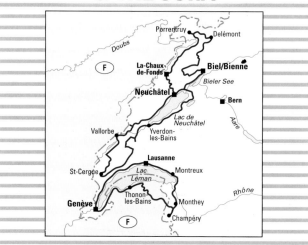

The strip of mountainous land which lies along Switzerland's western and northwestern borders is generally known as the Jura, after the mountain range of the same name which straddles the Franco-Swiss frontier. Comprising about 10 per cent of the country's surface area, these mountains rarely exceed 1,700m in height and have a softer and more rounded appearance than the jagged configuration of the Alps. Furrowed by attractively wooded valleys, and offering dramatic views over their Alpine neighbours to the south, the Jura mountains offer a wealth of striking scenery, and towns and villages of great charm which are easily accessible. The canton of Jura, formerly the northern part of the canton of Berne, was established in 1978 in recognition of popular sentiment that the districts of Delémont, Porrentruy and Les Franches Montagnes were a distinct entity which merited appropriate autonomy. But the Jura mountains themselves also cover large parts of the south-lying cantons of Neuchâtel and Vaud, as well as straying over the borders of cantons Basel (Basle), Solothurn and Bern (Berne).

Genève (Geneva) is the geographic anomaly lying at the southern ripple of the Jura's flattening folds, a large city within a tiny canton (of the same name), almost entirely surrounded by French territory, which is strictly part of none of the three component parts of the country – the Swiss Alps, the Swiss Plateau (or Mittelland), and the Jura. Cynics might claim that it is not really part of Switzerland either, because this is one of those few cities which could arguably claim to belong to the world. Truly international in apparently every facet of its activities, more than one in three of its residents is a foreign national and there are more international organisations based here than in any similarly sized community in the world. The citizens of Geneva are accustomed to hearing their city described in such terms as 'sterile, anonymous, dull and undramatic' – or, in Voltaire's words, as a place where '…One calculates but never laughs'. In answer they need do no more than point to the considerable appeal of the city's setting at the southwestern extremity of Lac Léman (Lake Geneva) – itself a feature of timeless beauty – and suggest that its critics spend some time sampling the extensive range of cultural and recreational facilities Geneva has to offer.

Genève (Geneva)

The famous landmark of this cosmopolitan city is the towering Jet d'Eau, a plume of water forced up to a height of about 150m from an off-shore site close to the south bank of Lac Léman (Lake Geneva). The city's other distinctive features are its elegant quays, promenades, parks and gardens. Prominent among the latter is the lakeside Jardin Anglais, with its celebrated flower clock, and the Jardin Botanique, which is host to a fine collection of exotic plants. The Promenade des Bastions is another fine open space, notable for its statues and monuments, and located on the fringe of the city's Old Town. Dominated by the 12th- to 13th-century St Peter's Cathedral, this charming old quarter, with the quaint Place de Bourg-de-Four at its centre, is distinguished by art galleries, antique shops and antiquarian book stores, as well as a comprehensive selection of bars and bistros. The city's other leading sights include the Tour de l'Ile, a 13th-century survivor of the original city fortifications, the 4th-century Eglise St Germain, the 16th-century Hotel de Ville, and the city's oldest house – the Maison Tavel. A generous choice of museums is devoted to natural history, old musical instruments,

clock making, and the Red Cross, and includes the famous Musée d'Art et d'Histoire.

Biel

The prosperous centre of Switzerland's clock and watch-making industry, Biel is home to such household names as Rolex, Swatch and Omega. The latter even has its own museum. A bilingual lakeside town of considerable appeal, it has a well-preserved old quarter with a charming square known as the Ring at its centre. The surrounding houses date from the 16th century, and are distinguished by arcades, turrets and stepped gables, as well as a generous number of wrought-iron signs. One of the town's most appealing features is its collection of medieval fountains; the Ring's Banneret (1546), and the Angel Fountain (1564) on the Obergasse among them. The mid-18th-century Fountain of Justice on the Burggasse is another fine example of the genre.

Notable among the town's museums is the Schwab Museum, one of the most important prehistorical and archaeological collections in the country. Biel is also well known for its weekend carnival on the Friday after Ash Wednesday.

Neuchâtel

This lakeside canton capital is one of the most demonstrably French-influenced of Switzerland's cities, with an air of relaxed charm which belies its commercial importance as one of the centres of Swiss clock and watch research technology. The Old Town (Ville Ancienne) is dominated by the city's three most striking buildings: the picturesque Château, the Prison Tower, built between the 10th and 15th centuries, and the 12th-century Collegiate Church of Notre-Dame. The old quarter itself is distinguished by a collection of charming fountains including the Banneret (1581), Fontaine du Lion (1664), La Justice (1545) and the famous Griffon (1664) which, legend records, was once filled with wine to welcome the French king to the city. Other striking buildings include the Maison des Halles, the Hotel du Peyrou, and the handsome patrician mansions which can be found near the latter. The city's museums include the Musée d'Art et d'Histoire, the Musée d'Ethnographie, and the Musée Cantonal d'Archéologie.

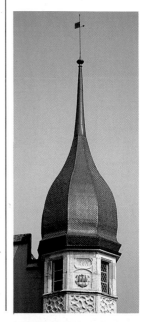

Right: characteristic stepped gables and onion dome in Biel's 'Ring'
Below: the graceful classical façade of Neuchâtel's 18th-century Hôtel du Peyrou

2 days: 241km (150 miles)

THE SWISS RIVIERA & SAVOY ALPS

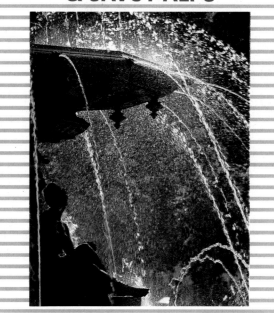

Genève (Geneva) • Coppet • Nyon • Rolle
Morges • Lausanne • Vevey • Champéry
Hermance • Genève (Geneva)

The crescent-shaped Lake Geneva (Lac Léman) shares its banks between France and Switzerland – with the latter having roughly two-thirds of the shoreline (and the fish). Some would also say that it has the best part of the deal. Most of the Swiss lakeside is on the sunny north bank in the canton of Vaud and the exclusive strip of land between Lausanne and Montreux has come to be known as the Swiss Riviera for reasons that will quickly become apparent. But the wider Lake Geneva Region is no less appealing, with its delightful blend of sloping vineyards, atmospheric towns and villages, and stunning waterscapes across the lake to the Savoy Alps of France. By way of contrast, the tour will take you through this high mountainous region, via the dramatic peaks of Switzerland's own Dents du Midi, before following the lake's south bank through the French spa towns of Evian and Thonon back to Geneva.

Cool waters cascade over a sculpted bather in Geneva's tranquil Jardin Anglais

ℹ️ Tour de l'Ile – also in station

Follow blue road signs for Lausanne, taking road 1 – also signposted as Route du Lac – for about 14km (9 miles).

Coppet, Vaud

1 Earning modest notoriety as the anti-hero's Swiss HQ in the James Bond novel Goldfinger, this atmospheric little village is distinguished by its imposing 18th-century **château**. Set amidst a classically-styled park, its most celebrated owner was Louis XVI's Minister of Finance, who acquired it in 1784 and lived here until his death in 1804. The decor and furnishings of the public rooms date from this period. Otherwise the building is notable for its elegant courtyard, comprising stables and an orangery. The village itself has a distinctive russet-coloured domed **church** built in the early 1500s, and a narrow main street of arcaded houses with brightly painted shutters. A **regional museum** is housed in a late Gothic building in the Grand-Rue.

Follow the lake road for 8km (5 miles) to Nyon.

Nyon, Vaud

2 A Celtic settlement, chosen by the Romans as the site for their first garrison town in this part of Helvetia, the former **Noviodunum** today owes much of its historical face to the influence of the Bernese. The 16th-century **castle** is their most obvious legacy, sitting squarely above the town with its five spired towers making a distinctive skyline. The view over the lake from the terrace is outstanding. One of the most important **porcelain collections** in Switzerland is housed within the castle walls – most of it

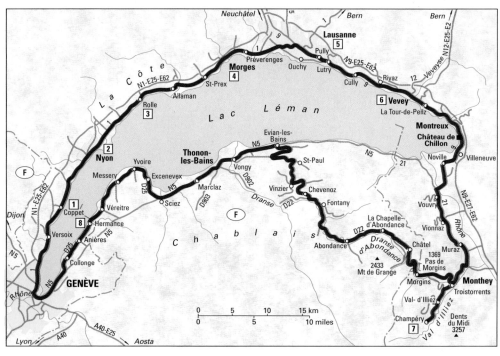

manufactured by an 18th-century factory which still stands in the **Rue de la Porcelaine**. The town's **Roman Museum** features the remains of a 1st-century **basilica**, discovered in 1974, as well as an extensive collection of artefacts recovered from local excavations. The church of **Notre-Dame**, dating largely from the 15th century, has some interesting paintings on the north interior wall – pre-dating the main body of the building by an estimated 200 years. Elsewhere in the town, the **Place du Marché** is notable for its fine arcaded buildings, again in the Bernese style. Behind the **Quai des Alpes** stands the 11th-century **Tour de César**, a remnant of the town's original fortifications.

Continue on the lake road for a further 11km (7 miles) to Rolle.

Rolle, Vaud

3 This busy little lakeside town has a typically Savoyard-style 13th-century **château**, of trapezoid design with a rounded tower at each corner. The church of **St Grat** is of early 16th-century origin, subsequently altered in the 18th century. The majority of the buildings in the **Grand-Rue** date from the 16th century, with the rambling vintners' houses standing out as amongst the most handsome. Lying a short distance off-shore is the man-made **Isle de Laharpe**, constructed in 1844 and surmounted by a monument to local hero Frédéric de Laharpe – the military leader who delivered the fledgling canton of Vaud from the Bernese in 1798.

Follow the lakeside road for a further 15km (9 miles) to Morges.

Morges, Vaud

4 Once one of the biggest ports on the lake, Morges is still a busy centre for the cantonal wine indus-

The unmistakeable plume of Geneva's famous 'Jet d'Eau'

try. Its commercial significance was somewhat reduced when freight began to be transported by rail rather than water, and now its 17th-century harbour is devoted predominantly to pleasure-boat traffic. The huge 13th-century **château** stands close to the lakefront and shows obvious Savoyard influences with distinctive rounded towers at each corner of a robustly fortified square. Inside is a **military museum** with a collection of armaments and uniforms dating from the late 1700s. In the **Musée Alexis Forel**, housed in one of a number of handsome baroque and late Gothic mansions on the **Grand-Rue**, is a comprehensive collection of antiquities including a unique set of engravings and etchings (20 of them by Rembrandt).

Continue for about 12km (7.5 miles) on road 1 into Lausanne.

Lausanne, Vaud

5 Capital of the canton of Vaud, the former Roman camp of Lousonna offers impressive views across the lake to the mountainous Haute-Savoie from its commanding hillside position. By no means all of its contemporary architecture does justice to its enviable location, however, but this is a minor cavil set against the city's many seductive qualities – not least of them being its infectious energy and cosmopolitan atmosphere. The acknowledged centre of commercial activity is the **Place St-François** which takes its name from the much-altered 13th-century church on its south side – the only surviving remnant of a Franciscan monastery which disappeared in the mid-16th century. North of the square, over a deep gorge, is the old **Quartier de la Cité** at the centre of

FOR HISTORY BUFFS

1 Coppet's château became the home of the celebrated Madame de Staël, who had been exiled by Napoleon for making unenthusiastic comments about his regime, on her father's death in 1804. For the duration of their respective lives, the French émigrée kept up an effective campaign of literary sniping against the diminutive emperor from a celebrated 'salon' she established here.

BACK TO NATURE

2 Nyon's **Musée du Léman** shows life in and around the lake over the centuries and features a remarkable aquarium which occupies the whole of one large wall. Fossils, fauna and fishing paraphernalia recovered from the lake, along with models of ancient fishing craft, comprise the core of a collection which offers an intriguing glimpse into this vital natural resource.

RECOMMENDED WALK

2 It is almost impossible to distinguish one lakeside walk from any other on this tour, but the leafy **Rive** lakefront sector of Nyon has a particularly charming promenade which is one of the more pleasant places for a stroll.

SPECIAL TO...

6 In Vevey's Grand Place, the famous fortnight-long **Fête des Vignerons** (wine growers' festival) is held every 25 years (next due in 1999). Reputedly the largest pageant in Europe, it is a Bacchanalian feast of extravagant proportions – lending the lie to the common misconception that the Swiss are a dour people.

FOR CHILDREN

6 Vevey has two excellent museums, both guaranteed to appeal to children of all ages. The Musée de l'Alimentarium, sponsored by Nestlé, is a thoroughly enjoyable hands-on experience about food with a variety of extraordinary exhibits including an 'essences display' where you try to match smells to foods, and a huge mouth to climb into to watch a cartoon video about teeth and tooth care.

The Musée Suisse du Jeu provides comparable fun; it is an absorbing 'games' museum where each exhibit is tailored to a different theme.

which stands the city's most famous landmark – the **cathedral of Notre-Dame** which has fine views from its south terrace. The 12th-century structure, arguably the most impressive Gothic building in Switzerland, is unusually sombre inside. Distinctive features include the rose window (13th-century stained glass), the crumbling tombs of bishops from the same era and the 13th-century choir stalls in the south aisle. At the end of the latter is the first of 232 punishing steps leading to the top of the south tower. The view is almost worth the effort. North of the cathedral square, via the charming medieval **Rue Cité Derrière**, is the **Château St Maire**, built in the late 1300s and extensively enlarged in the 16th century. A vast, squat structure of brick and sandstone, it is now the seat of the canton's government. West of the cathedral is the colourful market quarter of the **Place de la Palud**. Notable sights include the arcaded **Hôtel de Ville**, built in 1672, and the delicately sculpted **Fontaine de la Justice**. In the neighbouring **Place de la Riponne** is the handsome neo-classical **Palais de Rumine**, now the home of various museums (one of which contains the 12,000-year-old skeleton of a mammoth). Other interesting museums include the **Musée Olympique**, recording Lausanne's strong associations with the Olympic Games, housed in the new Cio building at Ouchy, and the extraordinary **Musée de l'Art Brut** in the Avenue Bergières which is a unique exhibition of unorthodox art by mentally handicappd artists and prison inmates. Southwest of the Place St-François is a funicular railway which runs the short distance to the old port of **Ouchy**, now a popular hotel and recreational suburb with a delightful leafy promenade. Sights include the **Elysée Museum** which houses a renowned photography collection in an elegant 18th-century mansion, and the stately **Hôtel d'Angleterre** built in 1775.

Excursion boats leave from the busy quayside to all points of the lake.

Take the old lakeside road 9 for about 18km (11 miles) to Vevey.

Vevey, Vaud

6 Splendidly sited high over the head of the lake, Vevey offers impressive views of the Savoy Alps to the south and the full sweep of the lake to the west. The most popular Swiss destination for English-speaking visitors during the 1800s, today it is one of the pleasantest of the larger Vaud Riviera resorts – an elegant town of considerable charm. The Gothic church of **St Martin**, a much-restored 13th-century structure, is the town's most distinctive building. Standing apart on a terrace, with fine views over the town and lake, it is notable for its 15th-century balustraded belfry. Inside, the choir dates from the late 1400s. Other interesting sights include the golden-domed **Russian church** in the Rue des Communaux, the **Musée Jenisch** in Rue de la Gare (natural history and Swiss art), and **La Grenette** – an early 19th-century grain market in the **Grande Place** on the lakefront. East of here are the discernible remnants of the old town; a short distance west of the centre are the unmistakable outlines of something rather newer – the sweeping 1960s glass and concrete headquarters of **Nestlé**, the world-famous chocolate manufacturer. Charlie Chaplin lived in the district of **Corsier**, north of the town centre, for 25 years until his death in 1977; he is now buried in the cemetery of **St Maurice's** church. Among its many arts-oriented events, the town hosts an annual **International Comedy Film Festival**.

Stay on road 9 through Montreux, following signs to

A jumble of russet roofs in Lausanne's ancient Quartier de la Cité

SCENIC ROUTES

Most of the north bank of Lake Geneva (Lac Léman), but particularly the stretch of road between Lausanne and Villeneuve, offers spectacular views south across the water. Later, the valley road up the Val d'Illiez to Champéry, and the pass road over the Pas de Morgins, afford breathtaking mountain views.

Aigle. About 4km after the Château de Chillon (conspicuous on your right), turn right on the road signposted Noville and Evian then follow signs to Monthey. The total distance from Vevey is about 31km (19 miles). Instead of entering Monthey take the road up the Val d'Illiez via Troistorrents to Champéry, about a further 13km (8 miles).

Champéry, Valais

7 A former mountain farming community, dramatically sited opposite the jagged peaks of the Dents du Midi, Champéry is now a year-round sports and leisure resort of great appeal. It is also one of the most fashionable resorts on the **Portes du Soleil** ski circus – the largest ski region in the world. Built on the western flank of the Val d'Illiez, where the valley descends from the impassable mountain barrier on the Franco-Swiss border, the village has retained much of its traditional Alpine feel. Although it is essentially a one-street community, it is none the less a long street, with some fine old wooden chalets still in evidence. One of the oldest structures is the quaint 18th-century baroque bell tower of St **Théodule's** church; one of the newest is the fine modern sports complex below the main street near the **Planachaux** cable car station.

Return to Troistorrents and take the main valley road up to the Pas de Morgins – about 22km (14 miles). Cross the border into France, then drive via the ski resorts of Châtel and Abondance

The colourful lakefront promenade of Ouchy below the city of Lausanne

*to just beyond Fontany where you diverge right, following signs to Evian-les-Bains via the village of Vinzier. At the exclusive French spa resort of Evian take the lakeside **N5** road to Thonon-les-Bains, then continue on the same road to Sciez and take the **D25** through Yvoire until the border and Hermance. The total distance from Pas de Morgins is about 76km (47.5 miles).*

Hermance, Geneva (Genève)

8 A delightful little fortified port some 15km northeast of Geneva (Genève), Hermance is the most attractive Swiss village on the lake's southern perimeter. Notable for its fine **beach** (children's play area) and picturesque narrow streets, it also has some fine old buildings including the 14th-century **keep** of the old castle, the 13th-century church of **St Georges** (altered in 1679) and the adjoining 15th-century **Mestral House**. Other houses in the village date from the same period and some are now used as artisans' studios.

Return to Geneva via Anières, about 15km (9 miles).

Geneva (Genéve) – Coppet 14 (9)
Coppet – Nyon 8 (5)
Nyon – Rolle 11 (7)
Rolle – Morges 15 (9)
Morges – Lausanne 12 (7.5)
Lausanne – Vevey 18 (11)
Vevey – Champéry 44 (27)
Champéry – Hermance 98 (61)
Hermance – Geneva 15 (9)

2 to 3 days: 307km (191 miles)

ROMAN JURA

Neuchâtel • Grandson • Baulmes • Vallorbe Lac de Joux • Aubonne • Romainmôtier La Sarraz Orbe • Yverdon-les-Bains • Estavayer-le-Lac Neuchâtel

The Romans left an indelible stamp on the country they called Helvetica (or Rhaetia). During a period of benign, and mostly peaceful, occupation between 15BC and AD455 they concentrated their settlements mostly in the north and west of the country. This tour takes you through some of the most visible legacies of the latter. You will also pass through the lovely Vallée de Joux (Joux valley), then over some of the highest peaks of the Swiss Jura through the serried vineyards above Lake Geneva (Lac Léman), returning between the lakes of Neuchâtel and Murten.

Time-conscious players take a break from their medieval role play in the fortress town of Estavayer-le-Lac

[i] 7 Rue de la Place d'Armes

Leave by the new autoroute, following signs to Yverdon and Lausanne, and join the existing lakeside road after about 9km (6 miles). Continue via St-Aubin to Grandson, a further 24km (15 miles).

Grandson, Vaud

1 After the famous Battle of Grandson in 1476 (see For History Buffs) the defeated Duke of Burgundy left the town's castle in such a hurry that his entire artillery and much of his ill-gotten treasure was abandoned. Today the huge and impressively sited **13th-century castle** still towers over the town from its elevated position on the bank of the lake. Inside is a **museum** commemorating the great battle, exhibiting a fine collection of the abandoned armaments, and – somewhat incongruously – an interesting selection of **vintage cars**.

The church of **St Jean-Baptiste** is Grandson's other most striking building – a handsome 12th-century Romanesque building with Gothic additions. The nave is supported by massive columns, themselves surmounted by what are said to be some of the finest examples of carved **Romanesque capitals** in the country. Behind the church is an impressive **fountain** dating from 1637.

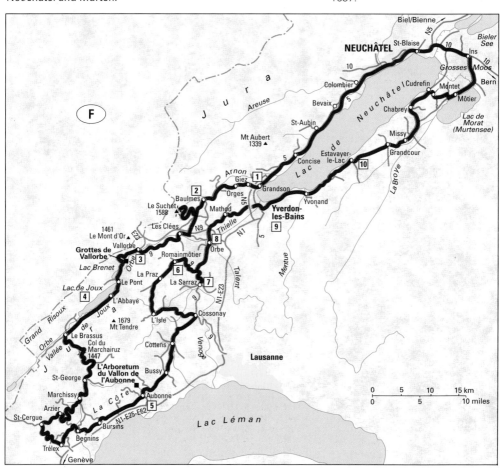

Drive up through the town on the narrow country road, via Giez and Orges, to Baulmes (12km/7.5 miles).

Baulmes, Vaud

2 A typical mountain settlement of the Jura, this quaint little agricultural village has earned modest celebrity recently due to the discovery of prehistoric remains on the flanks of the 1,285m Mont de Baulmes. Details of the find and exhibits are on show in the **Musée du Vieux-Baulmes** on Rue de Theu, itself a 17th-century building of some distinction. Note also the church of **St Pierre**, founded in the 13th century and rebuilt in 1871. In the church tower is a well-preserved **Roman altar** dedicated to Apollo.

Continue for 3km (2 miles) following signs to Vallorbe, and turn right up a winding mountain track signposted Le Suchet. This will take you through a dense pine forest to a marvellous belvedere at 1,588m, with fine views over the Jura and the lakes of Neuchâtel and Joux (about 8km/5 miles). Return via the same track and continue to Vallorbe, via Les Clées. Turn right shortly after Les Clées on road 9 (not the autoroute) for a further 16km/10 miles.

Vallorbe, Vaud

3 A hospitable base for excursions into the Vaud Jura and the Vallée de Joux, this unassuming and pleasantly sited town is best known for its proximity to the **Grottes de Vallorbe** (Caves of Vallorbe), a fascinating series of caverns a few kilometres west (see For Children). Vallorbe is also the home of a unique **Musée du Fer**, a small museum acknowledging the debt the town owes to the ferrous nature of its mountainous terrain. The collection includes examples of metal tools and implements through the ages, a working forge and four giant revolv-

ing paddles actually drawing power from the River Orbe outside.

i Grand-Forges 11

Drive west through Le Pont, following the south bank of Lac de Joux until Le Brassus (22km/13.5 miles).

Lac de Joux

4 The largest lake in the Swiss Jura takes its name from an old word for 'forest', which once surrounded it. The lake, 10km long and 1.5km wide, is still enclosed in a narrow basin protected by tree-covered mountains on all sides. For many years during the last century the lake is said to have provided much of the ice used by Paris hotels and restaurants. The ice was carved from the frozen surface of the lake in winter, and stored in underground chambers in the health resort of **Le Pont** – a small lakeside village which bridges Lac de Joux and the diminutive Lac Brenet. It was then transported by rail on the new Simplon railway connecting Paris and Milan. The south bank of the lake provides the most picturesque route west, passing through the small community of **L'Abbaye**, dominated by its 12th-century **Gothic church tower**, before the road leads into the old clock-making centre of **Le Brassus**.

The road ascends the Col du Marchairuz (1,447m) to the south, via the villages of St George, Marchissy, Bassins and Arzier to the climatic resort of St-Cergue (fine views). From here, take the steep, winding mountain road down towards Nyon, turning off left through the village of Trélex, passing through Genolier and Begnins, and from there continuing through a string of little farming villages,

FOR HISTORY BUFFS

1 In 1476 a famous battle took place in the little town of Grandson, ensuring that it would secure an important place in Swiss history. After a long siege and a spirited resistance, the town's garrison finally surrendered to the Duke of Burgundy who demonstrated his compassion by promptly executing them. Learning of this, the army of the early Swiss Confederation – outnumbered by the Burgundians nearly two-to-one – marched on Grandson and routed the invaders.

FOR CHILDREN

3 The Grottes de Vallorbe (Caves of Vallorbe) are a series of spectacular caverns forming vaults over the source of the River Orbe which surges beneath the viewing galleries and emerges into a picnic area outside. Stalactites and stalagmites reach out from the rock roof and floors and, together with the subtle lighting and hypnotic sound of rushing water, the whole experience is guaranteed to appeal to children of all ages.

9 In Yverdon-les-Bains, next to the castle, is Europe's first science-fiction museum – the 'Maison d'Ailleurs' (the House of Elsewhere). Among its eclectic collection are display cases devoted to toy robots (old and new).

BACK TO NATURE

5 Just north of Aubonne, in the Aubonne valley, is a vast 'botanical forest' known as L'Arboretum du Vallon de l'Aubonne. Created in 1968, it has more than 2,000 species of trees and shrubs in a lake and riverside setting of considerable beauty with marked paths. There are four access points: from the villages of Montherod, St Livres or Bière, or by foot from Aubonne.

3 Five kilometres west of Vallorbe, on the road to the Vallée de Joux, you will find one of the few herds of North American bison resident outside America. Entry is free to a splendid park beneath the Mont d'Orzeires.

Café society beside the baroque charm of Yverdon-Les-Bain's Place Pestalozzi

- including Bursins. This route, 64km (40 miles) in all, will take you parallel to, but above, the N1 autoroute to Aubonne.

Aubonne, Vaud

5 Another former Roman settlement, and one of the most appealing hill towns in the Swiss Jura, Aubonne is a bustling market centre of narrow streets and covered passageways. The town is dominated by its splendid baroque **château**, lent additional distinction by its 13th-century **onion-domed tower and arcaded courtyard**. The Old Town is remarkably well-preserved and remnants of the original 12th-century fortifications can be seen at intervals. The town's **16th-century church**, incorporating much of an earlier structure, is notable for its Gothic choir and adjacent 14th-century fresco.

Take the road to Cossonay, turning west in the town on the road signposted La Chaux and Col du Mollendruz. Follow the road west, turning north at L'Isle, leaving the col road about 5km (3 miles) later through the hamlet of La Praz to Romainmôtier (40km/25 miles).

Romainmôtier, Vaud

6 An ancient village clustered around the surviving **church** of the former **abbey of Saints Pierre et Paul** – considered to be one of the most outstanding buildings of its type in Switzerland. Founded in the 5th century by St Romanus, the present church was built in the early 11th century and shows predominant Romanesque influences. Particularly notable are the graceful Lombardian arches of the exterior, the 14th-century main door with roof paintings from the same period, and the 15th-century choir stalls.

North of the church is a 14th-century wall, and the Tour St Georges dates from the same period. Near by stands the former **prior's house**, dating from the 13th century and altered in the early 1600s. Note also the early 18th-century **Maison de la Dîme**, an old granary which is now a museum detailing the history of monastic life in the village (with slides and videos).

Drive 2km (1.25 miles) east to road 9, and turn right through Pompaples to La Sarraz (9km/5.5 miles).

La Sarraz, Vaud

7 The dominant feature of the village is the 15th-century turreted **castle**, set amidst landscaped gardens on an elevated site. Founded in the 11th century, it went through a turbulent period of destruction and reconstruction – usually at the hands of the Bernese who eventually decided to let it stand. Today it is a museum exhibiting mainly 18th-century furniture and paintings. In the chapel of **St Antoine**, built around 1360, is one of the more macabre exhibits in this part of Switzerland. The **tomb of Count François de la Sarraz**, dating from his death in 1363, depicts the dead man lying naked, surrounded by his wife and children, and – for some reason best known to them – being devoured by worms and toads.

In a nearby building in the castle grounds is an **Equestrian Museum** with over 1,000 items of horsy paraphernalia, and an interesting exhibition detailing the evolution of the horse over 70 million years.

Return via the same road for about 3km (1.8 miles), turning right to Arnex-sur-Orbe on a narrow country road to Orbe (9km/5.5 miles).

Orbe, Vaud

8 Once the Roman settlement of Urba, the present town has a seductive medieval atmosphere with mixed Burgundian, Savoyard and Bernese architectural influences. The view over the old town rooftops from the terrace of the 13th-century **château** is recommended. Only the keep and tower survive from this old fortress. The 15th-century church of **Notre-Dame** has fared better: note the Gothic portal dating from the early 1400s, and the four-turreted tower added in the 18th century. Inside are some splendid carvings. In the Place du Marché, outside the elegant **Hôtel de Ville** (1786), is a wide-basined **fountain**, built in 1753 and surmounted by a banner-carrying statue pre-dating it by two centuries. Note also the baroque 16th-century **Hôtel des Deux Poissons** in the Rue du Grand-Pont (formerly a monastery) and the pretty **bridge** (1421) at the end of Rue du Moulinet.

Take the road north for 13km (8 miles), signposted Yverdon and Mathod. Cross the autoroute and turn right at Mathod through Treycovagnes for Yverdon-les-Bains.

Yverdon-les-Bains, Vaud

9 As its name suggests, the town is a thermal spa which enjoyed considerable popularity in the 18th century. The Romans were rather keen on the waters, too, and gave it the name Eburodunum when they founded an outpost here on the site of a Celtic settlement. Today it has one of the biggest outdoor sulphur pools in the country, which you will find in the **Parc Thermal**. The **castle**, on the side of the broad cobbled Place Pestalozzi in the centre of the old town, is 13th-century and built in the Savoyard style with distinctive round pepperpot towers and a massive keep. It houses a **museum** with a curious collection of Victoriana and a room dedicated to the Swiss educationalist **Enrico Pestalozzi** who had used the building as the base for his famous **Institute** in the early 1800s. A monument to him stands near by. Next door, note the splendid **Hôtel de Ville** (1773) with its distinctive Louis XV façade. Also by the square is the church of **Notre-Dame** with an equally lavish baroque façade. Inside, the stalls date from 1499. Other fine façades can be found throughout the town.

ⓘ Place Pestalozzi

Follow the lakeside road for 19km (12 miles) to Estavayer-le-Lac.

Estavayer-le-Lac, Fribourg

10 One of the best-preserved medieval fortified towns in western Switzerland, this romantic lakeside settlement has retained much of its original 13th-century walled perimeter. The small, cluttered centre is characterised by hilly cobbled streets and a jumble of delightful 16th- and 17th-century buildings. At its core is the imposing Gothic church of **St Laurent**, built between 1379 and 1525 and notable for its fine carved choir stalls (1522) and wrought-iron screen separating it from the baroque high altar. At the

eastern end of the town is the splendid late 13th-century **Château de Chenaux**, one of the finest Savoyard castles of its type and still heavily fortified. Entered via a barbican and covered bridge, it is part public and part local government offices. Other notable buildings in the town include the **Dominican Convent** in the Grand-Rue, founded in the 14th century and rebuilt in the 18th century, and the nearby 16th-century **Hôtel du Cerf**. The local museum is installed in a former 15th-century tithe barn in Rue du Musée, now called the **Maison de la Dîme**. Among its exhibits there is a curious tableau depicting a group of frogs playing poker.

Take the minor road through Grandcour and Missy, rejoining the lakeside at the little fortified town of Cudrefin. From here turn south through Montet and Mur to join the north bank road of Lac de Morat. Follow this until the main road, turning left to join road 10 at Ins, then continue back to Neuchâtel (about 51km/32 miles).

The 15th-century barbican of Estavayer-le-Lac's Savoy-style Château de Chenaux

Neuchâtel – Grandson 33 (21)
Grandson – Baulmes 12 (7.5)
Baulmes – Vallorbe 35 (22)
Vallorbe – Lac de Joux 22 (13.5)
Lac de Joux – Aubonne 64 (40)
Aubonne – Romainmôtier 40 (25)
Romainmôtier – La Sarraz 9 (5.5)
La Sarraz – Orbe 9 (5.5)
Orbe – Yverdon-les-Bains 13 (8)
Yverson-les-Bains – Estavayer 19 (12)
Estavayer-le-lac – Neuchâtel 51 (32)

2 days: 233km (144.5 miles)

CLOCK COUNTRY

Biel • La Neuveville • Le Landeron
Neuchâtel • La Chaux-de-Fonds • St Ursanne
Porrentruy • Delémont • St-Imier • Biel

One of the more predictable images associated with Switzerland is that of the cuckoo clock. The fact that most of them are manufactured in Germany (and in particular the Black Forest) and imported exclusively for the tourist trade suggests that Swiss clock manufacturers are as disenchanted with the image as the majority of the Swiss people. Switzerland is proud of its clock- and watch-making tradition, but it would doubtless prefer to be recognised for the quality of its precision timepieces rather than a wooden bird on a stick. This tour enters the heart of the Swiss clock-making region, spanning the cantons of Neuchâtel and Jura, and passing through some of the most beautiful countryside of the Jura – Les Franches Montagnes. Many of the best-preserved towns of medieval Switzerland are also found in this north-west region.

BACK TO NATURE

1 St Peter's-Insel (Ile de St Pierre) is a nature reserve on a peninsula which used to be an island. It can be reached by foot from the town of Erlach, or boat from most of the larger towns on Lake Biel. The philosopher Rousseau had a room in the old hotel here (which is open for viewing) and the area is notable for the variety of its flora and fauna.

Two hirsute and heavily armoured soldiers on a wall in Biel's 'Ring' (marketplace) bear witness to the town's military past

☐ Silbergasse 31

Take the lakeside road 5 for about 15km (9 miles) to La Neuveville.

La Neuveville, Bern (Berne)

1 A charming old town on the upper leg of the curiously shaped Bieler See (Lake Biel), La Neuveville preserves a strong olde-world atmosphere. It is sometimes described as the 'Montreux' of the Jura, but it deserves a more imaginative comparison.

Lanterns, pretty fountains with banner-waving figures and the remains of medieval fortifications are among the historical features which characterise its cobbled streets. Two old gate towers, the **Tour Rouge** and the **Tour de Rive**, stand at either end of the main street, the Rue du Marché. The houses here were built between the 16th and early 19th centuries, and many of them have Gothic façades. Note particularly the baroque mid-18th-century **Dragon House**, so-called because of its scaly gargoyles, and the splendid 16th-century **Hôtel de Ville**. The latter contains the town's museum (fine Burgundian cannons from the Battle of Murten 1476). At the eastern end of the Old Town, the **Eglise Blanche** is a 14th-century building with notable Gothic frescos from the same era. A 13th-century **castle** overlooks the town from the north. A ruin for three centuries, it was restored in 1885 and again in 1931.

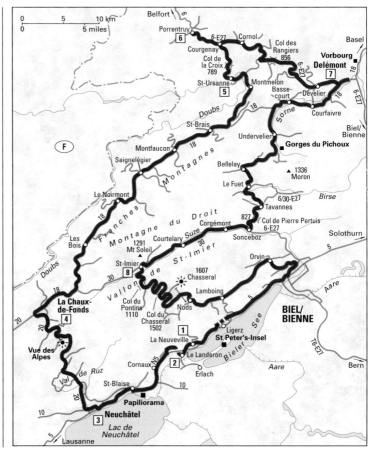

Follow signs to Le Landeron for about 3km (2 miles).

Le Landeron, Neuchâtel

2 Another fine old fortified town with a handsome collection of medieval houses, Le Landeron is particularly notable for its long and leafy main street with an ancient gate at each end. The oldest is **La Portette**, to the south, built in 1596. The other dates from 1659. Enhancing the fine collection of 16th- and 17th-century houses which line this central area are two colourful 16th-century fountains – the **Vaillant** and the **St Maurice**, both with bannerets. The 15th-century **Hôtel de Ville** has an even older chapel attached to it.

Return to the autoroute and follow signs for Neuchâtel for about 18km (11 miles).

Neuchâtel

3 Capital of its canton, Neuchâtel is a stately and pleasant city attractively situated on the north shore of the lake of the same name. Surrounded by vine-covered terraces, it is famous for its wine – thousands of gallons of which were poured into the city's **Griffin** fountain to celebrate King Henry II of Orléans' arrival in 1657. The fountain, then only three years old, still stands on the Rue du Château – apparently none the worse for the experience. This is one of the most French of Swiss cities, the Orléans inheritance and French University ensuring as much. It is also one of the big centres of Swiss clock- and watch-research technology, provid-

Tapered spires form a picturesque background to part of Neuchâtel's Old Town

ing the official time to the entire country from its Observatory. The **château**, built between the 12th and 15th centuries and perching picturesquely above the **Old Town**, is one of the city's most striking buildings. Formerly the seat of the Counts of Neuchâtel, it is now used as the cantonal offices, although the flower-decked courtyard is open to the public. Near by, the **Prison Tower**, built in sections between the 10th and 15th centuries, offers fine views. Between the castle and the tower is the **collegiate church of Notre-Dame**, a 12th- and 13th-century Romanesque-Gothic building of considerable distinction. One of the most notable features of the interior is the **Cenotaph** of the Counts of Neuchâtel, a 14th-century monument which comprises an intriguing group of many-coloured statues. The **Old Town** (Ville Ancienne) grew up beneath this triumvirate of buildings and is particularly notable for its many fine fountains, including the **Banneret** (1581 statue), **Fontaine du Lion** (1664 statue), **La Justice** (1545), as well as the wine-spouting Griffon (see above). Of the many elegant 16th- to 18th-century buildings, the Renaissance-style covered market hall, **Maison des Halles** (1569–75), stands out as the best example. To the east of this old quarter is the **Hôtel du Peyrou**, a magnificent Louis XVI structure with beautiful landscaped gardens. Neuchâtel is also well known for its

SCENIC ROUTES

Between Neuchâtel and La Chaux-de-Fonds the road reaches a height of 1,283m as it passes that section known as the **Vue des Alpes**. The views south and to the west are striking. Further on, between La Chaux-de-Fonds and St Ursanne, the route threads through the part of the Jura known as **Les Franches Montagnes**. This is one of the loveliest parts of the tour, characterised by distinctive Jurassian houses, rolling pastures and fir forests. Note also the stocky little mountain ponies and bay horses which are a feature of the region. After Delémont the road passes through the dramatic **Gorges du Pichoux** – a deep cleft in the landscape gouged by the Sorne river. Immediately to the south rises the unfortunately named peak of **Moron** (1,336m).

The early 18th-century Doubs Bridge spans the cool green waters of St-Ursanne's river

excellent selection of museums. They include the **Musée d'Art et d'Histoire**, close to the lakefront, the **Musée d'Ethnographie**, and the **Musée Cantonal d'Archéologie** (with tools dating back to the Stone Age).

Follow the old road 20 for 22km (13.5 miles), via Vue des Alpes, to La Chaux-de-Fonds.

La Chaux-de-Fonds, Neuchâtel

4 The third largest city in French-speaking Switzerland, La Chaux-de-Fonds is particularly proud of its most famous son – the internationally celebrated architect Le Corbusier. Little of his influence is evident, but that is probably because he spent the majority of his life in Paris. Although the late 18th-century grid-patterned city (the original was destroyed by fire in 1794) is a busy agricultural centre, La Chaux-de-Fonds is also in fact the thriving commercial hub of the Swiss watch-making industry. Unsurprisingly, then, it has Switzerland's largest museum devoted entirely to time-pieces. The **Musée International de l'Horlogerie** is located in an extraordinary underground building in the midst of a park, opened in 1973. Here, in an imaginative arrangement of rooms on different levels, connected by galleries, bridgeways and ramps, is arguably the world's definitive collection of anything that ever recorded the passage of time. Among the museum's many fascinating exhibits are primitive sundials, musical clocks, costume watches, early wristwatches, precision atomic time-keeping devices, and a vast 'carillon' – an elaborately sculpted construction of tubular bells and chimes. The town's other

fine museums include the **Musée des Beaux-Arts**, with its collection of fine art, the **Musée d'Histoire et Médaillier** (medals) and, just outside the town centre, the interesting **Musée Paysan** – an authentic early 17th-century farmhouse frozen in time.

Take the old road 18 through Les Franches Montagnes, then take the left fork after St Brais to St Ursanne (about 49km/30 miles).

St-Ursanne, Jura

5 Taking its name from the Irish hermit-monk Ursicinus who settled here in the 7th century, this pretty town retains much of its medieval appearance and is virtually unaffected by contemporary building. Its collection of fountains, turreted houses, ornate balconies and façades is as pleasing as that of any small town in the country, and is delightfully enhanced by ramparts and three ancient fortified gates which still stand guard at strategic points on the perimeter. The gates of **St Pierre**, **St Paul** and **St Jean** were largely rebuilt in the 16th and 17th centuries and are variously distinguished by bell turrets and heraldic statues. Porte St-Jean is incorporated into a terrace of riverside houses with overhanging roofs and balconies and stands at the end of the picturesque **Doubs Bridge** – a robust, many-arched structure of 1728. The Romanesque **collegiate church** was built between the 12th and 15th centuries, the oldest part being the choir beneath where the bones of St Ursicinus are said to rest. The south doorway is particularly notable for its polychrome figures (including the eponymous saint standing modestly by the Virgin Mary).

Take the old road over the Col de

la Croix, joining road 6 at Courgenay for Porrentruy, for 13km (8 miles).

Porrentruy, Jura

6 Best known for its largely unspoilt Old Town, Porrentruy has a picturesque château comprising buildings of various ages standing high above the Old Town. The château's oldest section is the 13th-century **Tour Réfouse**. Part of the town's original 16th-century fortifications, the **Porte de France**, stands just below; the most interesting of the estimable collection of historic buildings can be found in the Rue Pierre-Péquignat and the Grand-Rue. The **Hôtel de Ville** and the **hospital** (now a **museum**) were both built in the mid-1760s by the same architect. Elsewhere there are two old fountains of note; the 1564 **Fontaine de la Samaritaine**, near the hospital, and the 1558 **Fontaine du Suisse**, on the Rue des Malvoisins. The banner-carrying soldier of the latter stands astride a truculent-looking wild boar, an animal which features large on the town's coat-of-arms. Note also the churches of **St-Pierre**, an early 14th-century Gothic basilica, the 13th-century Romanesque **St-Germain**, and the **Jesuit church** of 1597 (finished in 1604). The latter's unusual octagonal **tower** is a century younger.

Take road 6 southeast for about 27km (17 miles) over the Col des Rangiers to Delémont.

Delémont, Jura

7 Capital of the canton of Jura, the town is another important precision instrument and watch-making centre. Like its neighbour, Delémont

An inscription on one of St-Ursanne's three medieval town gates

also has a fine **château** and an interesting **Old Town** sector with part of the original town fortifications still in evidence – notably the 13th-century **Tour des Archives**. The town gates are mid-18th-century reconstructions. The three most prominent of the municipal fountains – La Vierge, St-Maurice and Sauvage – all date from the 16th century. Other notable structures include the baroque **Hôtel de Ville**, St-Marcel's church and, just northeast of the town, the ruins of **Vorbourg Castle** and its still-intact pilgrimage chapel. To the west is the mid-16th-century **Château Domont**. The town's museum, **Musée Jurassien**, has the most comprehensive collection of regional artefacts in the canton.

Double back now on road 18, signposted La Chaux-de-Fonds, over the Col du Mont Crosin to St-Imier. Turn left about 2km beyond Bassecourt, signposted Gorges du Pichoux and Tavannes. At the latter, rejoin road 6 for 5km (3 miles) over Col de Pierre Pertuis to Sonceboz, then take road 30 to St-Imier (51km/32 miles).

St-Imier, Bern (Berne)

8 A splendid site on the southern flank of Mont Soleil (1,291m), this is a busy little town specialising in the design and manufacture of clocks and watches. Both the 12th-century **church** and the **Tour de la Reine Berthe** (the bell tower of the former church of St Martin) are fine Romanesque structures.

Return to Biel on the Biel/Neuchâtel road, turning left just beyond Col des Pontins for the Col du Chasseral. Note that there is a small toll to pay for use of the higher stretches of the Chasseral road (35km/22 miles).

Biel – La Neuveville 15 (9)
La Neuveville – Le Landeron 3 (2)
Le Landeron – Neuchâtel 18 (11)
Neuchâtel – La Chaux-de-Fonds 22 (13.5)
La Chaux-de-Fonds – St-Ursanne 49 (30)
St-Ursanne – Porrentruy 13 (8)
Porrentruy – Delémont 27 (17)
Delémont – St-Imier 51 (32)
St-Imier – Biel 35 (22)

RECOMMENDED WALKS

3 In Neuchâtel there are 4km of quayside walks which provide spectacular views of Lake Neuchâtel and the Alps. Osterwald Quay, immediately south of the Old Town, offers shady seating areas and a viewing table.

7 The tour will take you on the Chasseral road beneath the 1,607m peak of the same name, 12km southeast of St-Imier. The summit, the highest point of the northern part of the Jura range, affords a magnificent panorama in every direction – with the Alps to the south and the Black Forest to the northeast. Leave the car at the Hôtel du Chasseral and follow the easily ascended path to the top. Allow half an hour each way. Alternatively, there is a chairlift from the small hamlet of Nods, a little further on the road to Biel.

SWISS PLATEAU

Once a huge river of ice, the Swiss Plateau (also known to its occupants as the Mittelland) is the central belt of relatively low-lying land separating the Alps from the mountains of the Jura. Constituting about 30 per cent of the country's land area, it is the most populous of the three main geographical regions, not least because it is accessible, fertile and climatically agreeable. Most of Switzerland's major population centres are therefore found here, Zürich and Basle foremost among them, and nearly 80 per cent of Swiss citizens choose to make the region their home.

With the exception of the far west and northwest, the area is almost exclusively German speaking and the people are mostly of Germanic origin. The Rhine marks the border with Germany to the north, and the other great river of significance is the Aare, splitting the plateau diagonally from the pre-Alps of the Bernese Mittelland to the confluence of the two rivers in the north. One of the most features of this region is its beautiful valleys, the pastoral Emmental standing out as a particularly fine example. But arguably the Swiss Plateau's greatest appeal is the remarkably well-preserved medieval fabric of many of its towns and cities. It seems almost as if there is no population centre of any size on these tours which does not have a carefully protected old quarter and a collection of enviable historical treasures. Bern (Berne), Fribourg and Solothurn are just three outstanding examples of how a rich architectural inheritance need not be compromised by the demands of progress. Even the great financial and commercial centre of Zürich has apparently managed effortlessly to build a modern city around an historical core of substantial charm. The worst excesses of post-war architecture appear to have bypassed most of Switzerland, and the prosperous Mittelland is no exception.

Bern (Berne)

The Swiss capital is justly celebrated as one of Europe's most charming cities. It has a splendid Gothic medieval inheritance, most notably the 7km (4 miles) of 15th-century arcades which flank its narrow cobbled streets. Known as the 'Lauben', these precursors of the modern shopping mall are quite unique and jealously protected by the city authorities. Berne is also known for its two other outstanding landmarks, the series of 11 beautifully gilded thematic fountains, mostly erected during the 16th century, and its famously decorated clocktowers. Of the latter, the 12th-century Zeitglockenturm in the centre of the Old Town is probably the most impressive. Other notable sights include the early 15th-century Rathaus and its fine square, and the world-famous bear pits (Barengraben), found across the River Aare via the Nydeggbrucke. Near by is the Rose Garden (Rosengarten), with over 200 varieties of rose and a splendid view of the city from its elevated site. The city's finest building is the Munster (cathedral) begun in 1421, a Gothic structure of considerable distinction with what is said to be the country's highest spire at over 100m. Close by, the Bundeshaus, the seat of the Swiss government, is an imposing 19th-century building typical of the Renaissance style which characterises much of the city's contemporary public architecture. Berne's other main attractions include a fine choice of museums clustered around the Helvetiaplatz, and some excellent street markets.

Zürich

Switzerland's largest city is also its most wealthy. The name Zürich has become synonymous with banking and finance, and the so-called city 'gnomes' who oversee the private accounts of the world's super-rich. But Zürich is also an important cultural centre, attractively sited at the northern tip of the lake of the same name. The Old Town is best viewed from the shady Lindenhof, an elevated terrace on the west bank of the Limmat river where the Romans first built a customs post in 15BC. Beneath the Lindenhof, courtyards, squares and winding cobbled alleys lined by 16th to 17th-century guildhouses characterise both sides of the river, but the view is dominated by the towers and spires of the city's three churches to the south. On the left bank, the 13th-century tower of St Peterskirche has Europe's largest clock face, and the nearby 13th-century Fraumunster is notable for its delicate spire and remarkable stained glass by the Russian-born French artist, Marc Chagall.

A perplexed-looking sun points out the time on Berne's famous astronomical clocktower, the Zeitglockenturm

A view across the Limmat river to Zurich's Old Town

On the opposite bank, the twin towers of the Grossmunster are one of the city's most distinctive landmarks. Among a choice of over 30 museums, the Museum of Fine Arts (Kunsthaus) is one of the country's most important institutes, and the Swiss National Museum (Landesmuseum) one of its most entertaining. Other sights and attractions include the city zoo on the Zurichbergstrasse, the Opera House (Opernhaus) on the landscaped Utoquai, and the famous Emil Buhrle Foundation on the Zollikerstrasse, housing one of the world's most impressive collections of French Masters. And no visit to the city would be quite complete without a stroll down the Bahnhofstrasse, a famous shopping boulevard beyond the budget of all but the customers of the many banks which are also found here. The riches of the rich are securely contained in huge bank vaults beneath the street.

Basel (Basle)

The gateway to the northwest of the country, Basle is strategically located on the Rhine which marks the border between France and Germany. The cultural and architectural influences of both countries are seen to intriguing effect throughout this attractive old city. Home to the country's oldest university, founded in the mid-15th century, it is also host to Switzerland's most colourful carnival, the Fasnacht, a highly celebrated national institution which lasts for three days and nights beginning on the Monday following Ash Wednesday. Places of interest are found mostly in the Old Town, and include the Fischmarkt with its splendid Gothic fountain, the early 15th-century Spalentor gate tower, the 16th-century Rathaus in the Marktplatz, the picturesque 12th-century Munster (cathedral) overlooking the river, and the intriguing kinetic Tinguely Fountain on the Theaterplatz. Of the city's 30 museums, the Museum of Fine Arts (Kunstmuseum) stands out, and is said to be home to the world's oldest public art collection. Not to be missed is Basle's zoo, one of the finest in the country, laid out in a splendid park in the middle of the city with a collection of over 4,000 animals.

2 to 3 days: 292km (180.5 miles)

SOLOTHURN AND THE EMMENTAL

Basel (Basle) • Zwingen • Solothurn Utzenstorf
Burgdorf • Hasle • Langnau im Emmental
St Urban • Olten • Basel (Basle)

The first stage of this tour temporarily leaves the Swiss plateau and winds up through the most northerly part of the Jura, a mountainous region of striking beauty which affords magnificent views of the Bernese Mittelland and the Oberland beyond it. Various parts of the cantons of Basle, Berne, Jura, Solothurn and Lucerne are visited in turn, with the route following nearly the entire length of the Emmental. The Emme river originates beneath the 2,197m Hohgant on the north side of Brienzer See (Lake Brienz) and follows a course of 80km (50 miles) before joining the Aare near Solothurn. The valley it has cut affords a fascinating kaleidoscope of contrasting pastoral images, and offers some of the most rewarding scenery of the middle lands of Switzerland – not to mention a selection of fine cheeses for which it has become world famous.

An ancient timber chalet now used as a wood store, Emmental

ⓘ Chifflande 5

Take road 18 south from Basle, signposted Delémont, and turn off on the minor road for Zwingen and Passwang after about 17km (10.5 miles).

Zwingen, Basel Land

1 The little village is notable for one outstanding feature – its picturesque **castle** strategically positioned so that it is naturally protected on three sides by the Birs river. Built in the 14th century, it retains an appealing medieval appearance, notwithstanding major extension works carried out in the 16th and 17th centuries. The oldest part is the keep, abutting walls of the same age surmounted by a typically Bernese half-hipped roof dating from the later alterations. A pretty little stone **bridge** connects the tower to the opposite bank.

Continue south over the Passwang pass (943m), turning right soon afterwards and following signs for the Scheltenpass (1,051m). About 1km after the village of Courchapoix, turn left through

A 15th-century astronomical clock adorns the face of the 12th-century clocktower in Solothurn

SCENIC ROUTES

1 There are three spectacular stretches of road through the northern Jura between Zwingen and Solothurn. The first, via the Passwang pass, is approached from the desolate Lüssel valley. After the tunnel there are distant views south over the Emmental to the Bernese Alps. The Scheltenpass, next, up the Guldental, offers similarly pleasing views. But the most dramatic part of the tour is between Gänsbrunnen and Solothurn, through the peaks of the Weissenstein. The views across the Mittelland from here are the finest in the Jura mountains – but the road is perilous in parts, and it is a good idea to stop where possible to admire the scenery rather than risk distraction.

FOR CHILDREN

2 Solothurn's Naturmuseum in the Klosterplatz will prove to be a joy to children of a particularly tactile disposition, because they are allowed to touch many of the exhibits. The natural history collection, said to be among the most impressive in the country, is both educational and enjoyable.

*Vermes and Envelier.
At Crémines turn left for
Gänsbrunnen, and from there
take particular care on the
beautiful but narrow mountain
road through the Weissenstein
to Solothurn (about 78km/48
miles).*

Solothurn

2 Solothurn's relatively modest size belies its considerable range of sights, attractions and facilities. Although a busy commercial centre of some importance, it describes itself as the best-preserved baroque town in Switzerland, with good reason. The **Old Town** is a magical chrysalis of medieval alleys and squares, walls and moats, ornamental fountains and ornate baroque chapels. The centre is closed to motor vehicles, and pavement cafés and markets are therefore a popular feature of the appealingly quaint heart of this quarter – still enclosed by its original 17th-century walls. But perhaps its most engaging characteristic is the fact that Solothurn is effectively a window on the past: the architecture and decorative styles of the buildings embrace nearly every epoch of modern Swiss history. Perhaps the most famous of the town's landmarks is the **Krummturm**, the so-called 'crooked tower', which is part of the original town fortifications on the south bank of the river. But the richest collection of treasures lies in the heart of the Old Town, clustered in perfect symmetry on the north bank and entered via one of two splendid medieval gates, the **Bieltor** and the **Baseltor**. Here you will find the imposing baroque pile of **St Ursen cathedral**, built in the mid-18th century by an architect from Ticino. The Italian influence is demonstrable. A short distance further along the Hauptgasse is the 17th-century **Jesuit church**, with a magnificent stucco interior – also the work of Ticinese designers. Further on is the Marktplatz, dominated by the town's oldest building, the 12th-century **Zeitglockenturm**, a clock-tower with an astronomical face (added in the 15th century). Also in the Marktplatz is the elaborately decorated **St Ursen fountain** of 1530.

One of the town's other interesting features is its generous selection of museums. Of these, the **Altes Zeughaus** is the most impressive. A former arsenal, it was built between 1610 and 1614 to a design originally drawn up by Leonardo da Vinci. Inside a deceptively huge building (its lines were exaggerated to deter Bernese predators) is a splendid collection of weapons and armour. Solothurn's other museums include the **Kunstmuseum** (impressive collection of old masters), the **Naturmuseum**, and the **Historisches Museum Schloss Blumenstein** (French antiquities). The town's newest museum, the **Schloss Waldegg**, is in one of its most beautiful baroque manor houses, built in 1682 as a summer residence amidst sculpted gardens on the northern outskirts. A superb collection of 17th- to 19th-century

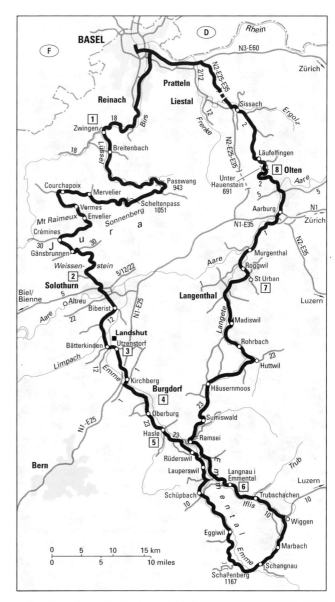

antiquities offer an intriguing insight into how Solothurn's patrician class of mercenary soldiers lived.

ℹ Hauptgasse 69

Take road 12 south for about 13km (8 miles), via Biberist, turning off at Bätterkinden for Utzenstorf.

Utzenstorf, Berne

3 If you are a hunting, shooting, fishing type, as many Swiss are, you may well want to stop at the **Schloss Landshut**, just outside this little town on the eastern bank of the Emme river. The castle was built in the mid-13th century, largely rebuilt in the 17th century, and has the unusual distinction of being the only fortress in the canton of Berne with a moat. Inside is Switzerland's only **museum** dedicated to hunting – although its full title pays lip service to the notion of 'protection of game' as well. The town itself has an old Gothic **church** dating from the early 16th century. Next door is a baroque presbytery of 1744.

*Take the minor road south for 12km (7.5 miles), crossing over the **N1** to Kirchberg, and continuing to Burgdorf.*

SPECIAL TO...

2 The Ticinese architect Matteo Pisoni, who built St Ursen cathedral , developed an obsession with the figure 11. The city's patron saints, Urs and Victor, were members of the 11th Roman Legion and were beheaded on the banks of the river. Pisoni designed the cathedral with 11 bells and 11 altars, and the structural measurements were all in multiples of 11. The figure recurs throughout the town: 11 fountains, 11 churches, 11 towers and 11 guilds. Solothurn was the 11th canton to join the Confederation, and there are even 11 official tour guides.

BACK TO NATURE

2 Switzerland's largest stork colony is just outside Solothurn, a few minutes' walk from the boat landing stage in the village of Altreu. The population of the distinctive black-and-white birds exceeds 200, and they can be reached within two hours by foot from Solothurn, or within 20 minutes by boat.

Burgdorf, Berne

4 The town stands at the entrance to the Emmental, and it developed around a 7th-century fortress built with the explicit purpose of deciding who went in and out of this desirable pastoral region. The present **castle** is of 12th-century foundation, but has been added to several times; it is said to be one of the earliest brick structures in the country. Now containing a local history **museum**, it is an imposing structure of characteristic Bernese style with the canton's shield painted on the white walls of the residential quarters. Part of museum's the permanent exhibition is devoted to the famous Swiss educationalist Pestalozzi who founded his school here in 1798. From the top of the tower there are magnificent views of the **Old Town** and its handsome guildhouses beneath. The town is also notable for its late 15th-century **church**.

Take the road south, signposted Oberburg and Hasle, for about 6km (4 miles).

Hasle, Berne

5 Stop here awhile to admire the unique covered **wooden bridge** which spans the Emme over a distance of nearly 70m. Built in 1839, it is the longest single span bridge in Switzerland. Take time to visit the 17th-century **pilgrimage church** as well. Inside are some splendid 15th-century frescos dating back to an earlier building. (Hasle should not be confused with the village of the same name in the Entlebuch, about 30km east.)

Continue on the same road southeast and just before crossing the Emme turn off on the minor valley road on the west bank of the Emme to Lauperswil, then drive up the Emmental through Schüpbach, crossing and re-crossing the river until you reach the hamlet of Eggiwil. Follow the signs for Schallenberg from here, but instead of turning right for the pass, continue up the head of the valley through Schangnau

and Marbach. Continue to Wiggen and turn left on road 10 for Langnau (about 57km/35 miles).

Langnau im Emmental, Berne

6 An ideal halfway point to break overnight, this lovely old dairy town is the chief settlement of the Emmental, and has a handsome centre of characteristic valley houses and taverns with huge half-hipped roofs. The **local museum**, housed in a 16th-century timber chalet known as the **Chüechlihaus**, is well worth a look. The collection includes local pottery, clocks, implements connected with the dairy industry over the centuries, and faithfully assembled rooms from different eras. Opposite is a fine country **church**, built by the celebrated church architect Abraham Dünz in 1673. Inside is a remarkable pulpit of the same era, with intricate baroque carvings.

Langnau owes its air of cheerful prosperity to the famous Emmental cheese, and the town is the principal exporter of the product. If you are planning on buying a 'wheel' of Swiss cheese, this is certainly the place to do it.

Take the main valley road north to Ramsei, joining road 23 here for Sumiswald and then Huttwil, where you should branch off following signs for Langenthal. Here, drive into the centre and

Medieval Petersgasse leads up to the late Gothic Church of St Peter (Peterskirche), Basle

Dizzy valley view down to the typical Emmental farming village of Trub

follow signs for St Urban. (About 49km (30 miles) in total from Langnau.)

St Urban, Lucern (Lucerne)

7 The most interesting feature of this little village is its disproportionately large **Cistercian monastery**. Founded in the late 12th century, it prospered throughout the Middle Ages and through a combination of good housekeeping and the revenue from a small brickworks, built an ambitiously grandiose **baroque church** in the early 18th century. The architectural style is known as Vorarlberg, after the western province of Austria where it originated, and where the two architects came from. The interior is particularly lavish, with an uplifting blend of white stucco and gilded adornments. The rococo pulpit is notable, and the carved choir stalls are quite exceptional. The monastery was extended about 20 years later in similarly extravagant fashion, but it was closed in 1848. Today it is one of the best appointed psychiatric hospitals in the country.

Follow signs to Roggwil, passing through it until you reach road 1. Turn right, following signs for Olten (about 20km/12.5 miles)

Olten, Solothurn

8 This is a lively little railway town with a well-preserved old quarter picturesquely set by the banks of the Aare river. It was founded on the site of a Roman camp, and the oval contours of the largely 16th-century old town follow faithfully the original lines of its predecessor. There are two outstanding landmarks: the **Alte Brücke**, a covered wooden bridge reserved for pedestrians, and the early 16th-century Gothic **tower** of the former church of St Martin (demolished in 1844), which rises above the rooftops. The neo-classical twin-towered town **church**, built in 1806, is also a relatively imposing structure. If you plan to explore a little, look in on the **Kunstmuseum (Fine Arts Museum)** on the Kirchgasse opposite. Its collection includes contemporary paintings and sculpture, and the collected works of the locally born painter and caricaturist Martin Disteli (1802–44). Near by is a good local history **museum**. The wider reaches of the town are less appealing, but as this is the central workshop of Swiss Federal Railways perhaps that is not so surprising.

*Return to Basle on road 2, joining the **N2** autoroute at Sissach (about 40km/25 miles).*

Basel – Zwingen 17 (10.5)
Zwingen – Solothurn 78 (48)
Solothurn – Utzenstorf 13 (8)
Utzenstorf – Burgdorf 12 (7.5)
Burgdorf – Hasle 6 (4)
Hasle – Langnau 57 (35)
Langnau – St Urban 49 (30)
St Urban – Olten 20 (12.5)
Olten – Basel 40 (25)

2 to 3 days: 293km (183 miles)

MEDIEVAL LOWLANDS

Zürich • Bremgarten • Lenzburg • Aarau
Brugg • Baden • Zurzach • Schaffhausen
Stein am Rhein • Winterthur • Zürich

Between the 11th and 16th centuries, many of the towns and cities on this tour were at various times under the control of the dynasties of the Kyburgs, Habsburgs and Bernese. The result is a fascinating medley of architectural styles accommodated within some of the best-preserved medieval towns in Switzerland. The cantons of Zürich, Aargau and Schaffhausen in which they are located are among the wealthiest in the country, and passing through them you will note that their administrators have spared demonstrably little expense in preserving their enviable cultural inheritance.

Cheerfully setting about his task, a straw-hatted farmer rakes hay on a roadside near Stein am Rhein

A battered painted sign outside Stein am Rhein's 16th-century Gasthaus Rothen Oschen

⃞ Bahnhofbrücke 1

Leave Zürich via the Bederstrasse, following signs to Zug and Adliswil on road 4. From Adliswil follow signs to the Albispass and, shortly after it, Mettmenstetten. Then drive north to Affoltern am Albis, turning west here for Muri to join road 25 for Boswil. Turn right here on to a minor road for Bremgarten. (about 48km/30 miles).

Bremgarten, Aargau

1 Once a prosperous Habsburg town, Bremgarten fell to the Swiss in the mid-15th century and first impressions suggest that progress has effectively bypassed it ever since. Among a pleasing medieval collection, the 16th-century **covered wooden bridge** over the Reuss holds the attention. Built on four pillars, two tiny **chapels** project from the third. Other interesting sights include the original 14th-century rampart towers of **Hexenturm** and **Hermansturm**. The **Spittelturm**, distinguished by its coat of arms, is 16th-century. Note also the 14th- to 15th-century Gothic church of St Nicholas.

Follow signs to Wohlen on road 1. Just beyond Wohlen turn off the main road towards Villmergen. From there follow signs for Sarmenstorf and then Seengen. At the latter take the road towards Boniswil and Hallwil. Continue north on road 26 to Lenzburg (about 29km/18 miles).

Lenzburg, Aargau

2 The dominant feature of this ancient town is the imposing medieval **castle** on a wooded hill above a huddle of 17th- and 18th-century baroque buildings. Founded in the 11th century and altered in the 16th, the castle was successively the property of the Kyburgs, the Habsburgs, the Bernese, and a certain Mr E E Jessup of Philadelphia, USA, who bought it at the turn of this century and substantially restored it. Now the property of the town, it houses a cantonal history **museum**. The Old Town was largely destroyed by fire in the late Middle Ages and of the more notable buildings constructed in its wake, the **church** (1667) and **Rathaus** (1677) stand out. When the N1 autobahn was being constructed to the north of the town in 1964, the remains of a 1st-century **Roman theatre** were uncovered and can now be visited.

Take road 1 west to Suhr, there joining road 23 north to Aarau (about 10km/6 miles).

Aarau, Aargau

3 Built by the Habsburgs on a hill above the Aare, the Old Town of this cantonal capital is one of the most picturesquely appointed in the north of Switzerland. A fine view of

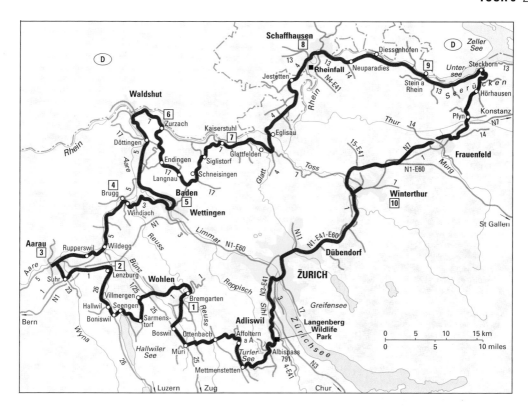

it can be had looking south across the river from the Neue-Aarebrücke (bridge). Many of the predominantly 16th- to 18th-century buildings are baroque in style and ornamental carvings and paintings are a repeated feature of the gables and façades of the old houses. Aarau's oldest building, the 11th-century **Schlössli**, now the **Stadtmuseum Alt-Aarau** (museum of Old Aarau), one of three museums in the town. Another ancient building, the 13th-century **Roreturm**, is incorporated into the 18th-century **Rathaus**. A short distance west is the 15th-century **Stadtkirche**, with an elegant 17th-century belfry and a contemporary **Fountain of Justice** adjacent. Near by is the **Oberer Turm**, another old tower which once formed part of the original town wall.

[i] Bahnhofstrasse 20

Leave Aarau via the Rohrerstrasse, road 5, signposted Brugg (and Baden) and continue for 19km (12 miles).

Brugg, Aargau

4 Another attractive old Habsburg town, near the confluence of the Aare and the Reuss rivers, Brugg takes its name from the original bridge (over the Aare) around which it developed in the early Middle Ages. Near its replacement stands part of the original town fortifications, the 12th- and 16th-century **Schwarze Turm** (Black Tower), thought to incorporate stones from the former 1st-century **Roman fort** of Vindonissa which stood about 1km east. Note also the late Gothic, 16th-century **Rathaus** and the charming Hofstatt Square where the 17th-century **Arsenal** (now the local history museum) and two 18th-century **storehouses** stand. The town's **Vindonissa Museum** contains a generous collection of artefacts from the remains of the Roman fort

near by, where an **amphitheatre**, which once held 10,000 spectators, has been uncovered.

Leave for Baden on road 3 and continue for 10km (6 miles).

Baden, Aargau

5 As its name suggests, this is a spa town – perhaps the best known in Switzerland. Although settled first by the Helvetians, the Romans, quick to spot the potential of a good bathing site, developed it into a prosperous town. Much of its present appearance dates from the time the Bernese almost destroyed it in 1712, although some former fortifications survive. The Old Town is picturesquely set on the west bank of the Limmat river, connected to the opposite bank by a charming **covered wooden bridge** of 1810. Here you will find the **Landvogteischloss**, a 15th-century Governor's castle which is now the local history **museum**. From the upper floors there are fine views of the steep-pitched roofs of the Old Town. The four-turreted **Stadtturm**, a 15th-century Gothic gatehouse, is conspicuous – along with the slimmer lines of the tower of the 15th-century Catholic **church** (much altered). Opposite stands a group of buildings which collectively make up the **Stadthaus** (town hall), the oldest part of which dates from the mid-15th century.

Among the town's cultural attractions, the **Langmatt Foundation** stands out. This was opened in 1990 on the Römerstrasse and comprises a renowned art collection which includes works by Pissarro, Renoir and Cézanne.

[i] Bahnhofstrasse 50

Leave via the Badstrasse, and cross the Schiefebrücke, following signs for Waldshut (Germany). Instead of crossing

BACK TO NATURE

Before the Albispass is reached, there is a forest region between the pass road and the village of Langnau am Albis to the east. This is now the site of the Langenberg Wildlife Park, where a variety of indigenous species – including wild boar – can be seen.

SCENIC ROUTES

There are two stages on the tour which offer excellent roadside views: the Albispass road provides a fine prospect south and east, and before Schaffhausen there is a stretch of riverside road between Kaiserstuhl and Glattfelden which is particularly pretty.

FOR HISTORY BUFFS

3 Between 1798 and 1803, when the French occupied the whole of the country, Aarau was capital of the short-lived Helvetian Republic – a Napoleon-inspired concept which was never accepted by the Swiss. When it lost its role as national capital, it assumed a more modest one as capital of the newly formed canton of Aargau.

SPECIAL TO...

5 Baden's thermal springs have the highest mineral content in the country and have long been a mecca for those seeking relief from rheumatic disorders.

Europe's most famous waterfall, the Rheinfall near Schaffhausen

FOR CHILDREN

5 The Schweizer Kindermuseum (Swiss Children's Museum) in Baden (29 Ölrainstrasse, near the station) is an intriguing toy museum with a fine collection of old wooden playthings.

9 Stein am Rhein has more than 500 antique dolls and kinetic figures in its Puppenmuseum, and there is a miniature steam railway by the boat landing stage.

RECOMMENDED TRIPS

8 Do not leave Schaffhausen without a visit to the spectacular Rheinfall near by. This is said to be the largest and most powerful waterfall in Europe, 23m high and 150m wide. Intrepid visitors can experience it at close hand by ascending a precarious-looking rock in the middle of the foaming waters, or standing on a platform at its base. It is also possible to bob about in a boat on the fringe of the heaving swell.

the Rhein (Rhine) and the border, follow road 7 east for Zurzach, keeping the Rhine on your left (27km/17 miles).

Zurzach, Aargau

6 Formerly the Celtic settlement of Tenedo and later the Roman fort of Tiberii, Zurzach was then an important bridgehead over the Rhine. Today it is better known for its hot springs, albeit ones which, uncharacteristically, the Romans apparently overlooked. There are some very handsome houses in the town's main street, mostly 17th- and 18th-century. The **church of St Verena** dates from the 10th century and contains the sarcophagus of the eponymous saint in a gloomy Gothic crypt under the choir. The **tower** is 13th- and 14th-century.

Head south on the minor country road to Tegerfelden and join road 17 for the villages of Endingen and Lengnau. About 3km (1.8 miles) beyond the latter take a left turn to Siglistorf and keep right for Kaiserstuhl (22km/13.5 miles).

Kaiserstuhl, Aargau

7 This peaceful little town has a particularly seductive medieval air about it, evoking the period when it enjoyed some strategic importance as a bridgehead on the Rhine. A significant part of the fortifications survive in the shape of two towers – the **Oberer Turm** and the **Storchenturm** – and part of the town wall. The 16th-century Gothic church of **St Katharina** shows later baroque influences, one of the few

buildings in the town to do so. The Hauptgasse has a number of fine old houses on it.

Continue east past Glattfelden, turning left on road 4 through Eglisau for Schaffhausen (about 30km/19 miles).

Schaffhausen

8 Almost completely encircled by the German border, the location of this beautiful old terraced town on the north of the Rhine did it no favours when stray American bombs killed 40 people in 1944 and destroyed a significant part of its ancient fabric. The fact that it still remains one of the best-preserved medieval towns in Europe, with a fabulous collection of historic buildings and sights, is testament to the remarkable wealth of its cultural inheritance. The majority of the town's 16th- to 18th-century buildings are found in the traffic-free alleys and streets of the characteristic Old Town and they are notable for their richly decorated oriel windows, frescos and reliefs. Among the most impressive is the famous **Haus zum Ritter** in the charming Vordergasse, with its magnificent Renaissance frescos painted in 1568 by the artist Tobias Stimmer (originals in the museum). Note also the unusually elaborate oriel on the late 16th-century **Haus zum Goldenen Ochsen** in the Vorstadt on the north side of the Old Town. Other beautiful old houses are simply too numerous to mention, but look out particularly for the old **guildhouses, fountains**, and the two fortified towers of **Obertorturm** (west) and **Schwabentorturm** (north). Dominating the whole is the outstanding surviving remnant of the original town fortifications – the **Munot** fortress, built between 1564 and 1585 on a vine-covered hill to the east. From the top of the distinctive tower there are excellent views of the town. To the west, in the heart of the Old Town, are two ancient churches: the **Münster**, a splendid Romanesque structure built about 1100, and **St Johann's**, founded about the same time but substantially rebuilt in the 15th century (although the tower dates from 1350). Note the famous **Hosanna Bell** in the chapel adjoining the Münster. Any walking tour of the town should also include the **Museum zu Allerheiligen** housed in the buildings of the former **Abbey of All Saints** behind the Münster. Among its comprehensive range of antiquities it has a celebrated prehistoric collection. In the cavernous confines of a former textile factory nearby is the **Hallen für Neue Kunst**, one of the country's leading museums of contemporary art.

i Vorstadt 12

Follow road 13 east for 19km (12 miles) to Stein am Rhein.

Stein am Rhein, Schaffhausen

9 Another lovely old medieval Rhineside town in an excellent state of preservation, Stein am Rhein has a splendid collection of

16th- and 17th-century half-timbered houses, exquisitely painted in characteristic fashion and dignified by decorative oriels. The compact Old Town nudges into a narrow ribbon of the Rhine where it leaves the Untersee, part of Bodensee (Lake Constance), and it is fair to observe that there is not a single building within it which could be described as ordinary. Particularly notable are the residential towers and gates of the 14th-century fortifications; the **Obertor, Untertor** and **Hexenturm** among a fine collection which includes parts of the old town wall. Note also the church and monastery of **St Georgen**, close to the bridge. Its buildings date from the 11th to the 16th centuries and the ensemble is said to be the best-preserved Benedictine monastery in German-speaking Switzerland. Note also the historical **museum** housed within the 16th-century **Rathaus**, which contains a valuable collection of banners and armaments, and the new **Museum Lindwurm** on the Unterstadt, a superb reconstruction of 'Bourgeois Life and Agriculture in the 19th century', housed in a 15th-century manor house.

ⓘ Oberstadt

*Continue on the lake road to Steckborn (see Tour 13) and then follow signposts to Frauenfeld (see Tour 13). Join the **N7** at Frauenfeld-West and drive west to join the **N1**, exiting at Winterthur-Töss, five junctions ahead (about 54km/34 miles).*

Intricate façade paintings depict contrasting scenes on a Gasthaus in Stein am Rhein's Rathausplatz

Winterthur, Zürich

10 This thriving industrial city is best known for its fine collection of art galleries and museums. The most celebrated is the 'Am Römerholz' Oskar Reinhart Collection, bequeathed to the town on the death of the hugely wealthy collector in 1965. Located in his former home on the Haldenstrasse, beautifully set in grounds overlooking the city, the collection includes works by Van Gogh, Cézanne, Manet and Renoir – among many others. In the city centre there is another collection inspired by the same collector, the **Oskar Reinhart Foundation** on Stadthausstrasse; it is equally illustrious but in less intimate surroundings. Art lovers should also visit the **Kunstmuseum**, with yet more astonishingly priceless Impressionist works. Winterthur also has a small Old Town, clustered around the 13th- to 17th-century **Stadtkirche** (town church). Among many handsome examples of 17th- and 18th-century burghers' houses, the baroque **Haus zur Geduld** stands out. Note also the nearby **Waaghaus**, a curious blend of Moorish and Gothic architecture built in 1503.

ⓘ Bahnhofplatz 12

*Return to Zürich on the **N1** (about 25km/15.5 miles).*

Zurich – Bremgarten 48 (30)
Bremgarten – Lenzburg 29 (18)
Lenzburg – Aarau 10 (6)
Aarau – Brugg 19 (12)
Brugg – Baden 10 (6)
Baden – Zurzach 27 (17)
Zurzach – Kaiserstuhl 22 (13.5)
Kaiserstuhl – Schaffhausen 30 (19)
Schaffhausen – Stein aim Rhein 19 (12)
Stein aim Rhein – Winterthur 54 (34)
Winterthur – Zurich 25 (15.5)

2 Days: 228km (141.5 miles)

BLACK LAKES & BATTLEMENTS

Bern (Berne) • Riggisberg • Schwarzsee
Fribourg • Bulle • Romont • Oron-le-Châtel
Moudon • Payerne • Avenches • Murten
Bern (Berne)

Some of the best-preserved fortified towns in Switzerland are found in the cantons of Fribourg and (northern) Vaud. Many of the historical landmarks on this tour demonstrate a mixture of Bernese, Burgundian and Savoyard influences – but those of the acquisitive rulers of Bern tend to prevail amongst the most outstanding examples of ancient buildings. But the Romans, as in so many parts of this country, have also inevitably left their mark – particularly in the ancient town of Avenches, once the capital of Roman Helvetia and still showing tangible evidence of a once thriving Roman city.

A child-loving ogre has a snack on the Kindlifresserbrunnen, one of Berne's many charming fountains

Take the old road south following blue road signs to Thun, through Wabern, bypassing Belp, then turning right to Riggisberg just after Kirchenthurnen (20km/12.5 miles).

Riggisberg, Bern (Berne)

1 The village is unremarkable except for the fact that it is home to one of the most celebrated museums in Switzerland. The **Abegg Foundation** (Abegg-Stiftung), in a modern building on the northern outskirts, was established by a wealthy industrialist and features a comprehensive collection of textiles and fabrics through the ages. The collection also includes Gothic furniture, Renaissance objects, Byzantine ivory carvings, Romanesque capitals and altars, and Egyptian sculptures. Open from the first Sunday in May to 1 November daily 14.00–17.15.

Take the road signposted Wattenwil out of the village, but branch right almost immediately for Rüti bei Riggisberg. From Rüti join the mountain road via Sangernboden and Zollhaus to Schwarzsee (33km/20 miles)

Schwarzsee, Fribourg

2 A sun terrace on one of the welcoming lakeside restaurants at this remote and tiny resort is a good place to break the journey. The name 'Schwarzsee' means black lake, and in certain conditions the ring of high tree-clad mountains around this pretty tarn lend a reflective sable gloss to its surface. The highest peaks are the 2,185m Kaiseregg and the 2,235m Schafberg, both to the southeast.

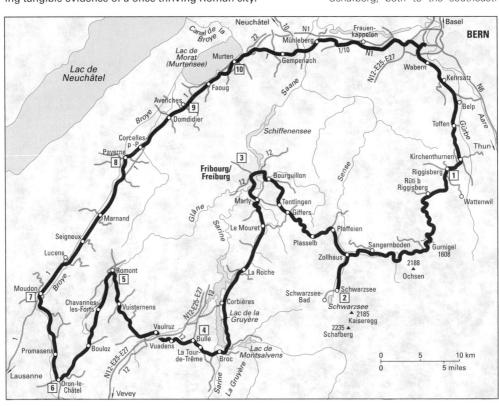

Return to Zollhaus and follow the country road via Plaffeien, Plasselb and Giffers. Bear right at Tentlingen to enter Fribourg from the southeast (26km/16 miles).

Fribourg

3 This cantonal capital is a city of curious ambiguity and considerable charm. The first characteristic arises from its inability to decide whether it is culturally and linguistically French or German inclined: the second, largely, from the resulting impasse. Over the centuries it has sought to resolve the matter by dividing itself into two distinct halves: the French-speaking community on the left bank of the River Sarine, and the German on the right bank. The **Old Town**, on the west bank, still shelters behind some of the original **fortified walls** built in the early medieval period. The cluster of ancient buildings is dwarfed by the substantial presence of **St Nicolas cathedral** and its magnificent 15th-century Gothic tower. This is the most impressive of the city's fine inheritance of churches. Dating from the 13th century, it has many remarkable features includ-ing a vivid 14th-century depic-tionof the Last Judgement above the main entrance, a 1433 group of sculpted figures in the chapel near the entrance, known as The Entombment, a world-famous 19th-century organ, and a late 15th-cent-ury font. A walk around the old quarter will reveal many fine old fountains, notably the **Fontaine St Georges** (1525) outside the splendid 16th-century **Hôtel de Ville** and the **Fontaine de Samson** (1547 – the original can be found in the museum) in the Place de Notre-Dame. Near by is the **Franciscan church** (Eglise des Cordeliers), largely rebuilt in the 18th century but dating from the mid-13th century. Inside is an extremely impressive altarpiece painted in 1480 by the 'Masters of

The view over the River Sarine of Fribourg's hilly Old Town from the Pont du Milieu

the Carnation' – two anonymous artists who habitually signed their works with a red and white carnation. More medieval and religious treasures can be found in the **Musée d'Art et d'Histoire** in an elegant hotel on the Rue de Morat.

[i] Square des Places 1

Take the minor road south through Marly, following blue signs for Bulle and Gruyères, to Corbières. From here follow the east bank of Lac de la Gruyère, following signs to Broc, then, shortly after, turn right to Bulle (31km/19 miles) .

Bulle, Fribourg

4 Best known for its cheeses, Bulle has managed to retain much of its traditional pastoral flavour with numerous cheese shops lining the main street. Its unusual museum, the **Musée Gruérien**, is located underground and is strongly influenced by the history of the cheese industry. The town has an imposing 13th-century **castle** with a large round keep, and near by is a 14th-century **Capuchin chapel**, formerly part of a long-vanished hospital.

Follow signs to Vuadens, cross under the autoroute and shortly after Vaulruz turn on to the country road through Vuisternens to Romont (18km/11 miles).

Romont, Fribourg

5 An imposingly located walled town, visible at a great distance on its conspicuous butte in the heart of the Glâne valley, Romont was chosen by Peter II of Savoy as a strategic military base in the mid-13th century. He built its fine **castle** and the **town walls**, much of which survive. The castle has since been altered, but strong Savoyard influences prevail. Inside its large courtyard is a huge **waterwheel** dating from 1772, and within the building itself is the national **Musée du Vitrail**, a museum devoted entirely to stained glass. Of the remaining town fortifications, the great 13th-century **Tour à Boyer**, which actually stands outside the town walls, is the most impressive. Less pugilistic architectural inheritances include the Gothic church of **Notre-Dame-de-l'Assomption**. Built by the House of Savoy in the 13th century, it was semi-destroyed by fire in 1434 and rebuilt with some notable works of stained glass. A number of charming 16th-century buildings survive throughout the town.

Take the road signposted to Chavannes-les-Forts and Oron-le-Châtel for 17km (10.5 miles).

Oron-le-Châtel, Vaud

6 Passing through this small village, you might well find time to stop at its imposing moated **castle**. Dominating the buildings beneath from a commanding hillside position, it was built at the end of the 12th century, sold to the Bernese in the mid-16th century and thence used as a bailiffs' residence until the early 1800s. Although it is heavily fortified, ironically it did very little fortifying and its exterior is thus little changed. Despite many alterations to the interior, the most recent changes taking place in the 18th century, the marvellous 15th-century Gothic **wood-panelled ceilings** remain in many of the rooms. A **museum** occupies much of the interior, and, for those of a more prurient disposition, the dungeons and torture chamber are also open to visitors.

Take the road north to Moudon for 12km (8 miles).

Moudon, Vaud

7 Formerly the important Roman staging post of Minnodunum,

Moudon's roots actually go back to Celtic times. This is a delightful little town with a surprising wealth of architectural treasures offering a convincing glimpse of history. Steep cobbled streets and overhanging roofs in the largely unspoilt **Quartier du Bourg** conspire to create a seductive medieval atmosphere, and it is not difficult to evoke images of the prosperous period when the town was one of the most important jewels in the Savoy crown. Only the **Tour de Broye** (1120) has survived from the original fortifications, but the 15th-century bell tower of the Gothic church of **St Etienne** was once part of the town walls. The largely 15th-century church interior is notable for its fine carved choir stalls (1502) and various frescos painted between the 13th and 17th centuries. The **Rue de Château** offers the most intriguing selection of buildings, with tiny little dolls' houses abutting the north wall, imposing merchants' houses such as the 14th-century **Maison d'Arnay**, with its massive 17th-century protruding roof, and the solid-looking **Château de Rochefort**, now the town's **museum**. Look out also for the pleasing 16th-century **fountain** adjacent to the museum. Other late Gothic houses are found throughout the town.

Return to road 1, following signs to Payerne and Bern (Berne). Note the magnificent 13th-century castle high above Lucens after 6km (4 miles) and continue to Payerne, turning off road 1 for the town (16km/10 miles).

Payerne, Vaud

8 This old Roman town is home to what is generally acknowledged to be among the most impressive Romanesque churches in Europe.

The remarkably well-preserved 1st-century Roman Amphitheatre in the former Helvetian capital of Avenches

Formerly part of a Benedictine monastery, the 11th-century **abbey church of Notre-Dame** was used as a barn from the mid-16th century until its restoration in 1926. Notwithstanding this unlikely role, its interior has now reassumed much of what must have been its original appearance. An inspiring blend of plainness and simple elegance lends it a somewhat austere air, but the golden quality of the light reflected from the yellow and grey sandstone walls more than compensates for the absence of ornamentation. The church is otherwise notable for its barrel-vaulted, pillared nave and the unusual block capitals on the pillars in the transept. Adjoining the south wall of the church is a 16th-century **chapter house** – the only other surviving building of the original monastery which was closed during the Reformation. Also close to the abbey church is the **Protestant parish church** of the same name, built between the 14th and 16th centuries. There is a painting of the Shroud of Christ (16th-century) in the southern aisle. Next door is the late **Gothic Law Court** (1571) and, also close by, two interesting **fountains** with figures dating from the mid-16th century. Some of the town's original fortifications remain, notably four **towers** which made up part of the town walls in the 13th and 14th centuries.

i Hôtel de Ville (Town Hall)

Return to road 1 and head for Avenches (12km/8 miles).

Avenches, Vaud

9 The home of Switzerland's most impressive **amphitheatre**, this little hill town was once the capital of Roman Helvetia. In the 1st century, Aventicum (as it then was) was considerably larger than it is today with a population ten times its present number and a massive 6km-long, 7m-high wall which encircled its hillsite. Notwithstanding the extensive fortifications, the town was destroyed around 259 by marauding Germanic tribes, and its fortunes progressively dwindled until it became the seat of a Bernese governor in the 16th century. Although there are many visible remains from the Roman period (despite the best efforts of local quarrymen to recycle the stone from the 16th to the late 19th century), the town is predominantly medieval in appearance. But much of the original town wall is still intact, including a number of the integral semi-circular observation towers. One of these, the **Tornallaz**, has been extensively but not altogether sympathetically restored. Much of the medieval fortifications have also survived – notably an 11th-century **tower** built into the bank of the amphitheatre over its main entrance. This now houses the **Roman museum**. Elsewhere in the town are some fine 14th- to 17th-century buildings, including the Renaissance-style **château** of 1565 in the marketplace (with aviation museum). Note also the 11th-century church of **Ste Marie-Madeleine**, altered in 1709.

Return to road 1 for 9km (5.5 miles) to Murten.

Murten, Fribourg

10 A gem of an ancient walled town, overlooking the lake of the same name, which has laudably preserved its enchanting medieval flavour. It is one of the few examples of its type where the **rampart walks** are freely accessible, giving spectacular views across the crooked rooftops to the lake below.

The Kadettenmusik youth band of Murten

Built between the 12th and 15th centuries, the distinctively roofed walls are in a remarkable state of preservation. Interspersed at regular intervals by 12 fortified **towers**, they were also cut by two main gates – one of which, the **Berntor**, is a splendid baroque reconstruction dating from 1777. Its **clocktower** bears one of the oldest timepieces in Switzerland. Leading west from the Berntor is the picturesque **Hauptgasse**, with its beautiful arcaded walks dating from the 16th century and many tall shuttered houses with late Gothic façades. On the Old Town's western tip is the 13th-century **castle**, built by Peter of Savoy. Beneath it is the old late 16th-century **mill** which now serves as the town's **museum**. Other interesting buildings include the late 15th-century **French church**, the 18th-century **German church** (with paintings of 1682), and the Gothic **Rübenloch** house on Hauptgasse.

i Schlossgasse 5

Stay on road 1, following blue signs for Bern (Berne). Cross over the autoroute, continue on road 1 and then join the autoroute at Frauenkappelen to enter the city. Exit the autoroute at Bern-Forshau or Bern Neufeld (28km/17.5 miles).

Bern – Riggisberg 20 (12.5)
Riggisberg – Schwarzsee 33 (20)
Schwarzsee – Fribourg 26 (16)
Fribourg – Bulle 31 (19)
Bulle – Romont 18 (11)
Romont – Oron-le-Châtel 17 (10.5)
Oron-le-Châtel – Moudon 12 (8)
Moudon – Payerne 22 (13.5)
Payerne – Avenches 12 (8)
Avenches – Murten 9 (5.5)
Murten – Bern 28 (17.5)

FOR HISTORY BUFFS

10 In 1476 the famous **Battle of Murten** took place between the Burgundians and the early Swiss Confederates. The former, who had been bombarding the town walls for the better part of two weeks, were surprised by a relief force from the Berne garrison which swept down from the high ground behind them. Armed with culverins, a rudimentary portable firearm, the Swiss left more than 10,000 Burgundians dead on the battlefield.

THE BERNESE OBERLAND

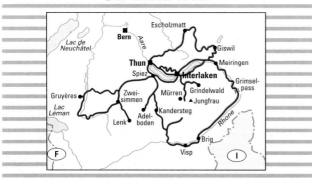

The Bernese Oberland constitutes more than two-thirds of the canton of Bern (Berne). The southern flanks of the highest of the Bernese Alps form part of the neighbouring canton of Valais, but the great peaks of the Jungfrau, Eiger, Mönch and Finsteraarhorn are all part of the Oberland. This strikingly beautiful mountain region has played a seminal role in the development of the winter sports and climbing industries, and some of the world's most famous skiing and mountaineering resorts are found here – Grindelwald, Wengen and Mürren foremost among them. Any tour of the Swiss Alps would be incomplete without visiting all three, not only because of their superb settings, but because of the one outstanding individual attraction that each possesses. At Mürren it is the Piz Gloria revolving restaurant on the summit of the Schilthorn, offering one of the finest Alpine pamoramas in the world; in Wengen it is the trip by cogwheel railway to Kleine Scheidegg, and from there through a tunnel behind the north face of the Eiger to the Jungfraujoch; in Grindelwald, the 'glacier village', it is the two huge glaciers which hang forbiddingly above the village (not to mention the forbidding north face of the Eiger).

Below this distinguished triumvirate of resorts is Interlaken, delightfully set between the two lakes of Thun and Brienz and traditionally (and understandably) one of the country's most popular holiday destinations. But the nearby town of Thun, on the west bank of the splendid lake of the same name, is a more than worthy rival. On Lake Thun (the Thuner See) and Lake Brienz (Brienzer See) are found a series of charming lakeside towns and villages; notable among the former are Spiez and Oberhofen, both renowned for their magnificent medieval castles. At the eastern end of the Lake Brienz, the pleasant old town of Brienz is not only a well-equipped holiday resort with a fine lakeside promenade, but also one of the most famous centres of wood carving in the world.

The thunder of waterfalls is a recurring feature throughout much of the Bernese Oberland, and one of them, the Giessbachfälle, discharges spectacularly into the lake opposite the town. Other captivating examples of this natural wonder include the famous Reichenbach Falls (Reichenbachfälle), close by in the precipitous Haslital (where Sherlock Holmes and Moriarty met their fictional watery deaths), and the Engstligen Falls (Engstligenfälle) near the old ski resort of Adelboden. Mountain lakes are another compelling feature of the region and there can be few more beautiful than the Öschinensee above the traditional resort of Kandersteg.

Interlaken

This elegant resort is celebrated for its wide tree-lined boulevards, stately Victorian hotels, tranquil waterscapes, flower gardens and – most memorably – dramatic mountain views of the Jungfrau massif. It was once famously dismissed by the 19th-century British travel writer John Murray as 'a sort of Swiss Margate', so popular had it become with English visitors.

Formerly known as Aaremühle because of its position on the banks of the River Aare, the town traces its origins to the founding of an Augustinian monastery in the early 12th century. All that remains of that structure, destroyed in the Reformation, are the east walk of the 1445 cloister, the chapter house and the 13th-century Gothic chancel of the present St Mary's church. This cluster of historic buildings is located on the east side of one of the town's showpieces, the massive 'meadow' of neatly manicured lawns and colourful flowerbeds known as the Höhematte. This is bordered to the north by the Höheweg, a wide and shady avenue lined by palatial hotels. In the built-up section between the Höheweg and the river is the famous pavilion-style Kursaal, a casino of 1859 with a splendid flower-clock in the midst of its landscaped gardens.

Thun

Partly built on an island between two branches of the Aare river, the

The fairy tale outline of the 12th-century Thun Castle is framed by a dramatic mountain backdrop

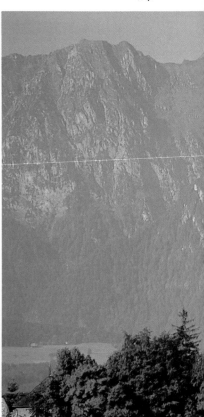

oldest quarter of this ancient Celtic settlement is sited on the east bank at the foot of a steep hillock known as the Schlossberg. The town's name is said to derive from the Celtic 'dunum', meaning fortified hill, although whatever ancient hilltop fortifications there might have been were long ago concealed by the formidable 12th-century castle which now dominates the town. The hipped roof, and various other additions, date from the 15th century but the four distinctive corner turrets pre-date them and are nearer to the keep in age. The chambers below are now home to a museum, exhibiting 14th- and 15th-century tapestries and a miscellaneous collection of uniforms, armour, weapons, furniture and ceramics. A flight of covered steps lead down to the Rathausplatz, with a central fountain and a handsome arcaded town hall of 1589, rebuilt in 1685. Arcades are also a distinguishing feature of the bustling Obere Hauptgasse which leads southeast from the square beneath the castle. An even more striking feature of this old street is the remarkable arrangement of footways actually built over the shops. From the top of the street there are more covered steps up to the church of St Mauritius, a baroque structure founded in the 10th century but dating mostly (except for the 14th-century octagonal tower) from 1738. There are two excellent parks in Thun which are worth exploring. The Jakobshübeli, east of the old quarter and a short distance beyond the town casino (Kursaal), is a hilly belvedere with spectacular views south towards the Oberland.

A picturesque roofed bridge spans the Aare river in Interlaken

On the west bank of the river is the suburb of Scherzligen, famous for its Romanesque church of St Maria, first mentioned in the 8th century but with a choir and tower dating from the 14th. The wall paintings were produced in the mid-15th century. Just beyond the church is the Schadau Park, laid out in the mid-19th century around the imposing Schloss Schadau of the same period. In an adjacent building there is a remarkable circular picture, on a strip of linen about 40m long, which depicts Thun around the time of the early 19th century.

LAKES, PEAKS AND PASTURES

Thun • Oberhofen • Spiez • Erlenbach
Zweisimmen • Lenk • Gruyères • Thun

Southwest of Thuner See (Lake Thun) the countryside offers intriguing juxtapositions of glacial scenery, rolling green pastures, deep valleys and high mountain passes. This tour traverses the cantons of Bern (Berne), Vaud and Fribourg and passes through the regions known as the Bernese Oberland, the Simmental, the Saanenland, the Pays d'Enhaut and the famous cheese area of Gruyère. At its start, it will also take you through one of the most fashionable areas of this part of Switzerland, the so-called Bernese Riviera between Thun and Interlaken. Few tours in this guide offer a such a large variety of scenery.

Leave Thun on the lakeside road to Interlaken. Oberhofen is about 5km (3 miles).

Oberhofen, Bern (Berne)

1 A popular bathing and sailing resort, the old village of Oberhofen is also the home of a picturesque medieval castle set amidst landscaped gardens on the lakeside. The oldest section is the 12th-century keep, but its present baroque

An ancient ivy-clad boathouse flies the Swiss flag over the placid surface of Lake Thun

appearance dates largely from the 17th century. Its chapel is 15th-century, with contemporary murals and an organ of 1800 transported from the village of Einigen across the lake. The castle is now a branch of the Bernese Historical Museum and has an interesting collection of period furniture, toys and musical instruments. There are delightful park walks along the shore.

Continue along the 'Bernese Riviera' in the direction of Interlaken, avoiding the town centre by following the green road signs to Luzern (N8). Once on the autobahn, follow green signs to Spiez and Thun (which appear very quickly), and you will shortly find yourself on the lakeside road (number 6/11) on the south bank of Lake Thun. Stay on this road through Faulensee to reach Spiez (about 35km/22 miles).

Spiez, Berne

2 This small resort town, on the south bank of Lake Thun, has a number of features to recommend it. Not least of them is its picturesque lakeside location in a natural amphitheatre at the foot of the brooding 2,362m pyramid of the Niesen. It is also notable for two important architectural works. The imposing 12th-century lakeside castle is a picturesque medieval pile of contrasting styles. Successively owned by different families, it has

The turrets and towers of Oberhofen Castle are reflected in the rippling waters of Lake Thun

been enlarged and much added to over the centuries. Today it houses a splendid **museum** containing some fine period furniture and armaments. Note particularly the low-beamed Bubenberghalle and the wine cellar. Directly under the castle walls is a shady **esplanade**, a pleasant place for a reflective stroll overlooking the lake. In the small garden under the castle walls is a statue of Adrian von Bubenberg, a resplendent figure in medieval battledress who was one of its first owners. Just beyond is the beautiful late 10th-century Romanesque **Schlosskirche of St Kolumban** containing a unique oval crypt and several notable frescos of curious origin. The spire is early 17th-century (restored in 1950), but the **tower** is thought to date back to the 8th century. Sitting somewhat forlornly in the churchyard is an old bell from the tower.

The village of Faulensee am Thuner See (Lake Thun)

> *Take the old road (number 11) out of Spiez, signposted Jaunpass, and follow it until Erlenbach (about 10km/6 miles).*

Erlenbach, Berne

3 A pretty old hillside village typical of the best of rural canton Berne and the Nieder-Simmental (lower Simmental), Erlenbach offers a pleasing glimpse into the authentic article. Many of the mid-18th-century timber houses here have distinctive saddleback roofs and colourful façades. The **10th-century church** (much altered) is slightly elevated above the village, accessed by a covered wooden stairway off the Dorfstrasse. Inside is a surprisingly extensive collection of murals – mostly dating from the 15th century. Erlenbach also has the distinction of providing access via foot or two-stage cable car to the 2,190m summit of the Stockhorn. This affords one of the best views in the Bernese Oberland, with almost the entire expanse of Lake Thun visible to the east, and the lower Simmental to the south.

> *Continue on the same road, branching left at Reidenbach to*

Zweisimmen, for about 24km (15miles).

Zweisimmen, Berne

4 Another pretty old village, Zweisimmen is probably better known as an overspill location for Gstaad (with which it shares its skiing area) than as the nominal capital of the Simmental. The church of **St Maria** is a mid-15th-century Gothic construction, notable for its wooden ceiling, stained glass and some fine frescos inside and out. On the west wall are interesting 15th-century representations of St George and the Dragon, and St Christopher. There is a small local **museum** in the old schoolhouse, and access by foot or mountain lift to the summit of the 2,079m Rinderberg which offers predictably fine views of this part of the Oberland. Still an important agricultural and market centre, Zweisimmen has many richly decorated timber chalets typical of the Simmental.

> *Take the valley road south, signposted Lenk, for about 13km (8 miles).*

SCENIC ROUTES

There are three stretches of road on this tour which typify the remarkably contrasting nature of Swiss scenery. The 'Bernese Riviera' route between Thun and Interlaken is a beautiful lakeside drive with a dramatic mountain backcloth; the Pays d'Enhaut between Rougemont and Montbovon is a pastoral region of exceptional beauty, and the Jaunpass road between Broc and Reidenbach manages to combine the key Alpine ingredients of lakes, peaks and pastures.

RECOMMENDED WALK

3 It takes about four hours to ascend the Stockhorn by foot – considerably less by mountain lift. If your knees are up to a steep but relatively easy descent of two hours or so, choose one of the marked paths past either of the two mountain tarns back to Erlenbach.

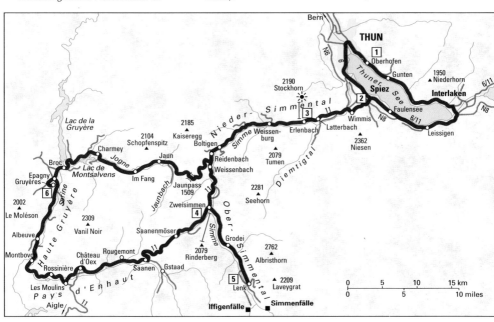

FOR HISTORY BUFFS

5 Strategically situated beneath the Rawil pass, on the Berne/Valais canton border, Lenk was often caught up in inter-cantonal skirmishing. Legend recounts that on one occasion in the 15th century the women of the village successfully repelled an attack by men of the Valais. In recognition of their valour, women have since been allowed the irrevocable right to leave the church before their menfolk.

BACK TO NATURE

5 One of Lenk's most enduring summer attractions is the Leiterli Alpine Flower Trail from the top of the Betelberg chairlift. Follow the green markings through fields of Alpine roses, and over 100 more indigenous mountain flowers. Lenk also has its own small nature reserve on the 'Lenkersee' a ten-minute walk outside the village centre. Here you will see a variety of waterbirds – including resident families of swans.

FOR CHILDREN

6 Wax museums are a perennial favourite with children, and the quaint little Wax Museum in Gruyères should not disappoint them. Located in the 12th-century tower of **Chupia-Bârba**, they may not recognise any of the 'famous' Swiss figures, but their original costumes are definitely worth a look.

SPECIAL TO...

6 Gruyère cheese is one of the most celebrated (and pungent) of Swiss cheeses – requiring substantially more milk than most other varieties. The dairy near the station in the town of Gruyères allows you to watch the most interesting phases of the production process – especially when the cheese is made into the familiar 'wheel'.

Lenk, Berne

5 For aficionados of waterfalls, this well-sited, all-year mountain resort is as good a place as any to appreciate them. The Iffigenfälle (**Iffigen Falls**) cascade for over 130m in the Pöschenried valley, 3km south of the village, and the Simmenfälle (**Simme Falls**) – shorter but more powerful – are a little further southeast. Both necessitate short walks from car parking areas where there are restaurants. The best vantage point for the Iffigen Falls is about 20 minutes by foot up a steep track; the Simme Falls, thundering down the northern face of the bulky 3,243m Wildstrubel, are only about five minutes from the car park and restaurant. The village of Lenk itself is a relatively successful blend of the old and new, with a cluster of colourfully decorated flower-decked chalets providing a pleasing foreground to the rugged glacial scenery. A century ago the town was a popular spa centre, famed for its sulphur springs. Today it is better known as a skiing and mountaineering centre (although it is still a popular health resort), and it shares its large skiing area with the village of Adelboden over the 2,209m peak of Laveygrat to the east. Lenk has a fully equipped sports centre and a variety of summer activities on offer.

Return to Zweisimmen and drive through the Saanenland, via Saanen (see Tour 25), into the pastoral Pays d'Enhaut via the resort of Château d'Oex (see Tour 25). Turn right at Les Moulins, through the old village of Rossinière (home to the painter Bathus and his 'Grand Chalet'), and into Haute-Gruyère. The town of Gruyères is reached after a total drive of 60km (37 miles).

Gruyères, Fribourg

6 Once an impregnable fortress town, never taken in battle, today Gruyères' sturdy walls are breached daily by thousands of visitors who throng its pretty cobbled streets and at times threaten to engulf it.

Diners enjoy a traditional fondue and a glass of wine in the fortress town of Gruyères

Founded in the 13th century by Peter II of Savoy, it is acknowledged to be one of the most beautiful medieval fortified towns in Europe. Occupying a hilltop site in one of the most scenic parts of the Sarine valley, its fairy-tale appearance belies the fact that it was once a feudal stronghold of great strategic importance. The main street, lined by fine 15th- to 17th-century Gothic and Renaissance houses which are protected as national monuments, leads up to the picturesque, typically Savoyard **Château de Gruyères** dating from the 12th century (but mostly 15th-century in its existing form). In the courtyard is a 14th-century **chapel** with some interesting stained glass and in the château itself there is a **museum** with a good collection – the highlight of which are three 15th-century **mourning robes**, relics of the Battle of Murten (1476) and once worn by the Knights of the Golden Fleece. From the castle's terrace there are spectacular views south and east. Back in the main street note the 14th-century **Maison de Chalamala**, formerly the home of the court jester to the Counts of Gruyère and one of the oldest buildings in the town.

Continue a short distance to Epagny, then follow the signs to Broc. Here, follow signs for the Jaunpass, crossing it and descending once more into the lower Simmental. Continue to the centre of Spiez and then take the old lakeside road (no 6) back into Thun. The total distance from Gruyères is 74km (46 miles).

Thun – Oberhofen 5 (3)
Oberhofen – Spiez 35 (22)
Spiez – Erlenbach 10 (6)
Erlenbach – Zweisimmen 24 (15)
Zweisimmen – Lenk 13 (8)
Lenk – Gruyères 60 (37)
Gruyères – Thun 74 (46)

2 days: 276.5km (171.5 miles)

The serpentine meanderings of the Grimsel and Furka pass roads, bisected by the Rhône river

ℹ️ Höheweg

Cross the river and take the Brienzstrasse 6/11 east along the north bank to Brienz (22km/13.5 miles).

Brienz, Bern (Berne)

1 One of the most attractive small lakeside towns in the region, Brienz is among the leading centres of **wood carving** in the country and many of the traditional timber buildings throughout the town's long main street are in some way connected with the craft. If you want an authentic hand-carved cuckoo-clock this is the place to get it, although Brienz woodcarvers would doubtless prefer to be better known for the quality of their furnishings and stringed musical instruments, particularly violins. There is a celebrated **school** here which is dedicated to teaching the skills involved in making the latter. The **church** on the hill on the western fringe of the village dates from the 12th century, although altered in the 16th, and is notable for its exterior paintings, particularly the depiction of St Christopher who maintains a watchful eye on the lake. The charming walk along the lakeside promenade, linking the two boat stations at either end of the village, has wooden sculptures of animals at various points. There are also swings and see-saws for children.

A couple of kilometres across the water are the spectacular **Giessbachfälle** (Giessbach Falls)

THE OBERLAND RING

Interlaken • Brienz • Meiringen
Lötschental • Kandersteg • Adelboden
Interlaken

This round tour takes in a variety of dramatic land and water-scapes, encircling the Berner Alpen (Bernese Alps) and actually passing beneath them on the return north through the Lötschberg train tunnel. Starting along the north bank of the beautiful Brienzer See (Lake Brienz), the route traverses some of the most spectacular valleys in the Alps. First climbing the spectacular Haslital to the eerie Grimselpass, it descends the Goms (Rhône valley) and then enters the wild and remote Lötschental before emerging from the tunnel at the head of the Kandertal. Finally, a brief diversion from the circuit takes you up the cataract-streaked Engstligental to Adelboden.

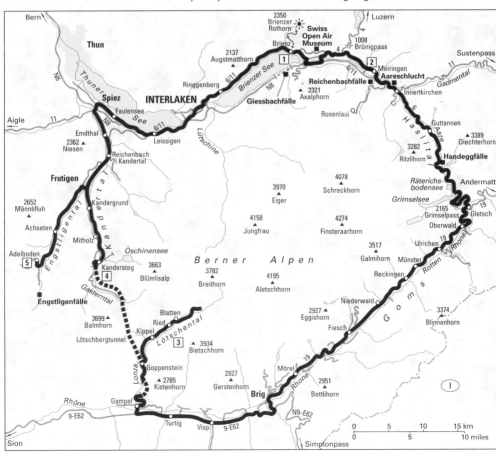

RECOMMENDED TRIPS

1 Of the many marvellous panoramas on offer in this part of the country, few are as pleasing as that from the summit of the 2,350m Brienzer Rothorn. Accessible by rack railway from the eastern end of Brienz (or cable from the Glaubenbüelen pass road to the north), the views of Lake Brienz (Brienzer See) and the Bernese Alps are well worth a fare almost as steep as the gradient.

3 The beautiful turquoise-green Öschinensee (Lake Öschinen), set in a natural amphitheatre of towering mountains, is reached by a combination of foot and chair-lift (about half an hour) from the resort of Kandersteg. There are delightful walks, beneath waterfalls and glittering glaciers, around the lake and it is possible to make the easy descent through the woods in about an hour.

FOR HISTORY BUFFS

2 The village of Ballenberg, just outside Brienz, is home to one of the most interesting museums in the country. The Swiss Open-Air Museum offers an intriguing glimpse into Swiss lifestyle and history throughout an attractive wooded park of 50 hectares (over 100 acres). Buildings from all over the country have been dismantled, transported and re-erected here – complete with traditional furnishings and fittings. In some cases, even their surroundings have been faithfully reproduced.

BACK TO NATURE

2 The 12km drive south of Meiringen, up the narrow **Rosenlaui** valley, offers a fascinating insight into the power of glacial movement. Close to the tiny climbing centre of Rosenlaui are the wild and rugged Glacier Gorges (Gletscherschlucht), great troughs in the rock gouged out by a moving sea of ice. Expect to do a little walking to see the best of this natural wonder, which is also accessible by foot (four hours including the return journey) on a well-marked path from the Reichenbach Falls (Reichenbachfälle).

A traditional paddle-steamer plies the distinctive turquoise waters of Lake Brienz

cascading through a deep wooded cleft in the 2,321m Axalphorn – and emptying into the lake in a turbulent fizz. Accessible by funicular from a platform by the lake, the pretty Giessbachsee station can be reached by car or boat. There is another, slimmer cascade which descends in a glittering streak down the mountainside behind Brienz.

☐ Hauptstrasse

Continue around the lake, cross the river, and join the N8 briefly until the turn-off for the Brünigpass. Re-cross the river and climb this road until the turn-off right to Meiringen (about 17km/10.5 miles).

Meiringen, Berne

2 Legend records that the 'meringue' was invented in this small town when Napoleon was passing through in the 1790s. Apparently the diminutive Corsican favourably received the glutinous puffballs which now carry the town's name. Meiringen is the main excursion centre for the part of the Oberland known as the **Haslital**, famous for its various natural phenomena including the **Reichenbach Falls** (Reichenbachfälle) and the eerie **Aare Gorges** (Aareschlucht). The former (reached by funicular from the outskirts of the town) were immortalised in the late 19th century when Sherlock Holmes and Moriarty plunged into the foaming waters after Sir Arthur Conan Doyle decided to kill off his fictional detective; there is now a museum in the town devoted to Holmes. The turbulent milky green waters of the Aare Gorges received no such helpful publicity, but are no less celebrated none the less.

Such is the appeal of Holmes that a museum featuring an accurate reconstruction of his Baker Street living room has opened in Meiringen's former English church. Although many of the town's buildings were destroyed in two serious 19th-century fires, the church of St **Michael** (rebuilt in 1684) survived, along with a number of traditional wooden houses. The detached

Romanesque **tower** of the church was built in 1351 and is the oldest dated in the canton.

Drive up the Haslital, following signs to Grimselpass on road 6. At Gletsch (see Tour 22), take road 19 to Brig (see Tour 20) via Goms valley (see Tour 22). Drive on through Visp (see Tour 22) for about 10km, then take the right exit to Lötschbergtunnel and Goppenstein. Before boarding the train take the diversion up the Lötschental. The total distance from Meiringen is about 132km (82 miles).

Lötschental, Valais

3 This is a wild and remote valley, approximately 13km in length, sheltering beneath the Jungfrau

A cattleshed overlooks the Oeschinensee, arguably Switzerland's most beautiful mountain lake

massif on the northern side of the Rhône trench. Largely isolated from the modern world until the early part of this century (when the Lötschbergtunnel opened at its mouth), the small communities which comprise it have retained much of their original identity. Kippel is the largest village of the valley and stands in the midst of some quite wonderful scenery. Its picturesque group of painted chalets and barns are clustered around the old church of **St Martin** (rebuilt in 1779) and it has a small **museum** which documents the traditions and folklore of this part of the Valais. Ried and Blatten, both similarly pleasing, are the two other hamlets of any appreciable size in this rugged mountain furrow.

Return to Goppenstein and drive the car on to the train for the 14.5km (9 miles) journey through the Lötschbergtunnel. Trains leave every half an hour, and no booking is necessary.

Kandersteg, Berne
4 At the northern end of the Lötschberg rail tunnel (opened in 1912), Kandersteg is a leading climbing and winter sports centre at the head of the Kandertal and at the foot of the imposing glacier-streaked Blümlisalp chain. It is a rambling, attractive old village consisting of one leafy street about 3km long, with many colourful wooden chalets and farm buildings (one dating from 1556). Note also the huge overhanging saddleback roof of the old section of the **Hotel Ritter** (1789) in the town's centre, and the **Rüedihus** restaurant – a quaint blackwood chalet of 1753 set alone amidst fields on the southern perimeter. One of Kandersteg's most enduring attractions is the dramatic nature of the scenery which surrounds it and its convenience as an excursion base for many fine walks, particularly around the spectacular Lake Öschinen (Öschinensee) – arguably the most beautiful mountain lake in the country.

Drive down the lovely Kandertal to Frutigen, taking the turning here up the equally impressive Engstligental to Adelboden (28km/17.5 miles).

Adelboden, Berne
5 This pretty old village lies near the head · of the thickly wooded Engstligental on a sunny terrace above the west bank of the Engstligen. Since its link with the nearby sports and spa town of Lenk it has become increasingly popular with skiing and winter sports enthusiasts. The long main thoroughfare retains an authentic Alpine feel with many old timber buildings leaning into the street. The village **church** dates from 1433 and has a 15th-century painting of the Last Judgement still tenaciously adorning the exterior south wall. The churchyard gates were presented by Allied servicemen interned here from 1943–45. Near by, below the Engstligenalp, are the impressive Engstligenfälle (**Engstligen Falls**) – two silvery spumes of about 150m.

Return to Interlaken via the main valley road to Spiez, then take the old lakeside road 6/11 (about 50km/31 miles).

Interlaken – Brienz 22 (13.5)
Brienz – Meiringen 17 (10.5)
Meiringen – Lötschental 132 (82)
Lötschental – Kandersteg 27.5 (17)
Kandersteg – Adelboden 28 (17.5)
Adelboden – Interlaken 50 (31)

SCENIC DRIVES

2 The road south from Meiringen, up the beautiful Haslital, leads to the ancient Grimselpass. After the village of Guttannen, as the valley walls close in and take on a curiously polished and greenish hue, look out for the impressive Handegg Falls (Handeggfälle) near the village of the same name. The pass itself, a bleak and desolate place with a Hospiz, lies at an altitude of 2,165m and offers magnificent views.

FOR HISTORY BUFFS

2 Although the Grimselpass has been used as a mountain crossing for millennia, the road was not built until 1895. A century before, the pass – more specifically, the gloomy Totensee lake just below it – was the scene of massive slaughter when the Austrian and French forces clashed here during the Napoleonic campaign. The name of the disturbing, khaki-coloured patch of water means 'Lake of the Dead'.

SPECIAL TO...

3 Every year on the Sunday following Corpus Christi, a celebrated religious festival takes place in the village of Kippel. Local participants, known as the 'Grenadiers of God', don colourful and exotic costumes and march through the streets to the church. Various other festivities accompany the procession.

FOR CHILDREN

3 The journey by motor rail through the Lötschbergtunnel is as exciting as any ghost train. Cars are driven on to what looks like a cattle wagon, following strict instructions to engage first gear and apply handbrakes, and the train then sets off into the black hole beneath the Lötschenpass. Do not expect to see much during the 20-minute journey apart from the lights of oncoming trains shortly before they thunder unnervingly past within inches. And do not attempt to get out of your car at any stage.

2 to 3 days: 204km (126.5 miles)

IN THE SHADOW OF THE JUNGFRAU

Interlaken • Unterseen • Beatenberg
Emmental and Entlebuch • Grindelwald
Lauterbrunnen • Mürren • Wengen
Interlaken

Making qualitative comparisons between different configu-rations of large lumps of rock is not easy, but those who have viewed the awesome spectacle of the Jungfrau massif are generally impressed enough to observe that it has few rivals on this continent. The triumvirate of the Jungfrau (4,158m), the Mönch (4,099m) and the Eiger (3,970m) are the highest peaks of the Bernese Oberland and their formidable presence states unequivocally why this region is acknowl-edged to be the jewel in the glittering crown of Switzerland's landscape. Their names translate, respectively, as the Young Girl, the Monk and the Ogre, and the presence of the Mönch is supposed to guard the Jungfrau from the dishonourable inten-tions of the Eiger (although, in fairness, she looks big enough to take care of herself). These mountains are viewed with vary-ing degrees of impact from a number of points on this tour, and to particularly fine advantage from the resort of Beatenberg across Thuner See (Lake Thun). From here you will drive along one of the country's few remaining toll roads, a delightfully forested track with magnificent views. And to prove that the Bernese Oberland does not have a monopoly on superb scenery, you will have an opportunity to admire one of the most picturesque pastoral regions of Switzerland – the Upper Emmental – before returning to the Oberland via the Panoramastrasse between the Entlebuch valley and Sarnersee (Lake Sarner). (Note that the resorts of Mürren and Wengen are not accessible by car.)

Sun-dappled hay fields on a mountainside near Grindelwald

ⓘ Höheweg 37

From Interlaken cross the Aare river to Unterseen, 1km (0.6 mile).

Unterseen, Bern (Berne)

1 This small village, just over the river from Interlaken, has determinedly maintained its character despite immediate proximity to its larger neighbour. Oddly enough, its German name means exactly the same as the Latin 'Interlaken', or 'between the lakes'. The tacit independence continues a centuries-old tradition dating from the time when the people of the vil-lage refused to pay homage to the Augustinian monks over the water. Many attractive buildings can be found here. They include a 15th-cen-tury Gothic **church** (rebuilt in 1674) and a jumble of 17th- and 18th-cen-tury timber houses with latticed win-dows. The regional **museum** is located here in a fine 17th-century building.

Follow signs to Beatenberg for 12km (8 miles).

Beatenberg, Berne

2 Beatenberg is a stately and well-sited village straggling for about 5km along the southern slope of the Güggisgrat. Fully equipped as a summer resort, with all the ameni-ties visitors might expect, perhaps its most obvious appeal is the splen-did view across Lake Thun to the Jungfrau massif. This prospect is actually surpassed by a trip by chair-lift to the summit of the 1,950m Niederhorn, from where a superb panorama of the entire Bernese Oberland awaits. In clear weather it is also possible to see Mont Blanc behind the Wildhorn's shoulder. The

Brightly painted shutters and ubiquitous cowbells adorn the façade of the Hotel Luegibruggli in Beatenberg

descent by foot, through forest and moorland, and back takes about an hour and a half.

ⓘ Hauptstrasse

There is a charge for a permit to use the private toll road ahead to Sigriswil, which can be bought from the tourist office or the Tea Room Primeli. Drive past the station under the barrier, through the secluded Justistal, and via the little resort of Sigriswil to Thun. Note that this road is closed from 8.30am to 4.30pm on Sundays, in which case you will need to return via the north bank of Lake Thun (24km/15 miles).
From Thun, take the road signposted Luzern (Lucerne) and Schallenberg through Steffisburg,

The infamous north face of the Eiger looms over chalets on the outskirts of the mountain village of Grindelwald

via Schallenberg and Schangnau to Marbach (26km/16 miles). At Wiggen turn right following signs to Lucerne, through Escholzmatt, turning right again just before Schüpfheim on the 'Panoramastrasse' for Flühli, Sörenberg and then Giswil 53km/33 miles).

Emmental (Berne) and Entlebuch (Lucerne)

3 The Emmental, probably best known for its famous Emmental cheese, is a region of rolling Alpine pastures and distinctive farmhouses

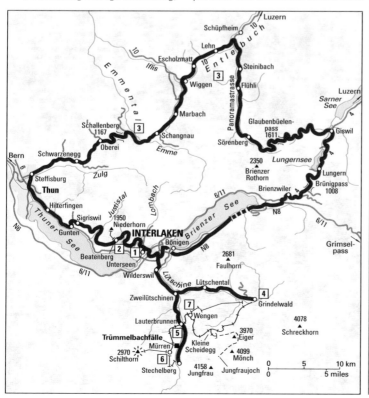

BACK TO NATURE

5 For connoisseurs of water-falls, they rarely get much more impressive than the Trümmelbachfälle (**Trümmelbach Falls**), about 3km further up the valley from Lauterbrunnen towards the small village of Stechelberg. These are the only glacier waterfalls in Europe actually inside a mountain which are accessible. Fed by the permanent snows of the Jungfrau massif, the swollen Trümmelbach forces 20,000 litres of water per second through a cavernous gorge with incredible ferocity – the noise rendering conversation impossible, and the powerful, almost horizontal, jets of icy water proving to be one of the most arresting sights in the Oberland. There are many separate cascades, with view-ing areas, some of them illu-minated. Admission charge.

SPECIAL TO...

6 The world's longest and oldest downhill ski race, the infamous annual 'Inferno', first took place in Mürren in 1928 with 17 (mostly British) entrants. Today there are over 1,500 amateur racers from every corner of the globe. The race, which starts just below the summit of the 2,970m Schilthorn, finishes more than 12km later (depending on snow conditions) in Lauterbrunnen. Traditionally held on the third Saturday in January, the Inferno is followed by a torchlit procession and the ceremonial burning of an effigy of the Devil.

with huge hipped roofs and massive hanging gables. The difference in building styles is marked, and noticeable almost as soon as you enter the Emmental region just after Schwarzenegg. After the pleasant little village of Marbach, you enter the Entlebuch valley via the dairy town of Escholzmatt which marks the watershed between the two valleys. This is a traditional farming area, but today it too has become popular as a holiday region – evi-denced by the profusion of camping sites and ski areas. The so-called 'Panoramastrasse' which runs from Schüpfheim via the resorts of Flühli and Sörenberg to Giswil is remark-ably beautiful – especially over the Glaubenbüelenpass (1,611m) after the jarringly modern outlines of Sörenberg.

From Giswil drive over the Brünigpass, following signs for Interlaken. Join the autobahn at the first opportunity, passing through a series of long tunnels and exit for Wilderswil and Lauterbrunnen. Drive through Wilderswil, turning left to Grindelwald ahead (60km/37.5 miles).

Grindelwald, Berne

4 The lure of the menacing north face of the 3,970m Eiger, which casts a semi-permanent shadow over the village, has helped to establish this cosmopolitan moun-tain resort as a mecca for climbers from all over the world. Not all of them have returned home; the Eiger having accounted for more climbing fatalities than most mountains. The village was first mentioned in a

document dated 1146, when it was a protectorate of the monks of Interlaken. Its subsequent history has been turbulent, with unhappy periods of destruction by force, plague and fire through the centuries. Since the late 19th centu-ry, after a disastrous fire, history has been kinder – helped in part by the patronage of the British early winter sports tourists who helped to establish it as an international skiing centre. Today it is one of the leading all-year sports resorts in Europe with a wide range of leisure amenities. It has come to be known as the 'glacier village', because of its unnerving proximity to two massive rivers of ice. Advancing and retreat-ing over the centuries, both frozen torrents roll remorselessly down upon the resort and can be seen at close hand by taking walks of varying length from the centre. The best vantage point from which to see the 'upper' (Oberergletscher) glacier is via a shady path past the precariously sited restaurant at Chalet Milchbach, itself a fine viewing position. But an even better view is gained by walking a further half-an-hour or so up a steep path to the ice grotto which over-looks the ice fall. Byron once described this phenomenon as a 'frozen hurricane'. Less active glacier-observers can make the shorter half-hour journey from the centre to the

The cascades of the Trummelbach Falls are impressively illuminated as the torrents of melting glacier water from the Jungfrau massif surge through the inside of the mountain

famous Gletscherschlucht (glacier gorge). Here, a path hangs off the vertical limestone walls of the gorge above the raging milky waters below. It continues through a tunnel for spectacular views of the Unterergletscher ice wall above.

i Sportszentrum

Return to the valley road, turning left to Lauterbrunnen (16km/10 miles).

Lauterbrunnen, Berne

5 Over the years many poets and writers have been drawn to this spectacularly situated town, each trying to do justice to the 'wreaths of dangling water smoke' which float from the precipitous valley walls enclosing it. The town's name means 'nothing but springs', and its meaning becomes quickly apparent. From the sheer 700m-high ramparts of the western valley wall, several waterfalls and mountain brooks cascade in spectacular fashion. The most celebrated is the **Staubbach**, variously translated as the 'spray brook' or 'dust stream', a silvery leap of 305m from a jutting ledge beneath the village of Mürren. Wordsworth described it as 'this bold, this bright, this sky-born water-fall'. Byron compared it to the 'pale courser's tail' of the Apocalypse. Visitors can try their hand at their own superlatives. The town itself is a pleasant, rambling arrangement of unpretentious hotels and blackwood chalets on both sides of the fast-flowing Lütschine river. Just below the village church, the old school-house has a local history **museum**.

i Hauptstrasse

Both Mürren and Wengen are accessible only by train or cable car, from Lauterbrunnen, Grindelwald or Stechelberg (for Mürren only).

Mürren, Berne

6 Perched precariously on a rocky shelf, high above the Lauterbrunnen valley, and opposite the Jungfrau massif, Mürren offers some of the most remarkably spectacular views in a country which has no shortage of them. Accessible only by funicular or steep mountain track from Lauterbrunnen, or cable car from the village of Stechelberg 6km down the valley, it is free from motor traffic – apart from the occasional Lilliputian farm vehicle, hotel luggage cart (or authorised 4WD vehicle). Formerly an isolated farming community, today it is an all-year mountain resort of pretty chalets and Victorian hotels, many of them teetering on the lip of the precipice. In winter it is one of the most traditional and charming of ski resorts; in summer it is a walker's and botanist's paradise. It owes its prominence in large part to the patronage of the British, who first adopted it in the mid-19th century and who, with the growth of skiing as a sport, popularised it in the early 20th century. Near the station is a monument to the skiing pioneer Sir Arnold Lunn who founded the Kandahar Club here in 1924.
The village is irregularly laid out on

A door cut into the frozen walls of the Ice Palace on the Jungfraujoch

a number of different levels and – perhaps not surprisingly – takes its name from a derivative of the word for 'wall'. On the uppermost of the pleasant chalet-lined streets is a large and well-equipped Alpine sports centre.

i Sportszentrum

Wengen, Berne

7 Like Mürren on the opposite side of the Lauterbrunnen valley, Wengen is a traditional village-resort of great character set on a mountain terrace in dramatic Alpine scenery. It too has had a long association with the British, illustrated by its traditional pubs and the presence of an English church. Perhaps unsurprisingly there is a tacit rivalry between the two resorts – each attracting fierce loyalties from different sections of the British winter sports fraternity. The DHO (Downhill Only Club) was founded here in the 1920s in opposition to Mürren's Kandahar Club. The DHO claims to have effectively conceived the notion of 'downhill only' skiing – taking the train uphill to ski down it, rather than taking the hard way up on seal skins. The resort centre is a charming cluster of shops, chalets and hotels – the best Victorian examples of the latter being on the southern fringe of the village by the railway up to the Kleine Scheidegg. The only access is by train up from Lauterbrunnen, or from Kleine Scheidegg (the mountain col between Wengen and Grindelwald). There is also a cable car link with Grindelwald via Männlichen. The village is also the venue for the International Lauberhorn Ski Race held every January on one of the oldest and most exacting courses in the world.

i Bahnhofplatz 12

Return to Interlaken in 12km (7.5 miles).

Interlaken – Unterseen 1 (0.5)
Unterseen – Beatenberg 12 (7.5)
Beatenberg – Emmental 50 (31)
Emmental – Grindelwald 113 (70)
Grindelwald – Lauterbrunnen 16 (10)
Lauterbrunnen – Interlaken 12 (7.5)

RECOMMENDED TRIPS

6 No visit to Mürren would be complete without the journey by cable car to the famous revolving restaurant on the summit of the Schilthorn. Beside its renown for the stunning panorama, the 'Piz Gloria' won additional fame as the mountain eyrie of the villainous Blofeld in the James Bond film On Her Majesty's Secret Service. A circular cinema shows clips from the film, repeated at half-hourly intervals throughout the day.

7 The railway trip to the Jungfraujoch from Kleine Scheidegg (above Wengen) is equally unforgettable. The tunnel is cut through the north face of the Eiger and there are remarkable windows actually in the mountain wall which afford spectacular views. The Jungfraujoch station itself is the highest in Europe, located in eternal snows at 3,475m, and as well as a superb panorama there are restaurants, an observatory and a fascinating ice palace.

FOR HISTORY BUFFS

7 A railway from Kleine Scheidegg to the summit of the Jungfrau was a Zürich engineer's dream in the late 19th century. Work started in 1896 to bore a tunnel nearly 1,500 vertical metres through the Eiger and the Mönch. It was completed in 1912 at huge cost, claimed a number of lives (including that of the man who conceived it), and ended in ultimate failure. When the funds dried up, the plan to continue the tunnel up to the top were shelved and the railway now finishes on the shoulder of the Jungfrau at 3,454m. The feat was, none the less, one of the most extraordinary in the history of engineering.

CENTRAL SWITZERLAND

The boundary of the central region of the country, marked by the cantons of Luzern (Lucerne), Uri, Unterwalden, Schwyz and Zug, is often referred to as the 'Cradle of Switzerland'. This is where the country was created and nurtured and, unsurprisingly, some of its most historic towns and villages are found amidst what are traditionally known as the 'forest cantons'. They not only form the physical heart of Switzerland, they also represent the historical embryo of one of the world's oldest democracies.

But the region has more than its illustrious past to recommend it. Long before the winter sports boom, the great majority of visitors headed directly for the ancient city of Lucerne and its environs. The 18th century had witnessed the beginning of educational travel, or the 'Grand Tour' as it was known, and Lucerne soon became a key point on the itinerary. But it was with the construction of the railway network in the mid-19th century that it really began to capture world attention. Within a short time Lucerne became one of the most popular destinations in Europe. With a rich medieval inheritance and a wealth of sophisticated facilities for the visitor, its appeal is understandable. But it has an additional ingredient which distinguishes it from other Swiss cities: the matchless scenery of one of Switzerland's most enchanting lakes, the Lake of the Four Forest Cantons ('Vierwaldstätter See'), better known to English speakers as Lake Lucerne. Two further reasons for visiting the Lucerne region are the great rocky sentinels of Mounts Pilatus and Rigi which stand on opposite banks of the lake, and which provide contrasting views of spectacular appeal.

The surrounding countryside of Lucerne varies from the fertile pastures of the Central Plateau to the steep mountain meadows of the Lower Alps. But the highest part of Central Switzerland lies immediately south of the lake, around the skiing and climbing resort of Engelberg at the foot of Mount Titlis.

Between the Titlis and the Sustenhorn to the south lies the Sustenpass, at 2,224m one of the country's most dramatic mountain roads. Spanning the Hasli and Reuss valleys, it connects the Bernese Oberland with the lower reaches of Central Switzerland beneath the St Gotthard massif. Here are the two ancient towns of Andermatt and Altdorf, the latter best known for its association with the William Tell legend. Further north, sheltering beneath the twin peaks of the Mythen, is the historic town of Schwyz, one of the oldest settlements in the country; and further north still is the beautifully preserved medieval lakeside town of Zug.

Luzern (Lucerne)

The unmistakable landmark of the city is the Kapellbrücke, the famous 13th-century wooden footbridge which connects both sides of the Old Town across the River Reuss. In 1992 it was extensively damaged by a devastating fire, but it was swiftly and carefully restored, although those of the unique ceiling paintings which survived undamaged have been removed to the museum (and replaced by copies). The bridge is also notable for its octagonal Wasserturm (water tower). The part of the Old Town on the north bank has a fascinating collection of ancient buildings from different eras. St Peter's Chapel is 12th-century, the Renaissance-style Rathaus early 17th-century, and the handsome merchants' houses of the impressive Weinmarkt late 15th century. Bordering this section of the city are the nine remaining Musegg towers of the original city wall – still largely intact – built between 1291 and 1513. Beyond them is the powerfully evocative Lion of Lucerne monument (sculpted in 1821 in memory of the largely Lucerne-born Swiss Guard who died in 1792 protecting the French royal family from the revolutionary mob). Beyond that is the equally famous Glacier Garden. On the south bank of the river, accessible by another old roofed bridge – the 15th-century Spreuerbrücke – the remaining part of this rich medieval collection includes the Jesuit church, built in 1666 (altered in 1895), the old 16th-century Arsenal (now the city's

An armour-clad warrior strikes a fetching pose outside the Redinghaus in Schwyz

museum) and the Franciscan church of St Mary built around 1270. One of Switzerland's most popular attractions, the Swiss Transport Museum, is also found in Lucerne, on the Lidostrasse.

Schwyz

The old town, which gave its name to the country it was instrumental in founding, has one of the most ornate baroque churches in Switzerland. Built between 1769 and 1774, St Martin's has an unusual two-storey underground crypt in the churchyard which dates from 1512. The town hall is an elaborately decorated building of 1645 and behind it is a 12th-century tower, the Archivturm, which houses one of the town's museums. Other notable sights include the 17th-century Capuchin Monastery, off the Hauptplatz, and the Zeughaus built in the early 18th century as a cornstore, but used subsequently as the town arsenal. Throughout the town there are several notable patrician residences dating from the 16th century, some of them, reportedly, still inhabited by families that can trace their roots to the foundation of the Confederation. In the impressive Bundesbriefarchiv on the Bahnhofstrasse visitors can see the original charter of 1291, marking the cantons' move to nationhood, and a collection of 14th-century banners.

Faithfully reconstructed after a recent fire, Lucerne's famous wooden Kapellbrucke looks none the worse for wear

1 to 2 days – 174km (107.5 miles)

SEVEN LAKES AND HORNBLOWERS

Luzern (Lucerne) • Willisau • Sursee
Sempach • Beromünster • Zug • Weggis
Luzern (Lucerne)

The American writer Mark Twain, one of many literary figures drawn to this part of the world, was fond of recounting an incident which took place as he descended Mount Rigi near Luzern (Lucerne). Finding the attentions of the ubiquitous hornblowers he encountered increasingly irksome, he paid them to go away. The news of his generosity was quickly spread by horn and the weary scribe found himself met by growing numbers of expectant hornblowers at every stage of his route back. The hornblowers are somewhat less in evidence today, but the fabled views from this celebrated viewpoint are as spectacular as ever. Known as the 'island mountain', it is almost entirely surrounded by water – which is the predominant feature of this tour. Through three cantons, seven separate lakes are passed, each surpassing the preceding one in scenic grandeur.

Top left: the powerfully emotive Lion Monument in Lucerne, erected in honour of the Swiss Guard who died to a man defending the French King from the mob
Above: Autumn clouds gather over Lucerne and its lake

Leave on road 10, signposted Bern. At Wolhusen leave this road and follow signs to Willisau (36km/22 miles).

Willisau, Lucerne

1 Although this little 13th-century town has been destroyed by fire on four occasions, much of its original town wall still stands. The **Obertor**, the town gate at the west end of the pretty Hauptgasse (with three picturesque **fountains**), dates

from 1551. The **Untertor** is of a similar vintage, but it has to some extent been rebuilt. Opposite the Obertor is the 17th-century **Heiligblut** pilgrimage chapel (literally 'precious blood'), a baroque structure containing a fine carved ceiling with Biblical paintings. The church of **Saints Peter and Paul** is a neo-classical building of 1804–10, retaining the 13th-century tower of an earlier structure. Note also the late 17th-

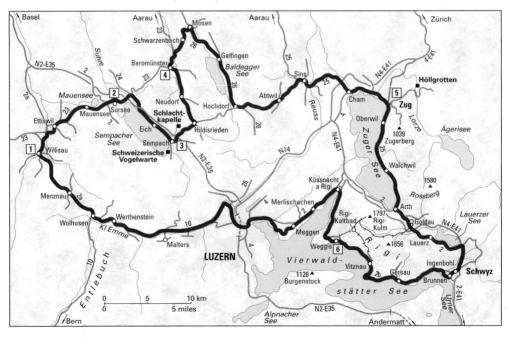

SCENIC ROUTES

There are many attractive lakeside roads on this tour, but two which particularly stand out are the east bank of the Zuger See (Lake Zug) between Zug and Arth, and the spectacular drive between Brunnen and Küssnacht which hugs the north bank of Lake Lucerne.

BACK TO NATURE

3 Just southeast of Sempacher See (Lake Sempach) is the Schweizerische Vogelwarte, Switzerland's foremost bird-watching station. As well as recording patterns of migration, the centre also houses an interesting ornithological museum.

FOR HISTORY BUFFS

3 The Battle of Sempach is remembered for more than simply the victory of a numerically inferior Swiss force over the Austrian enemy. The Swiss commander, Arnold von Winkelried, earned himself immortality by an extraordinary self-sacrifice when, at a critical moment in the battle, he launched himself single-handedly on the Austrian defences in an heroic attempt to breach their lines. His troops, galvanised by the spectacle of his valiant death, followed his example with renewed ferocity and thus turned the battle in their favour.

century **castle** above the church, once occupied by the family who first founded the town.

Follow signs to Sursee on road 23 for 12km (7.5 miles).

Sursee, Lucerne

2 This beguiling old lakeside town has more than a little in common with Willisau. Swept by fire on a number of occasions since its foundation in the 13th century, it too has managed to retain much of its original fortifications – including an imposing gate tower. The **Untertor**, also known as the Baseltor, is a 17th-century structure, substantially rebuilt. The late Gothic **town hall** of 1546 is a particularly handsome building and, standing at the head of a picturesque cobbled street of 17th-century burghers' houses, makes a charming scene. The baroque parish church of **St George** is another distinguished building, dating from 1641, and on the northern perimeter of the town is an early 17th-century **Capuchin monastery**. On the northern outskirts of the town, close to the route to Sempach, you might stop briefly at Mariazell where there is a 17th-century pilgrimage **chapel** founded in the 14th century. The altar and painted ceiling are worth the visit, and there is a fine view of Sempacher See (Lake Sempach) from the churchyard.

Follow the old lakeside road for 9km (5.5 miles) through Eich to Sempach.

Sempach, Lucerne

3 The main claim to fame of this pleasant old town is that in 1386 it was the scene of a pivotal battle between the Austrians and the victorious forces of the fledgling Swiss state. A couple of kilometres northeast, on a hillside, the **Schlachtkapelle** (battle-chapel) of **St Jakob** was erected immediately after the battle and marks the actual site where the Austrian commander, Duke Leopold, was killed. Inside is a painting of 1551 which commemorates the event. The best feature of Sempach itself is the charming main street, with the **Hexenturm** (witches' tower) – part of the surviving 13th-century town walls – and the half-timbered 17th-century **town hall**. Note also the 16th-century **Luzernertor** (town gate).

Drive past the Schlachtkapelle to Hildisrieden and turn on to the road for Beromünster (10km/6 miles).

Beromünster, Lucerne

4 Most of the present monastery buildings in this ancient monastic town date from between the 16th and 18th centuries, but the collegiate church of **St Michael** is an early 11th-century structure with baroque alterations. The **tower** is 13th-century and the fine choir stalls inside date from 1609. The church **treasury** contains some interesting pieces including a 14th-century silver book cover and a 7th-century reliquary. Beromünster's other great treasure, the first printed book in Switzerland, has long since departed but the building in which it was printed in 1470 – the **Schloss** – still survives just off the Hauptgasse. It is now a **museum** with a comprehensive local collection, including a reconstruction of the original print room.

Head north towards Reinach on road 23, branching right to Schwarzenbach after approximately 2km (1.25 miles).
Continue to Mosen, joining road

FOR CHILDREN

5 The famous Hell's Grottoes (Höllgrotten) can be found about 8km outside Zug on the road to Menzingen (following signs to Tobelbrücke-Höllgrotten). They comprise a series of spooky caves of varying size, imaginatively illuminated so that the stalactites and stalagmites take on a particularly diabolic appearance.

RECOMMENDED WALKS

6 Historically, the small 'island mountain' of Rigi is one of the most popular tourist destinations in the country – and deservedly so for the quality of its views. There are a number of different ways to reach the various summits. Half-hour journeys by cog railway start from Arth-Goldau, on the south shore of Zuger See, and the pleasant little resort of Vitznau on Vierwaldstätter See (Lake Lucerne) – both passed on this tour. Alternatively, a cable car leaves from Weggis to the little resort of Rigi-Kaltbad, where you can join the railway to Rigi-Kulm at 1,797m, the highest point of the mountain. A popular walk is back to Rigi-Kaltbad via the Kulmhütte, Rigi-Staffel and Staffelhöehe. There is a fine viewpoint over Lake Lucerne at Chanzeli and from there it is a short walk to the station at Rigi-Kaltbad.

26 and following the east bank of the Baldegger See to Hochdorf. Then drive cross-country to Sins via Abtwil. At Sins join road 25 to Cham, skirting the north bank of the Zuger See (Lake Zug) to Zug (about 40km/25 miles).

Zug

5 Capital of the canton of the same name, Zug is an ancient walled city with an atmospheric medieval core distinguished by original fortifications and slender spires. The old town, retaining a powerful Gothic flavour, is arranged in a semi-circle on the eastern bank of Lake Zug with many of the buildings clustered around the old Kolinplatz – a square named after Wolfgang Kolin, a standard bearer who died heroically preventing his banner from falling into the hands of the Milanese at the Battle of Arbedo (1422). His **statue**, holding aloft the cantonal banner, is overlooked by the picturesque blue-and-white tiled **Zytturm** (clocktower and gate). Near by in the Ober-Alstadt is the handsome early 16th-century **Rathaus** (town hall) with a fine Renaissance doorway. Typical Gothic houses line many of the surrounding streets and behind the Kolinplatz to the northeast is the 1526 **Capuchins' Tower**, close to the 17th-century chapel of a Capuchin convent. The other medieval tower of interest is the **Pulverturm** (powder tower) on the southern perimeter of the Old Town. The most dominant structure in the vicinity is the Gothic church of **St Oswald**, just south of the Kolinplatz. Built between 1478 and 1545, it is dedicated to the 7th-century Northumbrian saint who gave it its name. The choir stalls date from 1484. Between the church and the powder tower is the **Burg**, the 13th-century castle which was once the residence of the Habsburg governors. This simple old building is now a **museum** with a surprisingly extensive collection of local artefacts, armaments, uniforms and clocks. The **quaysides** between the **Fischmarkt** (fish market) and the **Alpenquai** are a particularly inviting

The village of Weggis at the eastern end of Lake Lucerne

feature of the town, offering fine views of Central Switzerland, including Rigi, Pilatus and the distant peaks of the Bernese Oberland. Zug's own mountain, the 1,039m flat-topped Zugerberg, is reached by car up a very steep and winding road southeast. From its terminus, there is a ten-minute climb to a terrace with an impressive panorama.

*Stay on road 25, heading south along the east bank of Zuger See to Arth. Continue past Goldau and Lauerzer See on old road 2, joining the **N4** at the first opportunity and leaving at the exit for Brunnen (see Tour 12). Continue on the lakeside road (2b) to Weggis (about 47km/29 miles).*

Weggis, Lucerne

6 Sometimes known as the 'garden of Lucerne', this village is one of the most charming resorts on the lake. The most exclusive of the hotels are magnificent 19th-century structures, built or adapted in various architectural styles, with wrought-iron balconies, wood panelling and carefully manicured lawns which stretch down to the water. Note the little **chapel of Allerheiligen**, built in 1623 and containing interesting late Renaissance frescos. The quayside walks around the village are particularly pleasing, with splendid views across the water to the sheer cliff of the Bürgenstock rising abruptly from the lake. Note the monument to Mark Twain who stayed in the village on a number of occasions.

Return to Lucerne on the lakeside road via Küssnacht am Rigi then Meggen (20km/12.5 miles).

Lucerne (Luzern) – Willisau 36 (22)
Willisau – Sursee 12 (7.5)
Sursee – Sempach 9 (5.5)
Sempach – Beromünster 10 (6)
Beromünster – Zug 40 (25)
Zug – Weggis 47 (29)
Weggis – Lucerne (Luzern) 20 (12.5)

A dragon's mouth makes an unusual drain for the gutter of St Peter's Church in the town of Stans

PILATUS, TELL AND TITLIS

Luzern (Lucerne) • Sarnen • Sustenpass Altdorf • Seelisberg • Beckenried • Stans Bürgenstock • Engelberg • Luzern (Lucerne)

*Take the **N2** south from Lucerne, following signs for Interlaken, Brünigpass and Sarner. Join the **N8** after about 9km to reach Sarnen (about 18km/11 miles).*

Sarnen, Obwalden

1 Founded in 1210, this historic lakeside town played an important role in the seminal days of the Swiss Confederation. In the baroque **Rathaus** (1729), the 15th-century White Book or **'Weisse Buch von Sarnen'**, the oldest chronicle of Swiss history, can be found. The building also contains some fine old portraits, including one of local hero Nicolas von Flüe, credited with banging heads together and saving the embryonic Confederation from dissolving in 1477. On a knoll opposite stand the few remains of the **castle** of the last Austrian governor, destroyed by popular revolt in 1308. The **Hexenturm** (witches' tower) is the only discernible remnant of the original fortifications. Near by is the ornate **Schützenhaus**, a grand old shooting lodge of 1752 with distinctive onion-domed twin towers. The former 16th-century **Arsenal** adjacent is now home to a regional museum. The town is also home to two important religious institutions, the **St Andreas Convent** and the sprawling **Benedictine College**, dating from the early 17th and mid-18th centuries respectively. Both now have modern churches built in the 1960s. Conspicuous on a hill above the town to the southwest is the twin-towered **church of St Peter**, founded in the 11th-century but dating in its present form from 1742. A 16th-century **ossuary** with a notable carved ceiling stands next door.

Take the Brünig pass road via the towns of Sachseln and Giswil, following the east bank of the Lungnersee. At the foot of the pass road, turn left for Meiringen, and thence follow signs for the Sustenpass. About 64km (40 miles).

Sustenpass Road

2 Much of this dramatic mountain road, particularly along the upper reaches of the beautiful Gadmental, was built between 1938 and 1946 by refugees from war-torn Europe – bearing testament to the Swiss discountenance of idle hands. A short distance beyond the Steingletscher Hotel there is a plaque on the left-hand side of the road, overlooking the spectacular glacier of the same name, which commemorates their efforts. The pass road is an impressive engineering achievement with countless tunnels and sinuous switchbacks, and there are excellent viewpoints at various intervals. One of the best is from the Swiss Touring Club **viewing table**, about

Fire lilies thrive in the rugged glacial environment of the Sustenpass

This part of Central Switzerland is one of the country's most historic regions. The cantons of Luzern (Lucerne), Uri and Unterwalden were three of the four 'forest cantons' which gave their name ('Vierwaldstätter See') to Lake Lucerne – which, with neighbouring Schwyz, they surround. More significantly, together they represent the kernel of the modern Swiss Confederation. During the 14th century it was the people of these forest communities who decided to throw off the Habsburg yoke and join together as 'confederates' to fight for freedom from their Austrian oppressors. It was here, in the old town of Altdorf, that the legend of William Tell's valiant rebellion against the Austrian governor was born, but – even as the power of the hated occupier waned – other neighbouring nations were already casting covetous eyes over the embryonic mountain state. The heart of historic Switzerland continued to be a battleground for many years to come – particularly towards the end of the 18th century when the French clashed repeatedly with Austrian and Russian forces in bloody fighting throughout Uri. Passing through the tranquil towns and villages of this beautiful Alpine region, it is hard to imagine that it was ever anything other than a haven of peace.

*Legendary Swiss marksman
William Tell rests a protective arm
on his son's shoulder in the town
square of Altdorf*

history, it was here that William Tell
split the apple instead of his son's
head. The intrepid crossbower is
commemorated by a suitably imposing bronze **statue** (1895) in the main
square beneath a 13th-century
tower. Behind is the classically
styled **Rathaus**, rebuilt in 1805 and
containing a colourful collection of
ancient banners. Throughout
Altdorf's narrow streets the 17th-
and 18th-century houses show
Lombardian influences (the canton
of Uri, of which Altdorf is capital,
once had extensive possessions in
Ticino). There are two **Capuchin
monasteries** on the north and south
of the town – the former was built
by the Bishop of Milan in the late
16th century and is the oldest in
Switzerland. Close to the main
square is an even older building, the
16th-century **Suvorov House** – so
called because it was the headquarters of the Russian General of the
same name during the bitter Franco-
Russian campaign of 1799. Near by,
in the Gotthardstrasse, a regional
museum is housed in a neo-Gothic
turn-of-the-century building. The **Tell
Museum** is located in the ancient
hamlet of Bürglen, the great man's
supposed birthplace, 3km southeast
of Altdorf.

2km before the summit of the pass,
on the right.

*Drive down the Meiental to
Wassen, joining the old road (2)
north to Altdorf (42km/26 miles).*

Altdorf, Uri

3 According to one of the most
durable legends in European

*Leave by road 2, signposted
Schwyz, and join the N2 after
about 3km. After the long tunnel,
exit at Beckenried and double
back taking the winding road via*

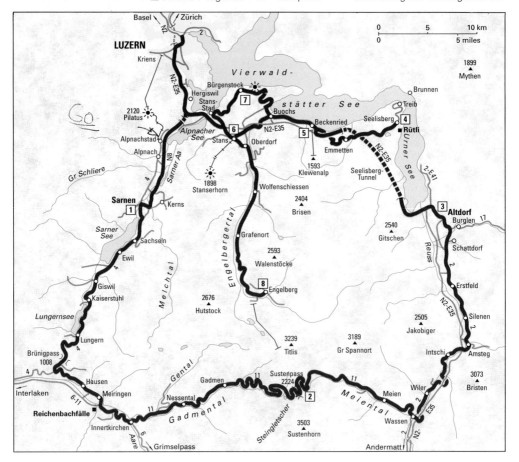

Emmetten to Seelisberg (30km/18.5 miles).

Seelisberg, Uri

4 Most impressively set on a mountain terrace amidst semi-Alpine pastures and woods, this secluded and exclusive summer resort has fine views over Lake Lucerne and the village of Brunnen below, and the twin peaks of the Mythen above the town of Schwyz to the northeast. Among the village's many amenities is a network of pretty gladed paths, one of which leads to the atmospheric old hunting castle of **Beroldingen**, founded in 1530 with a **chapel** of 1546. A steep, winding road leads a short distance north from Seelisberg to the hamlet of Treib, little more than a landing stage on the lakeside, but famous for its old **Boatman's House**, a former meeting place of the original Swiss Confederates. Although destroyed by fire in 1657, it was promptly rebuilt in the same style and has since been sympathetically restored a number of times. Treib can also be reached by funicular from the village.

Return by the same road to Beckenried (11km/7 miles).

Beckenried, Nidwalden

5 This agreeable lakeside resort has considerable historical significance as the original venue of the Diet of the Old Confederates who held their assemblies here between 1350 and 1554. The church of **St Heinrich** was built between 1790 and 1807 and the **pilgrimage chapel** of Maria im Ridli – high above the lake – dates from 1701. A cable car leads from the village to the 1,593m summit of Klewenalp from where there are pleasant

A belvedere in the mountain resort of Burgenstock provides a sweeping panorama of Lake Lucerne

walks. Not least of the resort's attractions are its beaches.

Follow the lakeside road west to Buochs, and from there to Stans (8km/5 miles).

Stans, Nidwalden

6 The famous democratic ceremony of voting in the cantonal government by a show of hands takes place in the town's impressive square, the **Dorf-und-Rathausplatz**, laid out after a fire in the early 18th century. The splendid baroque **church of St Peter** stands here, rebuilt in 1647 on the site of a 12th-century building. Its slender Romanesque **tower** is the most visible remnant of the earlier structure. Inside is an impressively ornate black marble pulpit. Adjacent to the church is a 15th-century **chapel and charnel-house**, containing some interesting murals. In front is a monument to the local hero Arnold von Winkelried, who died in a heroic but ultimately suicidal gesture at the Battle of Sempach in 1386. Behind is the **Rathaus**, a building of 1714 erected on the foundations of a much earlier structure. Other notable buildings include the medieval **Höfli** (also known as the 'Rosenburg', the house of the former monastery's 'steward'), and the 1775 **salt and corn store** on the Stansstaderstrasse, now the local **museum**.

The summit of the 1,898m Stanserhorn is reached by funicular and cable car from the town, then a short walk from the upper station. A marvellous panorama is the reward, with Lake Lucerne to the north and the peaks and glaciers of the Titlis and the Jungfrau massif to the south and southwest.

Follow signs to Stanstad, and from there climb a steep narrow road to the Bürgenstock (about 11km/7 miles). ·

SCENIC ROUTES

2 The stretch of road close to the summit of the Sustenpass, via the Himmelrank gorge, is the most dramatic of the tour. The descent of the Meiental towards Wassen is remarkable for the uniform V-shape of the densely-forested valley walls, and there are fine views of the pass road winding beneath to the Reuss valley.

RECOMMENDED TRIPS

Pilatus
This huge pyramid of rock was the first Swiss mountain to receive a name, the exact origin of which remains a mystery. Legend records that Pontius Pilate drowned in its small lake, but more prosaic versions suggest that it takes its name from the Latin word pileatus, meaning 'air-covered'. The summit, offering one of Switzerland's most famous panoramas, can be reached by mountain lift from the suburb of Kriens, or the steepest cogwheel railway in the world from Alpnachstad. Queen Victoria made the journey by mule but, sadly, that option is no longer available.

RECOMMENDED WALKS

6 The Felsenweg is a famous cliff path leading from the Bürgenstock resort around the Hammetschwand (1,128m). About halfway around, walkers will come across the highest and fastest outside mountain lift in Europe which ascends, intermittently through the rock face, to the summit. The panorama from here is stupendous, and there is a restaurant from which to enjoy it. The one-hour circular walk can be continued after descend-ing by the same lift.

FOR HISTORY BUFFS

4 On the tranquil lakeside meadow of Rütli, below Seelisberg, the Confederates of the three founder cantons met in 1307 to take an oath to drive the Austrians from their fledgling country. On 25 July 1940, when Switzerland was entirely surrounded by Axis powers, the highest ranking commanders of the Swiss army convened on this sacred ground to reaffirm their resolve to repulse any invasion.

6 It was at the Diet of Stans in 1481 that Niklaus von Flüe, the hermit and statesman, intervened with a combination of diplomacy and good sense to save the embryonic Confederation from dissolution at a sensitive time. He was canonised in 1947. Stans also has historical significance as the site of Pestalozzi's first orphanage. The 'father of modern education' resolved to do something for the children of the 400 men who were slaughtered in a courageous stand against the French in 1798.

SPECIAL TO...

6 Possibly the purest form of the democratic process occurs annually in the unassuming old cantonal capital of Stans, when on the last Sunday in April the citizens meet to elect their local government by a show of hands at the 'Landsgemeinde' in the town square. The town is one of only four places in the country where this 'open-air' vote takes place (always an excuse for a day of festivity).

BACK TO NATURE

8 If you are an early-rising nature lover, Engelberg's weekly nature treks, or 'Burgtours', every Wednesday between 6am and 2pm should prove to be of interest. Led by a mountain guide, the best examples of Alpine flora and fauna will be pointed out, and you will have an opportunity to watch the elusive steinbock at close quarters. Further details are available from the tourist office.

FOR CHILDREN

8 Engelberg offers a range of kinder-related activities during every week of the summer. Examples of events include a magic show on Sunday afternoons and a puppet theatre on Friday afternoons followed by trampolin-ing in the park. Further details from the tourist office.
Take the Brünigpass road via the towns of Sachseln and Giswil, following the east bank of the Lungernsee. At the foot of the pass road, turn left for Meiringen and thence follow signs for the Sustenpass (about 64km/40 miles).

Bürgenstock, Nidwalden

7 A traditional stamping ground for the rich and famous, this luxurious resort has been the home of many international celebrities, including Sophia Loren and Audrey Hepburn. Less of a natural community, and more of a large and sophisticated hotel complex, it was purpose-built at the end of the last century with the express intention of providing every conceivable amenity to its well-heeled guests. It is still privately owned and still very exclusive. Set on a plateau 500m up the wooded bluff of the same name, it offers a magnificent panorama of Lake Lucerne immediately below, the distant Jura and the twin rocky sentinels of Rigi and Pilatus. Its views, and the lovely walks in the vicinity, are the best reasons to visit this otherwise slightly unreal colony of affluent recluses.

Return to Stans by the same road, then take the valley road, to Engelberg (30km/18.5 miles).

Engelberg, Obwalden

8 The spectacle of monks in full habit mingling with brightly dressed winter and summer sports enthusiasts is one of the more arresting sights in this popular mountain resort. Another is the physical setting itself. Dramatically located in a wide, steep-sided valley shadowed by the dark precipices of the Titlis massif, Engelberg is an Alpine village of traditional appeal with some surprisingly monumental buildings. Foremost among these is the huge **Benedictine monastery**

The baroque church tower of the 18th-century Benedictine abbey in Engelberg

which has been here in one form or another since 1120. The present imposing group of buildings, dating from 1730, is still the dominant feature of the community. Located on the western side of the town, the great structure dwarfs nearby chalets and hotels. It includes a college and an impressive church which contains one of the country's largest organs. Queen Victoria attended her first (and only) Catholic mass here in 1868, a decision which so alarmed the British establishment of the day that questions were raised in Parliament. Guided tours of the monastery and its library are available every day except Sunday.

The town centre has some attractive old wooden buildings, elegant 19th-century hotels and a bustling main street. Inevitably, there are some unattractive examples of 1960s neo-Alpine architecture, but not in sufficient quantity to destroy the soul of the village.

There is a comprehensive range of sporting facilities in summer and winter, and a large sports complex. The trip to the top station of the 3,239m Titlis involves a thrilling aerial journey over the Titlis glacier. The final stage of the journey, from Stand, is courtesy of the world's first revolving cable car, the Rotair.

Return to Lucerne via Stans, joining the N2 at Stans-Nord (about 36km/22 miles).

Lucerne (Luzern) – Sarnen 18 (11)
Sarnen – Sustenpass 64 (40)
Sustenpass – Altdorf 42 (26)
Altdorf – Seelisburg 30 (18.5)
Seelisburg – Beckenreid 11 (7)
Beckenreid – Stans 8 (5)
Stans – Bürgenstock 11 (7)
Bürgenstock – Engelberg 30 (18.5)
Engelberg – Lucerne (Luzern) 36 (22)

An ornate gilded Madonna surmounts a fountain outside the splendid Benedictine abbey in Einsiedeln

THE MITRE AND THE BLACK MADONNA

Schwyz • Brunnen • Bürglen • Näfels Rapperswil • Einsiedeln • Schwyz

Follow signs to Brunnen for about 6km (4 miles).

Brunnen, Schwyz

1 Hans Christian Andersen used to stay regularly in this quaint former fishing village, observing that the fjord-like appearance of its setting reminded him of home. The impression of rugged Scandinavian waterscapes is at its most persuasive if you stand on the quayside looking down Lake Uri (Urner See). Directly across the elbow of water, where the two lakes of Lucerne and Uri merge, the Seelisberg rises sharply above the historic meadow of Rütli and towering over its shoulder is the 2,928m peak of Uri-Rotstock – one of the highest in the central Alps. Brunnen is now the next largest resort on these lakes – after Luzern (Lucerne) itself – and paddle-steamers make regular stops here for passengers to avail themselves of the many diversions the village has to offer. They include a variety of watersports, bowling, tennis and biking. Near the shady, chestnut-lined lakeside promenade is the **Bundeskapelle**, a baroque chapel built in 1632 with an altar of the same period. Overlooking the lakes are a number of elegant old hotels, and the waterfront is cluttered with attractive cafés and bars shaded by gaily coloured awnings. Winston Churchill chose to honeymoon here.

Drive south down the panoramic Axenstrasse, through Altdorf (see Tour 11), turning on to road 17 for Bürglen (18km/11 miles).

The tour is so-called because of the twin peaks of the Mythen (which translates as the 'Mitre') above the historic town of Schwyz, and the famous little statue of the Virgin which stands in the great abbey of Switzerland's most celebrated place of pilgrimage, Einsiedeln. But the religious significance of the route starts and ends there. In between you will pass through one of the country's most charming lakeside resorts, drive over one of its most scenic passes and linger in one of its most appealing medieval towns: and, because at least half of your journey takes you through the heart of the country, expect to see more than the occasional reference to William Tell.

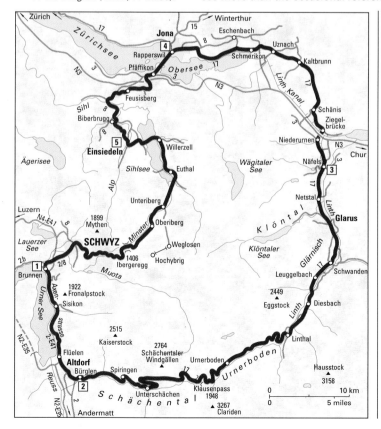

exact replica of the parish church in Schwyz. This is hardly surprising: they were designed by the same architect. An older ecclesiastical building is the **Capuchin monastery of Maria-Burg**, built in 1675. But Näfels' pride and joy is the **Freulerpalast**, a handsome palace built in 1645 for one Caspar Freuler, the commander of the Swiss Guard at the French Court in Versailles. Since 1942 it has been the **cantonal museum**, and in addition to its interesting collection of local textiles and fabrics, its pièce de résistance is an extraordinarily lavish Renaissance front door – which says a great deal about the financial prudence of being a 17th-century mercenary in the pay of the French king.

Continue on road 17 through Niederurnen and Kaltbrunn, following the north bank of the Obersee via Uznach and Schmerikon to Rapperswil (29km/18 miles).

Rapperswil, St Gallen

4 A small medieval town of great charm and seductive 'Swissness', Rapperswil is attractively located at the northern end of a causeway between the lakes of Zürich and Ober. Founded in the late 12th century, its atmospheric Old Town is dominated by a severe-looking **castle** with three towers, built in the mid-13th century and used as the residence of the Austrian governors. Inside are two **museums**, one record-ing the development of Swiss castles, the other devoted to Polish history and culture and commemorating the Polish uprising against the Russians in 1863. This curious anomaly is explained by the presence of a sizeable local Polish community which settled in the town in the mid-19th century. The **church** adjoining the castle dates from the same period, but was extensively rebuilt in 1883, although it retains two substantial towers from the

SCENIC ROUTES

2 The Klausenpass road, built at the end of the last century, offers magnificent views south over the Clariden range of mountains (up to 3,267m) and the 3,295m Scherhorn. Stop at the Klausenpass Hotel just before the pass for the best of the vantage points.

BACK TO NATURE

4 Rapperswil calls itself the 'City of Roses', and the aromatic bloom is much in evidence throughout the streets and public spaces – and the town's coat of arms. In the Rose Gardens, near the Capuchin monastery, over 6,000 rose bushes comprising 180 different species of rose flourish in delightful lakeside surroundings. Directly north, across the Lindenhof, is a small deer park which has been in this unusual town-centre location since 1871.

FOR CHILDREN

4 Rapperswil has an intriguing Kinderzoo, belonging to the Knie National Circus which uses the town as its base. It is located behind the railway station, on the lakeside road, and among its many attractions are a whale aquarium and a dolphinarium. Pony rides and a miniature railway are among the other diversions.

An organ grinder takes part in a convention of like-minded enthusiasts in Brunnen

Bürglen, Uri

2 Best known as the supposed birthplace of the legendary William Tell, this pleasant medieval village (not surprisingly) has a **museum** devoted to the great man. It is housed appropriately in a 13th-century Romanesque tower called the **Wattigwilerturm** – one of two impressive towers in the village. A separate chapel, the 16th-century **Tellskapelle**, occupies the site of the archer's reputed house and contains late 18th-century paintings commemorating his heroics. Note the **church of Saints Peter and Paul**, built in 1685, and two other old chapels on the outskirts of the village – the **Ölbergkapelle** (1693) and the **Loretokapelle** (1661). Near the bridge over the Schächenbach a stone cross marks the site of Tell's selfless gesture in hurling himself into the river to rescue a child. According to popular belief, the child survived but the ageing archer was swept away.

Continue for 70km (44 miles) over the Klausenpass (1,948m) and then down the Linth valley, through Schwanden and Glarus, to Näfels.

Näfels, Glarus

3 If ever there was a town which bears testimony to the Swiss predilection for being militarily outnumbered – it is Näfels. In 1388 a famous battle took place here in which 600 Swiss soldiers triumphed over an Austrian force variously estimated at anything between five and ten times their number. The respective losses each side suffered were recorded as 54 and 2,500. The Battle of Näfels is commemorated in the **Schlachtkapelle**, attached to the church of **Saints Fridolin and Hilarius**, built in 1778 and almost an

original structure. Below the Schlossberg, the upper part of the town has a number of distinguished buildings including the 15th-century **Rathaus** in the central Hauptplatz (remarkable carved doorway), and the early 17th-century **Bleulerhaus** on arguably the town's most appealing street – the arcaded Hintergasse. Note also the 15th-century **Breny-Haus** (with a 13th-century tower) on the Herrenberg, now the local history **museum**. Another interesting structure, by the lakeside, is the 16th-century **Heilig Hüsli**, once part of a wooden bridge built in 1358 which was dismantled 1878 and replaced by the present stone dam.

Cross the bridge on road 8, following signs to Luzern/Schwyz. At Biberbrugg take the country road via Bennau to Einsiedeln (19km/12 miles).

Einsiedeln, Schwyz

5 Describing itself as the 'jewel' of the Schwyz canton, the small town of Einsiedeln is an unexpected mix of the ordinary and the inspiring. Its location is particularly beautiful, comfortably sheltered beneath a green ripple of the lower Alps and surrounded by meadows and pine forests. But its fame springs chiefly from its reputation as one of the continent's most important places of pilgrimage.

The massive **Benedictine abbey of Maria Einsiedeln**, founded in 934, but dating in its present appearance from the early 1700s, is one of the most impressive baroque buildings in Europe. More than one respected authority has been moved to observe that the force of its visual impact lies not so much in its undoubted architectural merit, as in the sheer grandeur of a structure on

this scale in such an improbably rural setting. The buildings cover a total area of 34,000 sq m, and a façade of well over 100m presides over a graceful Lombardian-style square with a sweep of arcades around an ornate baroque fountain. A broad flight of steps leads up to the monastery church, flanked by twin clocktowers and surmounted by a monumental statue of the Virgin and child. The interior is richly decorated with intricately detailed stucco and rococo features, and the largest ceiling painting in the country – mostly the work of two brothers from Bavaria. The carved stalls and wrought-iron 17th-century choir screen, by a craftsman from Luzern (Lucerne), are particularly striking. But the goal of the estimated quarter of a million pilgrims each year is the **Gnadenkapelle** (Chapel of Grace), destroyed by French marauders in 1798 and rebuilt in 1816. This black marble obelisk, in the centre of the octagonal nave, contains the famous 15th-century **Black Madonna** – a surprisingly tiny wooden black statuette of the Virgin holding a black infant Jesus. Rather than signifying a novel approach to conventional theology, the colouration in fact owes its origin to the effect of smoke on the original Madonna, destroyed by fire in 1465. The town itself is of marginal interest, with a preponderance of religious souvenir shops and coffee bars.

Return to Schwyz by crossing the Sihlsee to Willerzell, following the east bank via Euthal, and taking the mountain forest road via Ibergeregg and Rickenbach (34km/21 miles).

Schwyz – Brunnen 6 (4)
Brunnen – Bürglen 18 (11)
Bürglen – Näfels 70 (44)
Näfels – Rapperswil 29 (18)
Rapperswil – Einsiedeln 19 (12)
Einsiedeln – Schwyz 34 (21)

The 12th-century castle towers above the town and lake of Rapperswil

FOR HISTORY BUFFS

4 Rapperswil Castle, built by a veteran of the First Crusade in about 1200, was saved from ruin in 1834 by a Polish resistance leader – Graf Plater. Using the castle as his base, Plater remained active in Polish politics for 40 years, co-ordinating resistance to the occupying Russian Czars. Effectively, Rapperswil was the seat of the Polish government in exile for much of the latter half of the 19th century.

RECOMMENDED WALKS

5 One of the most spectacular walking regions on this tour is around Hoch-Ybrig, a verdant mountainous area between Einsieldeln and Schwyz where there are over 100km of well-marked paths and hiking tracks to suit all timetables and levels of fitness. About 6km beyond Einsiedeln, turn south at Unteriberg and follow the road for 5km. The tourist office in Hochybrig will supply you with a walking map, and in addition to picnic areas (with barbecues), mountain restaurants, nature trails and trout lakes, there is also a zoo for the children.

SPECIAL TO...

5 Every five years one of the world's great amateur theatrical productions takes place in the abbey square of Einsiedeln. 'The Great Theatre of the World', first performed before the Spanish Court in 1685, is held under the night sky between the months of June and September. The cast of 600 are all local towns-folk, coached by the monks of the abbey. The most recent performance was in 1992, but the Festival of Miraculous Dedications is an annual torchlight procession which takes place every 14 September.

THE NORTHEAST

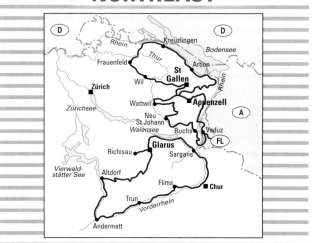

Comprising the cantons of Glarus, St Gallen and Appenzell, the northeast of the country is the lowest of the Alpine regions of Switzerland. Bordered to the north by the huge Bodensee (Lake Constance) across which lies Germany, to the south by the largest of the Swiss cantons, Graubünden, and to the east by Liechtenstein and Austria, it has two notable mountain ranges. The Glarner Alpen (Glarus Alps), the eastern section of the central Alpine chain, is the largest, almost completely encirc-ling the small canton of Glarus and including the highest peak of the region, the 3,614m Tödi on the border with Graubünden. The other is the Alpstein, standing alone between the Toggenburg and Rhein (Rhine) valleys and including the most famous vantage point of this area, the 2,502m Säntis. But it is probably more for its lush hilly countryside in the cantons of St Gallen and Appenzell that the region is better known.

St Gallen was, and remains, the natural focus of cultural and economic activity in the region, and during the Middle Ages was one of the leading educational centres in Europe. This part of Switzerland is the centre of the country's textile industry and from the early 16th century on St Gallen swiftly became the commercial hub of the northeast. A visit to any of the many textile museums, particularly in St Gallen, is recommended.

So is a visit to one of the thermal pools in the old spa town of Bad Ragaz, in the Rhine valley close to the southern border of the tiny principality of Liechtenstein. Linked to Switzerland by a common currency, language, diplomatic expedience and an absence of customs formalities, Liechtenstein is in fact a sovereign state with its own constitution and a royal family whose origins can be traced to the time of the Holy Roman Empire.

The relationship between the two countries has lasted since 1923, when Liechtenstein wisely decided that its future lay with Switzerland rather than the Austro-Hungarian empire. In the course of the past 50 years it has undergone a remarkable transformation from being a predominantly agricultural state to a highly industrialised producer. However, any idea that the small country is blighted by sprawling factories is misplaced; Liechtenstein has achieved the commendable feat of blending its industry unobtrusively with the surrounding mountain and valley scenery.

St Gallen
The old city owes its name to the Irish missionary St Gallus who had a hermitage near by. The monastery was founded in 719 and the present buildings rank among the finest of their era in the country. The cathedral is a magnificent baroque pile, built over a period of 14 years from 1755, and famous for its sumptuously decorated interior. The nearby abbey library, the Stiftsbibliothek, actually manages to surpass the level of lavish decoration. Its two-storey rococo hall, resplendent with gilded carvings, has over 100,000 rare manuscripts, many of which date from the 7th to 12th centuries. Among a number of fine medieval streets, the Gallusstrasse, Schmiedgasse and Multergasse stand out, and in a city which has no shortage of beautiful old Gothic buildings unquestionably the finest are found in a circle around the monastery precinct. The Textile Museum in the Vadianstrasse has the most comprehensive collection of embroidered fabrics and lacework in the country.

Appenzell
The old town has been since 1597 capital of the Catholic 'half-canton' of Innerrhoden. Along with its Protestant other half, Ausserrhoden, it is completely encircled by the canton of St Gallen. This is just one curious feature of many which distinguish Appenzell from other Swiss towns, another being the distinctive exterior decoration of many

The cantonal capital of Glarus shelters beneath the sheer granite walls of the Glarnisch

of the traditional wooden frame buildings which line its colourful streets. The busy Hauptgasse offers something of a contrast to the bucolic surroundings, and a variety of shops do a brisk trade in everything from the famous richly decorated Appenzeller cakes to the equally well-known embroidered lace. Many of the buildings date from the mid-16th century. The Rathaus is a fine Gothic building of 1561, the Löwendrogerie (chemist) is beautifully painted and the town church, founded in the 11th century, has a remarkable baroque interior.

Glarus

The most unusual feature of this impressively sited canton capital is its grid-pattern street plan, the result of a mid-19th-century fire which almost completely destroyed the old town. As the country's first example of 'town planning' it is interesting in itself and the generous use of squares and open spaces is imaginative. Some old buildings survived the fire and provide a pleasing contrast to the angular, sometimes functional-looking replacements.

The town museum, the Kunsthaus, has a fine collection of Swiss art, but probably the best reason to stay in the town is the spectacular nature of its mountainous setting and its convenience as an excursion centre.

A distinctive oriel, supported by tireless wooden figures, adorns the façade of the early 18th-century Haus zum Pelikan in St Gallen's old town.

ST GALLEN AND MARITIME SWITZERLAND

Part of the lavishly decorated rococo ceiling in St Gallen's magnificent Abbey Library

St Gallen • Wil • Frauenfeld • Steckborn Kreuzlingen • Bodensee (Lake Constance) Rorschach • Trogen • Herisau • St Gallen

The northern canton of Thurgau, throughout which much of this tour is routed, is a predominantly agricultural region hardly blighted by the concentration of busy industrial and maritime centres which help to make it one of the wealthiest areas in the country. Much of it borders Bodensee (Lake Constance), the great lake which forms a natural barrier between Switzerland and Germany. Subject to inexplicable changes of level, it is anything but constant, but in fine conditions a steamer trip from one of the many charming Swiss coastal towns and villages which border it is recommended. The remainder of the tour passes through the appealing rolling countryside of cantons St Gallen and Appenzell, as rich in pastoral scenery as any part of the country.

ⓘ Bahnhofplatz 1

Take the N1 for 29km (18 miles), signposted Zürich west, and exit at Wil.

Wil, St Gallen

1 Now a busy industrial centre, the medieval core of this small town was once the preferred summer residence of the prince-abbots of nearby St Gallen. Picturesquely perched on a hill in the middle of the Upper Thur valley, the impressively preserved **Old Town** has its houses arranged in a ring around the former abbots' palace – known as the **Hof**. This is a huge 12th-century castle, essentially rebuilt in the 15th century, which now houses the local **museum**. Both the Hofplatz and the Marktgasse have a fine collection of 14th- to 18th-century houses and the latter is notable for a row of pretty arcades. One of the town's most important buildings is the church of **St Nicholas**, built in the mid-15th century and commanding a fine view of the distant Säntis from its terrace. Note also the arcaded **Baronenhaus**, a four-storey neo-classical building of 1795.

Take the old road 7 for 17km (10.5 miles), via Wängi, to Frauenfeld.

Frauenfeld, Thurgau

2 Omitted from many tour itineraries, this riverside cantonal capital may have suffered marginal indus-trial blight, but, like Wil, it retains an **Old Town** of some charm which also happens to be host to two fine museums. Much of it was rebuilt after two fires in the late 18th century and what few medieval buildings remain are close to the **Rathaus** – a neo-classical structure built shortly after the second fire in 1788. Dominating the whole of this upper section of the town is the old **Schloss** – an old castle with a massive 13th-century keep sitting squarely on an ivy-clad sandstone rock above the river. Today it houses the **Cantonal Museum**, with a collection of primeval and medieval exhibits well worth a visit. Like many of the country's cantonal museums, it features reconstructed interiors of regional dwellings from the 17th cen-

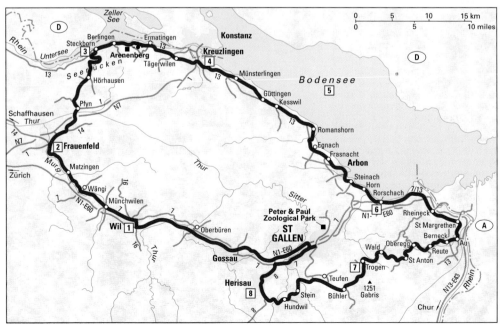

FOR HISTORY BUFFS

St Gallen owes its name to the peripatetic Irish hermit, Gallus, who arrived from Lake Constance in about 612 and settled in the Steinach valley. After his death, a monastery was founded on the site of his hermitage (which Gallus constructed, reportedly, with the help of a bear) and subsequently the city grew up around it. Thereafter, and throughout the Middle Ages, the city was the most important religious and cultural centre in Switzerland, losing its influence first with the arrival of the Reformation, and conclusively on the advent of the Helvetian republic in 1798.

BACK TO NATURE

About 4km north of St Gallen, the Peter and Paul Zoological park allows close surveillance of a variety of indigenous Alpine species including ibex, red deer, chamois, wild boar, marmots and lynx.
St Gallen's Botanical Gardens on the Stephanshornstrasse, east of the city centre, feature a fascinating variety of Alpine and tropical flora. There are two large greenhouses, and a network of paths lined with exotic blooms from all over the world.

FOR CHILDREN

On the outskirts of St Gallen, on the St Josefenstrasse, the Schiltacker amusement park offers a variety of rides and attractions including bumper cars, roundabouts, and the largest outdoor model railway in the country.
In Gossau, just outside St Gallen on the road to Wil, the largest zoo in northeast Switzerland is home to more than 500 animals, some of them staging regular 'performances' in the zoo's Big Top. There are also camel rides.

tury on. The town's other collection is kept in the **Luzernerhaus**, built in 1771 as the residence of the official cantonal delegate from Luzern (Lucerne). It is now the **Cantonal Natural History Museum**.

Follow signs to Steckborn, via the hamlet of Pfyn, for 17km (10.5 miles).

Steckborn, Thurgau

3 Situated on the southern bank of the Untersee – a narrow arm of Lake Constance – Steckborn is an ancient town built on the site of a Stone Age lakeside settlement. It grew up around the prison-farm of the monastery of Reichenau on a German peninsula across the water, but these days the locals are more likely to be engaged in less involuntary pursuits. Many of the original **town walls**, dating from the early 14th century, have survived along with a number of other mainly 16th- to 17th-century half-timbered houses. On the bank of the lake is the small castle of **Turmhof**, built at about the same time but using part of the original fortifications as its substructure. It is now home to a small **museum** with a collection of Stone Age and Roman artefacts. Note also the attractive 17th-century **Rathaus** (small historical collection of armaments), and the simple baroque church of **St Jakob** built in 1766 on the site of an earlier foundation.

Frauenfeld's castle lies above a bend in the wall-enclosed Murg river

Beyond the quiet village of Berlingen, 3km east, you will see signs to the 16th-century **Schloss Arenenberg** – formerly the home-in-exile of Louis Napoléon. It was later owned by the Empress Eugénie, who presented it to the canton of Thurgau in 1906. It has housed a **Napoleonic museum** ever since and the fine collection includes the various effects of Queen Hortense, the throneless emperor's mother, in an authentic period setting.

Take the lakeside road 13 for 16km (10 miles) to Kreuzlingen.

Kreuzlingen, Thurgau

4 One of the more curious characteristics about this busy industrial town is that only an invisible border line distinguishes it from the German city of Konstanz which adjoins it. Furthermore, rather than following an obvious geographical divide (like the Rhine), the border follows an indeterminate path through commercial and residential areas where you would least expect it. The town's most important historic building is the church of **St Ulrich**, a handsome mid-17th-century structure extensively restored after a fire in 1963. The interior is notable for its lavish rococo decor, wrought-iron screens and ceiling paintings. In a side chapel is a striking group of more than 300 small wooden figures representing scenes from the Passion – most of them original carvings from the 1720s. In the same chapel is a 14th-century Gothic cross, with what is said to be real hair on the head of Christ. Another impressive building is the teachers' college in the Hauptgasse, formerly an **Augustinian monastery** built in the 1660s and altered in 1765.

There is a **museum** just south-west of here in the 17th-century

FOR CHILDREN

4 Kreuzlingen is home to the oldest toy and dolls' museum in Switzerland. The Thurgau Doll Museum, in the Schloss Girsberg, contains more than 300 antique dolls and toys, many of them dating from the late 17th century.

RECOMMENDED WALKS

5 Nearly all of the old ports on the south bank of Lake Constance have attractive lakeside promenades, but unquestionably the most attractive is the long waterfront walk in the old town of Arbon. After a stroll around the historic centre, head for the Seeparksaal and follow the path alongside the lake.

SCENIC ROUTES

6 After leaving the south bank of Lake Constance, you will enter the low hills of the furthest northeastern corner of Switzerland. The country road above Berneck, especially between the villages of Reute and St Anton, offers spectacular views south over the Rhine valley.

Bodensee (Lake Constance)

Haus Rosenegg, with a collection of armaments and furniture.

Bodensee (Lake Constance)

5 Bordered by Austria, Germany and Switzerland, this is the third largest lake in Western Europe with a maximum depth of 252m and a total surface area of 545 sq m. Forming a natural border between Switzerland, which has all of the southern shore, and Germany which has most of the northern, it was occupied by the Celts before the Romans ousted them in the 1st century. The biggest Roman settlement was that at Arbor Felix, now Arbon, before the Alemanni removed them in turn in the 3rd century. Remains of all three civilisations are therefore a feature of the area, although evidence of the earliest human settlement has been traced to the Mesolithic period (8000–5000BC) and the remnants of whole Iron Age villages (c.800BC) – built when the water level was appreciably lower – can be seen at low tide. The road southeast along the south bank passes through a series of attractive villages and holiday resorts, many of them with boating harbours, and some of them with a surprising historical significance. Münsterlingen, for example, the second village reached, has a

former **Benedictine nunnery** which was reportedly founded by the ship-wrecked daughter of Edward the Confessor in the 10th century. The present **church**, an attractive early 18th-century baroque building, is host to the 16th-century bust of John the Baptist which, traditionally, makes the 8km journey to a church in Hagnau across the lake whenever it freezes over (this last occurred in 1968). The small village of Kesswil, notable for its pretty half-timbered houses, was the birthplace of the world-famous psychologist Carl Gustav Jung in 1875.

The port of Romanshorn, a good place to catch a steamer for a leisurely cruise, is followed by the former Roman settlement of Arbon, the first town of any size on this easterly lakeside route. It has a fine lakefront promenade of nearly 3km and a collection of handsome old buildings, including a medieval **castle** built on the remains of a Roman fort. There is a small **museum** inside. The neighbouring church of **St Martin** has a choir of 1490 and a tower of 1457. Note also the chapel of **St Gallus**, founded in the 7th century in memory of the saint who died in the town in 645. It contains some interesting, but faded, 14th-century frescos.

Follow the south bank of Lake Constance to reach Rorschach in 33km (20 miles).

Rorschach, St Gallen

6 One of the most attractive ports on Lake Constance, this old town has traditionally been the most important conduit of maritime trade with Germany. Founded in the 9th century by the monks of St Gallen, Rorschach reflects a similar level of medieval charm to its near neighbour. One of its ecclesiastical benefactors' most enduring legacies is the splendid baroque **Kornhaus**, a stately old granary built close to the harbour in 1746. It now houses an intriguing **museum** illustrating in vivid detail the history of the region, with particular emphasis on the lace and weaving industries. Just east of here is a pretty park with a lakefront promenade and fountains. The main street, the Hauptstrasse, has a number of interesting 16th- to 18th-century buildings, with the late 17th-century **Rathaus** standing out as a particularly fine example. Close by is the baroque mid-17th-century church of **Saints Columban and Constance**. On the southern outskirts of the town, prominent on a hillside, is the former **Benedictine abbey of Mariaberg**, another inheritance from the monastery at St Gallen. Now a teachers' seminary, it has a lovely early 16th-century Gothic **cloister** with an intriguingly interwoven vaulted roof.

Continue on road 7/13 through St Margrethen, then after 3km Au, and then look carefully for a sign to Berneck on a minor road to the right. Follow the narrow country road through Reute, Oberegg, St Anton and Wald until Trogen (about 40km /5 miles).

Trogen, Ausserrhoden

7 A beautifully sited small hilltown, with its handsome 18th-century mansions visible from some distance, Trogen is the elegant former capital of the half-canton of Appenzell-Ausserrhoden. At the centre of the town, the stately Landsgemeindeplatz – bordered by palatial merchants' houses – is the venue for the cantonal assembly which meets in even-numbered years. This apparent eccentricity is explained by a scrupulously democratic power-sharing arrangement with nearby Hundwil which acts as the seat of government in odd-numbered years. Among the many fine buildings which surround the square is a **church** of 1779, the neo-classical **Rathaus** of 1803 and the **school** of about 1650 – which is the oldest structure in this group. Note also the **Gasthaus zur Krone**, an early 18th-century tavern with fine painting on its façade. Just south of the town on this tour is the **Kinderdorf Pestalozzi**, a famous children's 'village' founded after World War II for war orphans from all over the world.

Take the mountain road south to Bühler, then join route 150 northwest to Teufen and take the mountain road south to Stein and Hundwil before joining route 8 to **Herisau** *(27km/17 miles).*

The elegant eastern façade of the mid-18th-century cathedral in St Gallen looks out over the monastery precinct

Herisau, Ausserrhoden

8 Capital of the half-canton, this bustling market town is characterised by some charming wooden houses and, like Trogen, an impressive central square surrounded by elegant 18th- to 19th-century buildings. Outstanding amongst them is a fine old church of 10th-century foundation, but dating in its present form from the early 1500s. It retains a 14th-century **tower**, and some intricate Gothic vaulting in the choir. Next door, the **Rathaus** is now home to a local **museum**. It is worth wandering through the old streets leading off the square to admire a mixture of building styles, and some unexpected treasures in a town that has traditionally been overshadowed by nearby St Gallen. The Oberdorfstrasse has some particularly handsome structures. On two hills overlooking the town are the remains of two 14th-century **castles**, the **Rosenberg** and **Ramsenberg** – to the north and west respectively. According to legend these were once connected by a bridge.

Return to St Gallen (10km/6 miles).

St Gallen – Wil 29 (18)
Wil – Frauenfeld – Steckborn 17 (10.5)
Frauenfeld – Steckborn 17 (10.5)
Steckborn – Kreuzlingen 16 (10)
Kreuzlingen – Rorschach 33 (21)
Rorschach – Trogen 40 (25)
Trogen – Herisau 27 (17)
Herisau – St Gallen 10 (6)

1 to 2 days: 217km (135 miles)

STAMPS AND SÄNTIS

An unusual wall sign in Appenzell spells out a cryptic message to cats and builders

Appenzell • Gais • Altstätten • Vaduz
Malbun • Wildhaus • Säntis • Urnäsch
Lichtensteig • Appenzell

You can expect plenty of variety on this tour which starts in the lush pastoral environs of Appenzell, follows the wide Rhein (Rhine) valley to the tiny principality of Liechtenstein, climbs above the valley floor to just beneath the mountainous frontier with Austria, before finally entering the Toggenburg district – a region of low mountain meadows and fir-clad slopes furrowed by the Thur river. Along its course is a string of pleasant farming villages, market towns and health resorts. But perhaps the highlight of the tour is the brief diversion to Mount Säntis – offering unquestionably the finest mountain panorama of northeast Switzerland.

ⓘ Hauptgasse 19

Follow signs to Altstätten, stopping at Gais after 6km (4 miles).

Gais, Ausserrhoden

1 A pleasantly sited health resort offering fine mountain views south towards the Säntis, this little town earned international fame in the last century as the first centre specialising in the 'whey cure' – a sometime fashionable treatment

involving the consumption of large quantities of milk. Gais has an exceptionally beautiful square, surrounded by late 18th-century baroque residences with many-windowed white façades and distinctively curved gables. Most of this group was built after a fire in 1780 which destroyed the heart of the old town. In the parish church, built at the same time, the designer has been unusually generous with the stucco brush and you will note that elsewhere in the town rococo is a popular decorative feature. A good excursion is to the summit of the 1,251m Gäbris, immediately above the town, where there are inspiring views in all directions. This is also true of the summit of the Stoss pass, 4km east on this tour, where there is a 15th-century chapel built in memory of a battle in 1405 in which 400 Appenzellers defeated a vastly larger Austrian army, thus liberating the region from the unwelcome occupiers. Legend records that Appenzeller women-folk played a significant role in the action. Near by is a monument commemorating the same historic victory.

Continue on the same road to Altstätten for 10km (6 miles).

Altstätten, St Gallen

2 Located on a broad fertile plain on the western side of the Rhine valley, this charming medieval town is protected by the Appenzell Hills to the south and west – providing ideal conditions for farming and vine growing. Its most appealing feature is the distinctive Marktgasse, a picturesque arcaded street lined with 18th-century houses characterised by the high rounded gables typical of this part of the country. Two

BACK TO NATURE

About 7km south of Appenzell, a cable car ascends from the small resort village of Wasserauen to the 1,640m Ebenalp. Some way beneath the summit, reached by a cliff path, is a former 17th-century hermitage in the caverns of Wildkirchli. The prehistoric remains of cave lions, bears and wolves which once inhabited this deep grotto (although not presumably simultaneously) have been found here. So too have human remains, making it one of the oldest prehistoric settlements in the country.

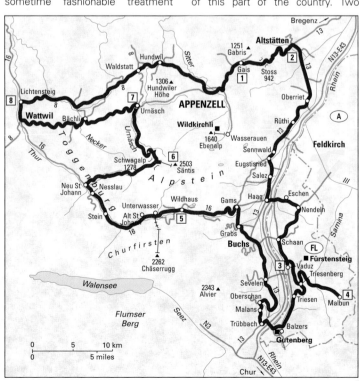

anomalous structures disturb the harmony of the sweep of raised and pillared arcades: the small 17th-century Placidus chapel was erected by those indefatigable builders – the monks of St Gallen – long before the main part of the street took shape. Opposite is a late 15th-century building which, although clearly much changed, is still identifiable as belonging to an earlier period. Note also the neo-classical late 18th-century Catholic church of St Nicholas. The pretty Engelplatz is the natural heart of the old town and retains one of four original town gates. The square also has an attractive fountain and a cluster of pleasingly asymmetrical old buildings. On the Obergasse, in a 15th-century mansion, there is a local history museum.

Follow road 13 south via Oberriet. At Eugstisriet the road forks to Haag. From Haag follow signs to Nendeln, crossing the **N13**, *and then take the road south to Vaduz (37km/23 miles).*

Vaduz, Liechtenstein

3 The distinguishing feature of this otherwise surprisingly ordinary little capital town is the imposing and impressively sited castle which dominates the surrounding area from its rocky shelf overlooking the Rhine. This is home to the Liechtenstein royal family (celebrated for their common touch) and is not open to the public. Its position, immediately next to the winding mountain road up to the ancient village of Triesenberg, means however that it can be viewed at close quarters. Its origins date back to the 12th century and the keep and those buildings on the eastern section are the oldest surviving parts. The walls of the northeast round tower, built at the beginning of the 16th century, are up to 4.5m thick in places.

In terms of architectural and aesthetic merit, there is little to recommend the town below it but, unusually in view of its size, Vaduz

A typically painted wooden façade of an Appenzeller house

has three world-famous museums – all on the Städtle, the larger of the two main one-way streets which comprise the centre. The **Liechtenstein State Art Collection**, in the Engländerbau (the 'Englishmen's building') has works by Rubens, Van Dyck and Breughel; in the **Landesmuseum** (National Museum) you will find an interesting collection of ancient artefacts, weapons, coins, jewellery, folk art and a large relief model of the principality; and in the **Postal Museum** you will learn why Liechtenstein is practically synonymous with the world of philately.

As a base for entertainment and excursions the town has much to recommend it, offering most of the sports facilities associated with a major resort and a network of picturesque paths through delightful countryside. A pleasant, well-marked walk from the centre leads to the ruins of the old robber-barons' castle of **Wildschloss**, a steep but scenic hour-long route through the Schlosswald woods to the north.

i Staedle 37

Take the Schloss-strasse just north of the town centre for 15km (9 miles), via Triesenberg, to Malbun.

Samina and Malbun valleys, Liechtenstein

4 The mountain road behind Vaduz Castle winds towards the upper Samina valley through the old village of Triesenberg, spectacularly positioned on a terrace high over the Rhine valley. A charming little church with an onion-domed tower is poised precariously over a vertiginous drop just to the side of the road. The village, in common with other small settlements in the vicinity and Austria's neighbouring Vorarlberg region, was populated by

SPECIAL TO...

3 The tiny state of Liechtenstein's somewhat disproportionate influence in stamp collecting circles means that Vaduz's post office, in the Städtle, is as much a focus of interest for collectors as the postal museum itself. Various commemorative issues are permanently on sale here.

RECOMMENDED WALKS

4 On the road to Malbun from Vaduz, just after the villages of Rotenboden and Masescha, you will see a signpost to Gaflei. This is the base for the famous 'Fürstensteig', a marked path said to have been cleared on the orders of Prince Johann II in the late 19th century. It now offers competent walkers the opportunity to marvel at magnificent views of the principality and the Rhine valley. You will need good walking boots, a head for heights, and a walking map from one of the local tourist offices. Park by the hotel (where there are excellent terrace views) and allow three to four hours.

FOR HISTORY BUFFS

5 Ulrich Zwingli, who died in 1531 aged 47, is one of Switzerland's most dominant historical figures. The son of a peasant, born near the small mountain village of Wildhaus, he was educated at Basel (Basle) University and later became instrumental in effecting the Reformation throughout the country. He was both an army chaplain and priest in the Grossmünster in Zürich, and he was killed at the Battle of Kappel (near Zug) between the Reformist and Catholic cantons. As a result of the battle, a treaty provided that each canton could choose its own faith.

SCENIC ROUTES

5 The road which descends the Toggenburg valley from Wildhaus to Neu St Johann is exceptional for its views of the seven peaks of the Churfirsten range south, but is equalled in scenic grandeur by the road which climbs from Neu St Johann up the northern flank of the valley past the Säntis to Urnäsch.

A distinctive onion dome forms the focus of the Liechtenstein village of Triesenberg, high above the Rhine valley

members of the Walser community who emigrated from the Valais in the 13th century. There is a small museum devoted to the Walser people (who tend to keep their language and customs very much alive wherever they have settled). The most eastern settlement in Liechtenstein is Malbun, at the head of the beautiful tributary valley of the same name, and close to the mountainous Austrian border. This is a small and relatively exclusive ski resort located at 1,599m, where both the Liechtenstein and British royal families have regularly taken winter breaks. There are plenty of restaurants with sunny terraces here and the helpful tourist office will give you a list of local walks timed to fit your schedule.

On the return to the Rhine valley floor you will pass through the old Celtic settlement of Triesen, notable for a 15th-century Gothic chapel. On the road south to Balzers you will see the imposing pile of the 14th-century Gutenberg castle ahead, and in the village itself is a small local museum detailing its history.

Return to Triesenberg and take the winding road to Triesen, then go south to Balzers. Cross the **N13** *to Trübbach, then via Malans, Oberschan and Sevelen to Buchs follow signs to Grabs, joining road 16 at Gams to Wildhaus (about 53km/33 miles).*

Wildhaus, St Gallen

5 Straddling a wide mountain pass and framed dramatically by the seven jagged teeth of the Churfirsten range to the southwest and the great ridge of the Alpstein massif immediately north, this old village is now one of northeastern Switzerland's largest sports resorts – albeit one that is not widely known outside the country. It is an unpretentious, straggling arrangement of hotels and traditional old chalets with one notable feature. Possibly the country's oldest surviving timber house is found near here (in the neighbouring hamlet of Lisighaus) –

an unexpected gem lent additional distinction by the fact that it was the birthplace of Ulrich Zwingli, the famous 16th-century reformer, in 1484. Wildhaus also has a fine late 18th-century baroque church (**St Bartholomew's**) with interesting ceiling paintings. In winter the resort is a popular base for some fairly friendly skiing in the midst of beautiful scenery; in summer it provides ample scope for testing ascents of the Säntis, and less testing long summer walks assisted by a large network of mountain lifts. These link Wildhaus to the smaller resorts of Unterwasser (**Alpine Dairy Museum**) and Alt-St Johann, which you will pass through shortly by road. From the former there is a funicular to the midway station at Iltios (good views of the Säntis), and from there a cable car ascends to a fine viewpoint on the 2,262m Chäserrugg. From the restaurant terrace you will be able to look south over the Walensee and the Flumser Berg.

Continue on road 16 to Neu St Johann then turn east, following signs to Säntis (28km/17.5 miles).

Mount Säntis

6 If you allow yourself only one aerial excursion to a mountain top on this tour, put this at the top of your list. At only 2,502m, there are much higher mountains in Switzerland, but Säntis can rival any in terms of the quality of its panoramic views. To the north lies the broad glassy outline of Bodensee (Lake Constance);

to the east, over the Rhine valley, are the Vorarlberg mountains of Austria; to the south, beyond the Churfirsten range, the Glarus and Graubünden Alps; and to the southwest, the unmistakable configuration of the Bernese Alps. Zürichsee (Lake Zürich) is also visible and beyond it, in fine conditions, a distant prospect of the Jura. The journey from Schwägalp by cable car covers nearly 1,200 vertical metres in about ten minutes, followed by a short walk to the summit where an observatory has been built. There is also a panoramic restaurant near the top.

Continue on the same road north to Urnäsch for 11km (7 miles).

Urnäsch, Ausserrhoden

7 One of the most attractive villages in the half-canton, Urnäsch has a charming square surrounded by fine 17th- to 18th-century timber buildings, a mid-17th-century church, and a sense of tradition which is almost tangible. If a ringside seat at the spectacle of authentic folk dancing is one of your cherished ambitions, then you need look no further than this typical Appenzeller community (if you choose your time carefully). Holidays and religious feast days are guaranteed to have the locals performing – and it is fair to say that whatever the occasion the dance represents something rather more than an elaborate pastoral cabaret for the benefit of tourists.

The creamy folds of the Säntis

Follow the mountain road west via Bächli and Hemberg to Wattwil, then turn north on road 8 to Lichtensteig (25km/15.5 miles).

Lichtensteig, St Gallen

8 Principal town of the Toggenburger district, this is a gloriously sited medieval town on a woody spur above the right bank of the river Thur. Founded around the turn of the 13th century, it was once owned by the monks of St Gallen and some of the prosperity they engendered is reflected in the elegant Hauptgasse, lined by handsome half-timbered arcaded mansions dating from the 16th to 18th century. One of the most distinctive is the old **Rathaus**, built in the early 16th century and altered in the next. Close by is the Toggenburger Heimatmuseum, with a good collection of old musical instruments among its exhibits. And if you are an admirer of 1960s church architecture, pay a visit to the **church of St Gallus** – a particularly striking example of the genre.

Continue on route 8 to Waldstatt, then go through Hundwil on the return to Appenzell (32km/20 miles).

Appenzell – Gais 6 (4)
Gais – Alstätten 10 (6)
Alstätten – Vaduz 37 (23)
Vaduz – Malbun 15 (9)
Malbun – Wildhaus 53 (33)
Wildhaus – Säntis 28 (17.5)
Säntis – Urnäsch 11 (7)
Urnäsch – Lichtensteig 25 (15.5)
Lichtensteig – Appenzell 32 (20)

FOR CHILDREN

7 There is an excellent museum of local folklore in Urnäsch, housed in an old timber-frame building, which is notable for its comprehensive and colourful collection of ancient hats and costumes. Children should be intrigued by the extraordinarily unwieldy head-dresses painted with a variety of different pastoral scenes.

2 days: 290km (180 miles)

THE RING OF TÖDI

Glarus • Klöntaler See (Lake Klöntal)
Andermatt • Disentis/Mustér • Vorderrhein
Valley (Ilanz, Flims-Waldhaus) • Bad Ragaz
Sargans • Flums • Walensee • Glarus

The 3,614m mount of Tödi is the highest of the peaks which collectively form the Glarus Alps (Glarner Alpen). Marking the boundary line of the cantons of Glarus and Graubünden, the summit also lies just about a kilometre east of the historic canton of Uri. After a short diversion into the picturesque Klöntal valley, this tour takes you through all three cantons as it circles the Tödi – best viewed from Linthal as you drive south from Glarus – and peripherally into the canton of St Gallen, via the beautiful Walensee, on the return leg. En route you will cross the scenic Klausenpass, stop at the old staging post of Andermatt, enter the Graubünden via the dramatic Oberalppass and return to Glarus via the Vorderrhein and Rhein (Rhine) valleys.

A jagged cataract-streaked precipice beside the scenic Klausenpass

[i] Kirchweg 18

Follow signs to Klöntaler See and Richisau for 13km (8 miles).

Klöntal, Glarus

1 This beautiful, narrow Alpine valley west of Glarus leads to the small and pretty hamlet of Richisau at its head. The road follows the north bank of the pale green Klöntaler See (Lake Klöntal), which doubled in size since the construction of a dam some years ago, and there are many pleasing viewpoints en route – especially of the great rock of the Glärnisch which rises abruptly from the southern shore. This lovely spot gave inspiration to the 18th-century Swiss poet Salomon Gessner who kept a summer chalet here.

Return to Glarus and drive up the Linth valley, over the Klausenpass (see Tour 12) to Altdorf (see also Tour 12) then taking the old road south up the Reuss valley to Andermatt (111km/69 miles).

Andermatt, Uri

2 This ancient crossroads town is located at the junction of four famous old mountain roads (Furka, Oberalp, St Gotthard and Reuss valley), three of which are closed for more than half of the year. Its historical importance as a staging post is therefore reflected in the design of the buildings, many of which show Italian and Valaisian influences. The busy main street is flanked by mainly 17th- to 18th-century buildings, some of which bear the curious scale-type cladding common to this part of Switzerland. The **church of St Peter and Paul**, between the

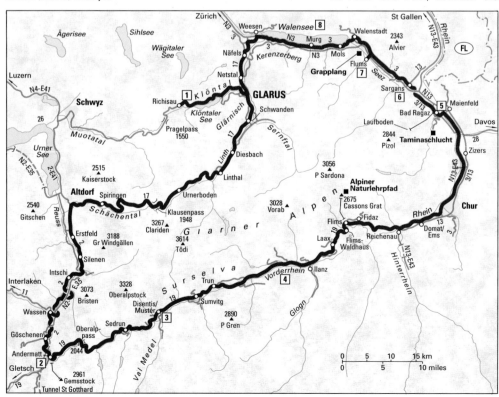

TOUR 15 71

main street and the river, is a fine baroque structure of 1695 with a rococo interior and a font of 1582. Near by is the **Rathaus**, an attractively arcaded stone building of 1767 incorporating parts of a 16th-century predecessor in its structure. In front is an old fountain, usually decked with flowers in the summer. Two other buildings merit mention: on the northern entrance to the town is the church of **St Columban**, rebuilt in the 16th century on the site of an earlier church of 766, and high on a hill above the village to the south is the mid-18th-century chapel of **Maria-Hilf** with excellent mountain views.

Andermatt – literally 'on the meadow' – has achieved worldwide fame as a ski resort, and its terrain is reputed to be among the most challenging in Europe. During the summer it is equally popular with climbers and walkers, with over 500km of paths. From the summit of the 2,961m Gemsstock, reached by two-stage cable car from the southern outskirts of the town, there is a magnificent panorama of the St Gotthard massif.

Take road 19 for 34km (21 miles) over Oberalppass to Disentis/Mustér.

Disentis/Mustér, Graubünden

3 This old regional capital looks down from its woody mountain terrace on the confluence of the two rivers flowing down from the Lukmanier and Oberalp passes; and because it lies at the meeting place of these two historic routes, over the centuries Disentis has played unwilling host to a succession of retreating and advancing armies – not always to its advantage. The town, now a popular holiday resort and spa, grew up in the shadow of a **Benedictine abbey**, founded in the 8th century but repeatedly destroyed by foreign aggressors. The present imposing abbey buildings, on the

Late autumn in the village square in Andermatt is still mild enough for outside refreshment

original site, date from the 17th century, and the intrinsic abbey church of **St Martin** is a substantial baroque structure which resisted the best French efforts to level it in 1799. Flanked by two distinctive onion-domed towers, it contains a 17th-century altar and other fine period details.

The 'Mustér' suffix is the Romansch translation of Disentis.

Continue east on road 19 up the Vorderrhein valley, via Ilanz, Flims and Reichenau, for 52km (32 miles).

Vorderrhein Valley, Graubünden

4 The main road east from Disentis follows the north bank of the Vorderrhein (Rhine) and passes through a string of charming old villages in what is also known as the Surselva region. The first village of significance is Trun, where members of the 'Grey League' – founders of the canton of Graubünden – swore their famous oath of loyalty in 1424. The maple which now stands close to the 18th-century baroque chapel of **St Anna** is the direct progeny of the original tree under which the swearing ceremony took place. If you are an admirer of early 20th-century painting, you will find some fine frescos (1924) in the vestibule of the chapel which commemorate the sacred oath. The main town of the valley is Ilanz, a picturesque old place which became the official capital of the Grey League in the 15th century. The medieval quarter lies on the south bank of the Vorderrhein (Rhine). In common with many of the churches in this valley, the late Gothic **St Margarethen** has some splendid ceiling paintings dating from the early 1500s. The belfry is early 15th-century. Among

FOR HISTORY BUFFS

1 The Pragelpass above Lake Klöntal, which leads into the Muotathal, has proved to be virtually impassable to all but feet, hooves or skis. In 1799 the Russian General Suvorov took his army over here on his way to Schwyz, and in 1892 two Norwegians completed what is thought to be the first crossing on skis of a Swiss mountain pass.

4 After the bloody battle of Reichenau in 1799, Napoleon's exhausted troops recovered on the meadows beneath Flims. Despite their anxieties, the villagers were left unharmed by their unexpected visitors.

FOR CHILDREN

4 If the weather is amenable, why not take the children for a cool swim in one of the charming mountain-ringed lakes in Flims. Lake Cauma, deep in the Flims forest, can warm up to a perfectly bearable 23°C. But if the water temperature proves a little too cool, there are plenty of boats and pedalloes to bob around in on both Cauma and Cresta lakes. If all else fails, try the indoor skating rink.

BACK TO NATURE

4 Accessible by three-stage mountain lift from Flims-Dorf, the Alpiner Naturlehrpfad is a sprawling nature reserve spectacularly set in the lee of the 2,675m Cassons Grat. Here you will find a variety of Alpine flora (and resilient fauna) flourishing at an altitude not far beneath the eternal snows.

RECOMMENDED TRIP

5 A highly rewarding excursion from the town, via car or foot, is to the dramatic Tamina gorge (Taminaschlucht) (entrance fee) where the hot springs – which feed Bad Ragaz's thermal baths – emerge. A narrow path winds down through a cleft in the rock to a wooden gallery where, centuries ago, apprehensive patients were lowered on ropes into the steaming, bubbling waters.

SPECIAL TO...

4 The Vorderrhein valley, which cuts through the heart of the Surselva region, is one of the main cultural and linguistic centres of the Romansch-speaking peoples. Divided into five principal dialects, Romansch is an ancient hybrid of Latin and Celtic tongues. It is the 'Surselvan' variant which is taught in all of the schools of the valley, Although only about one per cent of Swiss people speak Romansch, 22 per cent of Graubündners (about 40,000 people) use it as a first language.

the handsome collection of 17th-century baroque houses here, note particularly the **Casa Gronda**, built in 1677, in which the ubiquitous Russian guest, General Suvorov, once stayed in 1799. The **Surselva Regional Museum** is housed in the **Casa Carniec** and has an interesting collection of exhibits reflecting the culture of the Romansch-speaking peoples.

The major resort of the valley is Flims, a sophisticated all-year playground beautifully located on a wooded terrace high above the valley floor. A sprawling village, it is in fact divided into two distinct halves about 1km apart. The older, Flims Dorf, has some fine old buildings including a fine 17th-century parish hall and an early 16th-century church, but traditionally more popular with the international skiing set is Flims-Waldhaus, a cluster of elegant hotels and apartments attractively set amidst conifers with three pretty lakes close by. Flims enjoyed modest fame in the late 19th century as a spa, but it was not until the installation of Europe's first chairlift just after World War II that it became a major resort. Because of the scarcity of steel, this primitive form of mountain transport was constructed entirely from wood. Today, the lift network is as advanced as any in the country, and if you put aside time to take the three-stage lift (two chairs and a cable car) via Foppa and Naraus, you will be rewarded with a lovely panorama from the summit of Cassons Grat (2,675m). Above the hamlet of Fidaz, a short distance east of Flims, note the ruins of the medieval castle of **Belmont**, formerly the judicial centre of this part of the Graubünden. Last of the major settlements in the valley is Reichenau, once the scene of bitter fighting in the

Napoleonic campaign. The village church is late 15th-century, and **Reichenau Castle** dates from 1616, substantially rebuilt 200 years later.

*Join the **N13** Autobahn at Reichenau, following it to Bad Ragaz for 27km (17 miles).*

Bad Ragaz, St Gallen

5 One of the country's most famous traditional spa towns, Bad Ragaz enjoys a beautiful location on the bank of the Rhine and is complemented by an agreeable mix of modern resort facilities (including a golf course) and a variety of stately old buildings. The older of the town's two churches, St Pancras (built in 1703) retains a medieval tower and has some interesting 18th-century ceiling paintings. Of more interest, however, is the early 15th-century chapel of St Leonard with a splendidly painted choir of the same period. This can be found near the northwest exit of the town, beneath the ruins of the 13th-century Freudenberg Castle which was destroyed by the Swiss Confederates in 1437.

More recently, Bad Ragaz has acquired an additional reputation as a winter sports centre. A cable car ascends to the 1,630m peak of Pardiel to the west of town, and from there over the snowfields of Pizol to the higher station of Laufböden (2,224m). From both points there are fine views of the Ratikon massif to the east and the Rhine valley beneath, and there are good summer walks from the latter.

*Take the old road north to Sargans, passing under the **N3**.*

Sargans, St Gallen

6 Although the old core of this small town was completely destroyed

A weir's mirrorlike surface contrasts with the turbulence of a rocky stream in the Bisisthal valley

by fire in 1811, it retains some interesting features. The 18th-century church of Saints Oswald and Cassian, protected by an unseen Divine hand, survived largely unscathed – although alterations in 1892 and the addition of a new roof in 1934 fundamentally changed its appearance. Another survivor, the 13th-century town castle, has also undergone various rebuilding works, but since they took place over 500 years ago the old 'Schloss Sargans' still preserves its solid medieval appearance. Dominating the town from a woody bluff, it was the seat of the regional governors until 1798. Today it houses a local history museum in its keep. Below, in the 'new' town, the Rathaus is a pleasing neo-classical structure.

Continue on the old road, following signs to Flums, for 9km (5.5 miles).

Flums, St Gallen

7 Pull off the main road to take a closer look at this delightfully unspoilt old village at the mouth of the Schils valley. Above it to the northwest, conspicuous on a hill over the Seez valley, is the spectacular ruin of the 13th-century Castle of Gräpplang framed against a jagged mountain background. The village was once the location of a small iron-ore smelting industry, and its legacy is reflected in the mid-16th-century ironmaster's house

Framed by Alpine forests and meadows, the 13th-century ruins of Burg Grapplang above Flums withstand the ravages of time

(Eisenherrenhaus). Note also the ancient church of St Justus, rebuilt in the 12th century on the site of Roman remains. The Romanesque tower, and the choir, are of 15th-century origin. Near by is the former dower house of the castle, built in 1524, and another old house of 1624. Between the village and the castle is the chapel of St Jakob, a part-Romanesque structure with late 13th-century wall paintings.

Return to the main road, following signs to Walenstadt. Then follow the south bank of the Walensee (part of it on the N3) to Weesen (25km/15.5 miles).

Walensee, St Gallen

8 This lovely lake is one of the most frequented spots in the eastern Swiss Alps. Splendidly situated beneath sheer green cliffs on its northern shore, they in turn are dwarfed by the jagged teeth of the Churfirsten range behind. At each end of this 15km stretch of emerald water lie two popular holiday centres. Walenstadt, on the east bank, is an old garrison town with some fine 16th- and 17th-century buildings, and parts of the old town wall still much in evidence. The road which follows the south bank to Weesen is very appealing, and the charming little town at its end does it full justice. Not least of its attractions is a pleasantly shady lakeside promenade offering fine views, but it also has a collection of interesting old buildings including the 13th-century church of the Holy Cross which, together with the former convent and some other old Gothic structures, form a delightful square in the heart of the village.

Return via Näfels (see Tour 12) to Glarus (12km/7.5 miles).

Glarus – Richisau (Klöntal) 13 (8)
Richisau – Andermatt 111 (69)
Andermatt – Disentis/Mustér 34 (21)
Disentis/Mustér – Vorderrhein Valley – 52 (32)
Vorderrhein Valley – Bad Ragaz 27 (17)
Bad Ragaz – Sargans 7 (4.5)
Sargans – Flums 9 (5.5)
Flumes – Walensee 25 (15.5)
Walensee – Glarus 12 (7.5)

SCENIC ROUTES

Apart from the Klausenpass (see Tour 12), the scenic high points of the tour include the 2,044m Oberalppass road between Andermatt and Disentis, the mountain road up to the sun terrace of Flims, and the beautiful lakeside road around the Walensee.

GRAUBÜNDEN

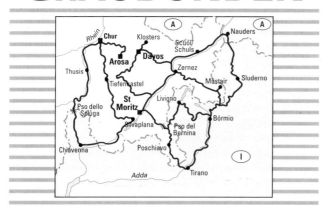

The largest of the Swiss cantons, Graubünden is also the most sparsely populated with less than one-sixth of the national average of inhabitants per square kilometre. The Graubünden Alps extend from the watershed of the St Gotthard massif in the west to the Rätikon range in the northeast, and to the Bernina massif on the border with Italy in the south. Also known by their French name of 'Grisons', these mountains comprise the Adula, Silvretta and Albula ranges and are criss-crossed by an intricate network of more than 150 valleys, one of the canton's most appealing features. The longest and most beautiful is the famous Engadine, which stretches for over 100km from the source of the En (or 'Inn') river near the Passo di Maloja (Maloja pass), via St Moritz, to Martina on the Austrian border.

Whereas the name of the canton may be unfamiliar to those who have never visited this southeastern part of the Swiss Alps, the leading international resorts of St Moritz, Davos, Klosters, Arosa and Flims may be more easily recognised. These are the great showpieces of the canton's flourishing winter sports industry. However, the region is by no means geared exclusively to its international playgrounds. In fact of all the Swiss regions, the southeast is the place where visitors will be most likely to find peace and seclusion. Against powerful competition, the Graubünden offers some of the most beautiful countryside in the country, rich in mountain scenery, sprawling forests and glittering Alpine lakes.

And for those who seek tangible reminders of the region's illustrious past, the medieval city of Chur, the oldest recorded settlement in Switzerland, offers a splendid collection of 14th- to 18th-century buildings, and three fine museums. But the most unusual characteristic of Graubünden is less to do with its scenery, history or architecture, than with its extraordinary mix of tongues. Even by Swiss standards this area is a veritable modern-day Babel, where the 170,000 population speak three different languages, one of which is fragmented into five dialects. Sixty per cent of the 'Bündner' speak German, 22 per cent speak Romansch (and its dialects), 14 per cent Italian, and the remaining 4 per cent a mixture of all three.

Of all the Swiss regions, Graubünden is arguably the most rewarding from a motorist's point of view. With three of the country's great Alpine passes – the Julier, the Splügen, and the Bernina – and with other, but no less dramatic mountain routes, there is no shortage of spectacular altitude driving.

St Moritz

The exclusive resort town of St Moritz is one of the most famous in Switzerland. A measure of how fashionable it is perceived to be throughout the world is the fact that in 1986 it took the unusual step of copyrighting its name, the first geographical location anywhere in the world to do so. In the mid-19th century this leading international playground was a sleepy Alpine village, with a growing reputation for its healing mineral springs. As the direct result of a bet between a local hotelier and a group of British tourists (that they would not be disappointed if they returned in winter) it single-handedly began the winter sports boom.

The town is divided into two parts, Bad and Dorf. The latter consists of a collection of unremarkable buildings, tightly packed above a lake on a steep hillside overlooking the Engadine valley; little remains of the original village apart from a 16th-century bell tower. The Engadiner Museum makes a laudable effort to show what the town was like a century ago, and near by another museum commemorates the Graubünden-born painter Giovanni Segantini. But it is for the extensive range of sporting and recreational facilities that St Moritz is best known, and for six months of the year St Moritz Lake is the venue for a remarkably inventive range of ice-sports including horse-racing on snow, ice polo, winter golf, ice hockey, curling – and skating.

As winter approaches, a tree stubbornly retains its autumn foliage in the mountain resort of Arosa

popular features, and for six months of the year it is the venue for a remarkably inventive range of ice-sports including horse-racing on snow, ice polo, winter golf, ice hockey, curling – and skating.

Arosa

Situated at the end of a steep and winding 30km cul-de-sac, at the head of the beautiful Plessur valley, Arosa was first settled by monks in the 13th century. Today it is one of Switzerland's leading ski and health resorts. In Inner-Arosa, the older and higher part of the village, many of the traditional wooden chalets still retain their delicate fretwork and elaborate inscriptions and there is a fine example of a late Gothic mountain church. Among a comprehensive range of sporting facilities there is, unusually for such a secluded spot, a casino. The Schlanfugg Museum has a section devoted to winter sports, effectively inaugurated when Sir Arthur Conan Doyle arrived on skis over the mountain from Davos in 1894.

A grizzled fisherman looks across the lake to the exclusive resort of St Moritz

2 days: 257km (160 miles)

BERNINA AND THE ENGADINE

St Moritz • Passo del Bernina (Bernina Pass) Poschiavo • Brúsio • Bórmio (Italy) Unter-Engadin • Zuoz • Celerina • St Moritz

No tour in this guide will provide you with more relentless scenic distraction than this – or a more breathtaking (in the literal sense) journey. Starting from the Ober-Engadin (Upper Engadine), one of the highest inhabited valleys in Europe, you will shortly enter an even higher one – the Val Bernina – before crossing the historic Passo del Bernina (Bernina pass) and beginning the dizzy descent to Poschiavo in the south of the Graubünden. Entering Italy, the mountain scenery is no less dramatic as you turn north through the old spa town of Bórmio and approach the glacier-streaked Órtles range in the Parco Nazionale dello Stélvio. Shortly, the Stélvio – the highest mountain pass in the Alps – is crossed before commencing the steepest descent of the tour down to the Val Venosta. Briefly crossing into Austria, you will return to St Moritz along the spectacularly beautiful Unter-Engadin (Lower Engadine) valley floor – celebrated for the timeless charm of its string of enchanting towns and villages.

Do not forget passports, and take particular care to ensure that your car brakes are in good working order.

Skiers descend a mountain path above the Italian resort of Bórmio

ⓘ Via Maistra 12

Follow signs to Passo del Bernina for 22km (13.5 miles).

Bernina Pass (Passo del Bernina), Graubünden

1 The pass, and the road leading up to it via the Val Bernina, offer some of the most arresting scenery in the canton. Before you reach the summit, at 2,328m, you might take a cable car to one of two excellent mountain-top vantage points (both with restaurants). The 2,973m col of Diavolezza is reached from a base station to the right of the road midway between Pontresina and the pass – about 7km from both. A popular starting point for skiers, it offers magnificent views of the Bernina massif and its glaciers. Alternatively, there are similarly fine views from the 2,959m Piz Lagalb, the base station for which is slightly ahead on the left (the latter summit is slightly cheaper to reach). The road over the pass itself, reached after passing three pretty lakes on the right, was completed in the early 1840s, although the crossing has been used since the 13th century. Leave the car at the hospice car park and explore a little. You will be rewarded with magnificent views of the Val di Poschiavo, into which you will shortly be travelling.

Drive down the Val di Poschiavo for 14km (9 miles) to Poschiavo.

Poschiavo, Graubünden

2 In view of its proximity to the Italian border (virtually encircling it) it is hardly surprising that this little

Panoramic views south down the Poschiavo valley from the Passo del Bernina

town – effectively six separate villages – is predominantly Italian in character. The most emphatic illustration of this is provided by the central Piazza surrounded by handsome patrician Italianate houses. The late Gothic church of San Vittore dates from 1497, although the slender five-storey bell tower is much older. The building is distinctly Lombardian in style, with a fine main portal. Note also the two baroque churches of Santa Maria Presentata (17th-century) and Santa'Anna (rebuilt in the early 18th century) with a striking ceiling painting in the nave. One of the most intriguing characteristics of the town is its Spanish Quarter, built in the early 19th century by people of local descent returning from voluntary exile in Spain. The Spanish influence is demonstrable, with many of the houses adorned with gaily painted façades.

Continue for 10km (6 miles) to Brúsio.

Brúsio, Graubünden

3 The last (scattered) settlement of any significant interest in this part of Switzerland, 3km before the frontier village of Campocologno, Brúsio is attractively situated amidst tobacco fields, walnut and chestnut plantations. Two old churches lift it above the ordinary. The catholic church of St Carlo is 17th-century early-baroque, the village Protestant church is mid-17th-century, rebuilt in 1727. Just over the border ahead, as you enter the fertile Valtellina (part of Graubünden until 1797) you will pass the celebrated early 16th-century pilgrimage church of Madonna di Tirano.

Cross the border, and in Tirano follow signs to Passo dello Stélvio and Bórmio (48km/30 miles).

Bórmio (Italy)

4 If you ignore the dispiriting modern suburbs of this old Roman spa town, you will have some idea of why it has become such a popular winter and summer sports resort. The medieval core is seductively pleasing, with a typically Italian potpourri of bustling markets, pavement cafés, antique shops, and predictably expensive leather goods and clothes shops. It has its fair share of charming historic buildings as well. Head for the cobble-stoned Via Roma if you are planning to stop here for a while, and join the locals in watching the world go by over a cappuccino or a glass of Merlot.

*Drive over Passo dello Stélvio, at 2,757m the highest pass in the Alps, and head down the valley road to Spondigna. Head north on the **SS40** via the east bank of Lago di Résia to the Passo di Résia, crossing the border into Austria. Just before of Nauders, turn left on the narrow road to the Swiss border village of Martina (about 94km/58 miles).*

Unter-Engadin, Graubünden

5 The Engadine valley stretches for nearly 100km from the border with Austria to the Malojapass, which marks the watershed between it and the Val Bregaglia. It takes its name from the En (or 'Inn') river which is fed by the glaciers and tributary mountain streams of the upper part of the valley and which flows, eventually, into the Danube. It

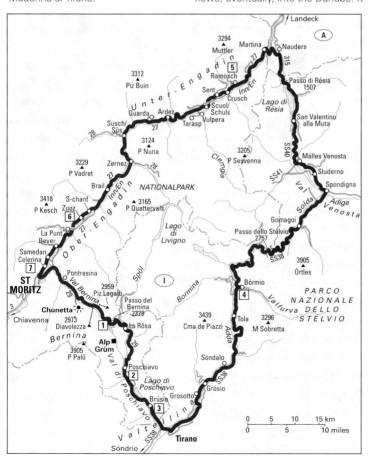

SPECIAL TO...

5 Many old houses in the Engadine bear distinctive floral or geometric patterns on their façades, known as sgraffito. Although it looks like paintwork, it is in fact a method of etching plaster using skilled techniques acquired over centuries.

SCENIC ROUTES

The drive up the Val Bernina at the beginning of the tour is one of many scenic high points en route, but the Val di Poschiavo road from the pass is equally dramatic. Thereafter, the road from Bórmio up to the Passo dello Stélvio will (literally) take your breath away. At 2,757m it is one of the highest mountain roads on the continent and the views south of the Ortles range and its glaciers are magnificent.

is divided into the Ober- and Unter-Engadin (Upper and Lower Engadine), with the boundary marked by a point just west of the village of Zernez, more or less halfway along its length. The valley floor of the former rarely drops much below 1,500m and is characterised by a chain of glorious lakes and sentinel peaks which average well over 3,000m. The Unter-Engadin is narrower, lusher and has a rich catalogue of charming old villages along its route. This is the soul of the 'real' Engadine, with its own unique Romansch culture, architectural style and language. Starting at the frontier village of Martina, you will shortly pass through some of the most beautiful countryside in eastern Switzerland, and some of the most remarkably unspoilt village communities anywhere in Europe. In Ramosch, note the early 16th-century late Gothic church, and the imposing ruins of the 13th-century Tschanüff castle high up on your right. At Crusch leave the main valley road to climb briefly to the little village of Sent with its 15th-century Gothic church, sgraffito-covered houses, and enchanting ruin of the 12th-century church of St Peter (with Romanesque tower) as you follow the road to Scuol. This is the cultural centre of the Unter-Engadin, a spa town with a fine early 16th-century church and some captivat-

ing examples of 17th-century Engadine architecture built around two paved squares. In one of these buildings, known as the Chagronda, is a museum of this part of the Engadine. The town, also known as Bad Scuol, has contrived to become part of a larger spa complex with nearby Tarasp and Vulpera – both attractively situated villages with mineral springs. The three are linked by bridges over the Inn river and pleasant walking paths (as well as roads). Together they have become one of the most popular climatic health resorts in the country. The imposing white building you will see above the valley to the southwest is the Schloss Tarasp, dating from the 11th century but much altered between the 16th and 18th centuries. Until 1803 it was still an Austrian possession, and after falling into disrepair it was restored by a German philanthropist in the early part of this century. Although still privately owned, it can be visited by arrangement with the Scuol tourist office. Back on the valley road Ardez is next entered, and together with Guarda (high off a side road to the right ahead), this remarkable old-world village offers some of the finest examples of the Engadine

The pretty village of Sent occupies a lofty position high above the Lower Engadine valley floor

architectural genre in the entire valley. Note also the 16th-century church and the ruins of the 12th-century Steinsberg castle on a hill to the east. The road now continues to Susch and Zernez (see Tour 17) before entering the Ober-Engadin.

Drive down the Unter-Engadin, entering the upper valley at Zernez and leaving the main road for the lovely old villages of S-chanf and Zuoz (58km/36 miles).

Zuoz, Graubünden

6 The influence of the Planta family in this ancient village of the Ober-Engadin is again clearly seen. The cobbled streets are very narrow, admitting little sunlight and lined by ancient 16th-century buildings shuttered and decorated in the distinctive Engadine style. The fountain in the main square is surmounted by a bear, the heraldic symbol of the Plantas, and a motif you will see repeated throughout the valley. The family coat of arms comprises a bear's paw with the sole (planta in Romansch) turned upwards. This is seen to interesting effect in the decorations of the village's Romanesque church, rebuilt in the 16th century, and providing a conspicuous landmark with its tall, finely tapered spire. One of the most imposing buildings in the village is the former Planta residence with its

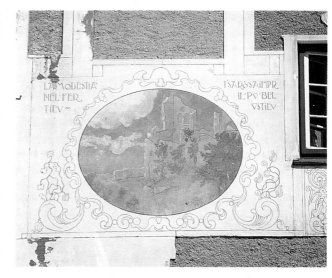

Part of the sgraffiti etched into the plaster of the mid-17th-century Chesa Juvalta in S-chanf

13th-century tower connected by arcades. Formerly the capital of the Ober-Engadin (now somewhat overshadowed by St Moritz) Zuoz is now a summer resort of considerable charm. It is also traditionally a centre of education in the valley, and is the home of the Lyceum Alpinum. In the mid-19th century it was host to the Engiadina boarding school for 'delicate' boys.

Continue on the old road, rejoining the main valley road at La Punt. Keep ahead until the turning for Bever (right) then drive via Samedan (see Tour 17) to Celerina (15km/9 miles).

Celerina, Graubünden

7 Often perceived as a satellite resort to St Moritz, this does an injustice to this pretty old village. It may provide the base station for a significant part of the region's skiing (from Marguns, 2,279m), and some modern and incongruous hotels, but the old quarter near the river has a pleasing traditional character which eludes many larger resorts. There are some characteristic Engadine houses here, and standing on a bluff a short distance east of the centre is the 11th-century Romanesque church of San Gian. The tower was struck by lightning in 1682 and has remained roofless ever since. Inside is a remarkable series of frescos dating from the late 1400s, including a cycle of the life of John the Baptist. Note also the painting of St Mauritius (who gave his name to the neighbouring super resort) on the choir wall.

Celerina has one other claim to fame: it is where the celebrated Cresta bobsleigh run ends.

Drive up the hill for 3km (2 miles) to St Moritz.

St Moritz – Passo del Bernina 22 (13.5)
Passo del Bernina – Poschiaro 14 (9)
Poschiaro – Brúsio 10 (6)
Brúsio – Bórmio 48 (30)
Bórmio – Unter-Engadin 94 (58)
Unter-Engadin – Zuoz 58 (36)
Zuoz – Celerina 15 (9)
Celerina – St Moritz 3 (2)

2/3 days: 276km (172 miles)

THE SEVEN PASSES

Davos • Susch • Zernez • Santa Maria
Müstair • Pontresina • Samedan • Klosters
Davos

Lovers of narrow, twisting mountain roads will be thrilled by the selection presented on this tour. With five Alpine passes in Switzerland and two in Italy, the lowest at 2,149m, the highest at 2,501m, there is no shortage of opportunities to challenge lungs, brakes and gears: and if you count the Wolfgangpass between Davos and Klosters, a mere 1,631m high, eight mountain passes are crossed in total. En route, you will pass through the beautiful Swiss National Park, a completely natural environment that is home to the largest congregation of animal and botanical species in the country. By way of contrast you will also visit two of Switzerland's most exclusive resorts, Pontresina and Klosters. Do not forget passports.

A Swiss milk producer from the Bernese Oberland

ⓘ Promenade 67

From Davos-Dorf, drive up road 28 to the Flüelapass, then down the pass road into Susch (27km/17 miles).

Susch, Graubünden

1 A pretty little village on the Unter-Engadin valley floor, overlooked by the ruins of an old castle, Susch sits picturesquely by the side of the Inn river in a small clearing surrounded by densely wooded hills. In 1925 it was all but destroyed by fire, but the church and an old tower survived. The former, with a conspicuous clocktower, is a stately Gothic building of about 1515, large enough to suggest that Susch was once a village of some importance. The adjacent tower is surmounted by an impressive baroque onion dome.

Continue for 6km (4 miles) on road 27/28 to Zernez.

Zernez, Graubünden

2 As an ideal base for exploration of the Swiss National Park, this attractively situated village, largely rebuilt after a fire of 1872, has inevitably developed into a major resort. But in addition to its sporting and recreational facilities, it also has some intrinsic features of historical interest. The most visible of these is the legacy of the ubiquitous Planta family which stamped its influence on the Engadine valley for the better part of 1,000 years. Among a number of handsome 16th-century houses (which survived the fire) lining the pleasingly cluttered streets, possibly the most appealing

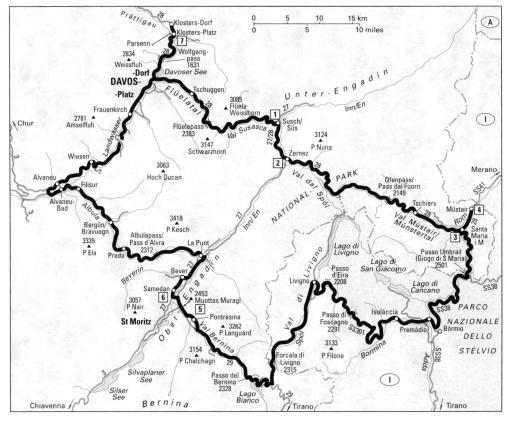

SCENIC ROUTES

1 The scenic road over the 2,383m Flüelapass road was opened in 1867 and commands impressive, if somewhat bleak, views from the hospice. The descent through the rocky Val Susasca to Susch is arguably its most impressive stretch, with fine views to the right up the tributary valley of Grialetsch soon after the pass.

2 The road down the Val Müstair, between the spectacular pass roads of Ofenpass (Pass dal Fuorn) and the Passo Umbrail, is remarkably beautiful. Be prepared to remain in low gear for the ascent of the tarmac track which passes for a road up to the Passo Umbrail. At 2,501m this is the highest of the Swiss mountain passes and one of the most dramatic.

6 Approached by a steep, narrow and, even by Swiss standards, serpentine road from La Punt, the 2,312m Albulapass has been in regular use since the early Middle Ages. The road ahead from Preda to Tiefencastel is the most rewarding of the drive, particularly through the typically Engadine village of Bergün (note the 12th-century church and cluster of prettily painted buildings).

BACK TO NATURE

2 The Swiss National Park is one of the world's most spectacular nature reserves in a monumental setting of extraordinary, solitary beauty. Entrance is free, but rules are rigidly enforced by a team of permanent wardens. Walkers must keep to marked paths, motorists may not deviate from the Ofenstrasse, flowers must not be picked or minerals collected. All that you are permitted to do is to walk, drive and enjoy the scenery and wildlife, which is compensation enough. About one-third of the 169 sq km is forest, another third Alpine meadow and the remainder rock, scree and water. There are 650 species of wild plants, 30 species of mammals, 100 species of birds and 5,000 species of invertebrates. Marmots, red deer, ibex and chamois proliferate, and occasionally white hares, foxes, martens and ermine can also be spotted.

RECOMMENDED WALKS

2 A number of walks through the Swiss National Park are recommended by the National Park House in Zernez, where you can pick up a walking map. All routes are carefully plotted with marked paths to take you to the best vantage points for observing wildlife in their natural habitat.

is the splendid Planta-Wildenberg castle with its 13th-century corner tower, ornate iron grilles and geometric wall patterns. This was one of the principal residences of the family for over 400 years. There are also two fine churches: conspicuous on a slope on the edge of the village is the 17th-century parish church with a tall, slender clocktower (and rich stucco decor), and the little 15th-century chapel of St Sebastian (interesting Gothic wall paintings). Before you leave the village it is worth stepping into the National Park House which gives a comprehensive overall impression of what you can expect next.

Stay on road 28 and drive through the Swiss National Park over Ofenpass (Pass dal Fuorn) to Santa Maria (35km/22 miles).

Santa Maria, Graubünden

3 At the foot of the Val Müstair you will enter the charming old village of Santa Maria, the chief settlement of the valley and one that is particularly notable for its traditional 17th-century houses painted in a style which is clearly reminiscent of the Engadine some 35km north. Short distances can make fundamental differences in style and culture in Switzerland, but clearly not in this case. The village church is a 15th-century late Gothic structure with a

The distinctive juxtaposition of an onion-domed residence tower and early 16th-century campanile in the village of Susch

tower that dates from 1400. There are fine interior murals painted around 1492, an exterior wall painting of St Christopher and some unusual (and ancient) tombstones with coats of arms in the churchyard. Elsewhere in the village there is a small local museum which, among other themes, recalls the life and work of the poet Simon Lemm who was born here in 1511.

Make a brief diversion of 4km (2.5 miles) to Müstair.

Müstair, Graubünden

4 History recounts that the Emperor Charlemagne founded a monastery in this ancient frontier village in the 8th century. Around the 12th century the monastery became a Benedictine nunnery (for reasons that elude ecclesiastical historians) and the medieval group of buildings which were then assembled rank among the oldest in Switzerland. For that reason alone the brief excursion to this old village is worthwhile, but there are others. The adjacent church of St John has a series of remarkable frescos, some of them thought to date from the 9th century, others from the late 12th

RECOMMENDED WALKS

5 Close to the main road between Pontresina and Samedan is a funicular station leading to the 2,453m peak of Muottas Muragl (with hotel and restaurant). The summit provides a superb view of the Bernina massif, the Ober-Engadin (Upper Engadine) and its lakes, and the towns and villages of the valley. It is possible to return to Pontresina by a well-marked, gently sloping path within a couple of hours and this makes a marvellous excursion if you are planning to interrupt the tour here.

FOR CHILDREN

5 In addition to the many activities offered by the 'children's holiday pass' (Kinder-Ferienpass) offered by the larger Ober-Engadin resorts, Pontresina has a large children's playground, the 'Jon e Din', at the Sports Pavilion Roseg (end of Via Maistra). There is a miniature golf course near the Surovas railway station and a large public swimming pool close to the tourist office. If all else fails, take them on a horse-drawn omnibus from the main railway station up the beautiful Roseg valley.

century. Arranged in circular bands, they depict Biblical scenes including the Last Judgement, the crucifixion of St Andrew and the stoning of St Stephen (in graphic detail). Some of the better preserved (depicting the life and Passion of Christ) have found their way to the Zürich National Museum. Note also the 12th-century statue of Charlemagne. Other features of note in the village are the Carolingian Museum (in the convent) and the Romanesque chapel of the Holy Cross with its unusual 16th-century carved ceiling.

Return to Santa Maria, taking the twisting road south for the Passo Umbrail, a distance of 20km (12.5 miles). On entering Italy drive down SS38, turn off to Premádio and follow signs to Passo di Foscagno and Livigno. Drive via the two passes of Foscagno (2,291m) and Eira (2,208m) to the mountain resort town of Livigno. Then climb the Val di Livigno, re-entering Switzerland and joining the Bernina pass road 29. Drive over Passo del Bernina (see Tour 16) to Pontresina (98km/61 miles).

Pontresina, Graubünden

5 Sedately different from its close neighbour St Moritz, Pontresina is far enough removed in style and character to give it a distinct and alluring identity. Formerly a peripheral village on the Bernina pass road, this is now a major year-round resort in its own right with excellent skiing and walking facilities, plus an air of Edwardian grandeur which gives the distinct impression of having changed little over the course of this century. Delightfully set on a southwest facing terrace, surrounded by scented pines and larch woods, its narrow streets

Above the serried ranks of stone and pines, Pontresina's elegant hotels look south west across the Bernina valley floor

demonstrate a successful mix of elegant hotels and typically sgraffiti-decorated Engadine houses with window grilles. Although first documented in the 12th century, it is essentially an early 20th-century resort in appearance – largely dating from the advent of the railway in 1908 when most of the hotels were built. But its earlier character is pleasingly illustrated by the tiny Romanesque church of Santa Maria, mostly 15th-century but with beautifully preserved murals dating from 1230 to 1497. The adjacent pentagonal tower known as La Spaniola dates from the 12th century. Inscriptions on headstones in the graveyard indicate the presence of a surprising number of British remains, suggestive of Pontresina's popularity (if not efficacy) as a health resort in the early 1900s. In an old Engadine house on the Via Maistra there is an Alpine Museum containing the collection of the Bernina Division of the Swiss Alpine Club.

Continue down the valley road for 6km (4 miles) to Samedan.

Samedan, Graubünden

6 Set back off the north side of the main valley road between Zuoz and St Moritz, Samedan occupies a delightful site at the foot of the Val Bernina facing the glittering peaks of the Bernina massif. Finding international fame as a haven for golfers in the 1920s, the core of the largely 18th-century village is none the less essentially unspoilt and much of the Engadine architecture is authentically intact with a variety of historical treasures. Foremost among them is yet another former residence of the Planta family, the 17th-century Chesa Planta, which is now a centre of Romansch culture and history. The church in the village centre is a 17th-century structure with a distinctive late 18th-century belfry. A little higher and to the west is a late Gothic church of 1492, with a simple Romanesque tower of about 1100. Inside is the family vault of the Plantas. The Engadine golf course here was laid out in the early part of this century, one of the first (and highest) altitude courses in the world.

Regain the main valley road, turning left to La Punt and there taking the road over the Albulapass. Continue driving northeast and, just after Alvaneu Bad, take the right turning to Belfort and drive up the Landwasser valley back to Davos. Continue through Davos to Klosters (about 85km/53 miles).

Klosters, Graubünden

7 At first glance it is difficult to see why this resort has become so voguish (especially with certain members of the British royal family). Straggling along a narrow wooded valley, under the brooding Gotschna, it is no more exceptional than many similar-sized Alpine villages and, moreover, it receives very little sunshine.in mid-winter. Added to that, it has a very busy main street which does little to enhance tranquillity. In common with many old-established Swiss resorts it is divided into two distinct parts: Dorf and Platz (the latter also known as Zentrum, which

The 'royal' resort of Klosters lies scattered about the Landquart valley

is where the better-heeled congregate). For all they have in common, they could well be separate villages.

But what Klosters has that others do not is access to some of the most famous ski terrain in the world on the wide snowfields of Parsenn to the southwest. This is accessed, incidentally, by a cable car which bears the name 'The Prince of Wales', the only mountain lift in the country named after a foreign dignitary.

The village takes its name from the cloisters of a 13th-century monastery which has long ceased to exist. The 15th-century church in the centre of Zentrum is one of the few buildings of any historical significance, retaining some fine wall paintings from the same period. There is also a local history museum housed in a restored mid-16th-century farmhouse called the Nuttlihüsli, on the north side of the Monbielstrasse. Although best known as a winter sports resort, Klosters has many advantages as a summer destination. Not least of them is its delightful hiking possibilities, with one famous 27km trail known as the 'circuit'. There is also a network of mountain-biking paths (bicycle rentals can be arranged in Zentrum) and on the Doggilochstrasse there is a fine outdoor heated swimming pool with excellent mountain views.

Return to Davos in 10km (6 miles).

Davos-Dorf – Susch 27 (17)
Susch – Zernez 6 (4)
Zernez – Santa Maria 35 (22)
Santa Maria – Müstair 4 (2.5)
Müstair – Pontresina 118 (73)
Pontresina – Samedan 6 (4)
Samedan – Klosters 85 (53)
Klosters – Davos 10 (6)

SPECIAL TO...

7 Although Klosters is best known as a winter sports resort, it has recently gained popularity as a mountain-biking centre with five hire centres and seven established trails, each comfortably accomplished within a day and ranging from 7 to 25km. The maximum climb is about 800m.

FOR HISTORY BUFFS

7 As you wander through Klosters, some of the older architecture may strike you as reminiscent of another part of Switzerland, the Valais. Once an exclusively Romansch-speaking area, this part of the Graubünden – known as the Prättigau – was settled by German-speaking immigrants from the upper Valais in the late 13th century. The settlers had much to cope with over the next 400 years. A famine in 1622 was followed by the Black Death in 1630, both of which decimated the local population. Those who survived then had to face the next deadly plague; the witch-hunts which remorselessly affected remote farming communities throughout Switzerland accounted for hundreds more deaths.

2/3 days: 277km (172 miles)

THE KEY TO
THE PASSES

Arosa • Chur • Lenzerheide/Valbella
Julierpass • Sils • Val Bregaglia
Splügenpass • The Domleschg • Arosa

Starting in the German-speaking altitude resort of Arosa, this tour takes you via Switzerland's oldest town and then through the Romansch-speaking valley of the Oberhalbstein before crossing the ancient Julierpass into the Ober-Engadin (Upper Engadine valley). As you approach the Italian border through the romantic Val Bregaglia, Italian progressively takes over as the principal language and the culture and architecture becomes noticeably Latin in flavour. Briefly entering a part of Italy which once belonged to the Graubünden, you will pass through the Roman town of Chiavenna, the 'key' to the Julier and Splügen passes, before crossing the latter to follow the Hinterrhein through its beautiful valleys and gorges to the Rhein (Rhine). Do not forget passports.

FOR HISTORY BUFFS

1 The earliest signs of human habitation in Chur have been traced to a neolithic settlement on the left bank of the Plessur river in about 3000BC. This is now covered by the Welschdörfli area of the city. Bronze Age and Iron Age remains have also been found on the same site, but the principal influence on the city's early development was Roman. By the end of the 4th century it was an important bishopric and until the late Middle Ages the Bishops of Chur exercised power far beyond the limits of the city, governing much of the present canton of Graubünden.

SPECIAL TO...

1 Chur's ingenious system of red and green footprints throughout the romantic Old Town allows visitors to follow a 'guided' tour at their convenience via all the most historic sights. Explanatory leaflets (appropriately coloured) are available from the tourist office and give potted histories (in English) of the principal buildings, museums and parks.

[i] Postfach

Drive down the Plessur valley for 29km (18 miles) to Chur.

Chur, Graubünden

1 Signs of human habitation as long ago as 3000BC have been discovered in this old cantonal capital and as a result Chur (pronounced 'kooer') claims to be the country's oldest population centre. But it was the Romans who laid the foundations of what was then known as Curia Rhaetorum, around which the medieval town subsequently developed. Its core is the Martinplatz, a short walk north of the Plessur river, with the 15th-century church of St Martin on its eastern perimeter. Behind this is Rätische Museum, housed in a fine 17th-century mansion and containing a noteworthy collection of prehistoric artefacts and later cantonal antiquities. Above is a fortified group of buildings known as the Bischöflicher Hof, the Bishop of Chur's former court which is reached via the Torturm, an ancient gate tower. The outstanding edifice among them is the Bishop's Palace, an early 18th-century baroque reconstruction with parts of an earlier palace incorporated in the structure. All of this is dominated by the city's cathedral, a 12th-century Roman-esque building which was built on the site of a Roman temple.

Left: a clump of hardy wild flowers withstands the ravages of the bleak and rocky Julierpass Right: the baroque dome of Chur's cathedral

Inside there is a late 15th-century carved altar and four notable early 13th-century statues of Apostles on either side of it. The old town has many other interesting buildings, narrow cobble-stoned alleys and flower-decked courtyards, and the city authorities have thoughtfully painted red and green footprints for you to follow through the most picturesque parts. Let them lead you past the 15th-century Rathaus in the Poststrasse and the 16th- to 17th-century patrician mansions in the Reichgasse which runs parallel. Try also to find time to visit the Kunstmuseum, on the corner of the Postplatz. Housed in a building known as the Villa Planta, it contains the best collection of works by Graubünden painters in the canton, including some alarming science fiction works by the same artist who dreamed up the monster in the film Alien (which has pride of place). A short distance west of the Martinplatz are two interesting vestiges of the city's original fortifications, the Obertor and Pulverturm.

[i] Grabenstrasse 5

Take road 3 south, via Churwalden, for 18km (11 miles) to Lenzerheide/Valbella.

Lenzerheide/Valbella, Graubünden

2 The two health and sports resorts of Lenzerheide and Valbella, only a couple of kilometres apart (and sharing a common ski region) are very beautifully sited on a high mountain road in the heart of the Lenzerheide valley. The timber line is unusually high on the surrounding mountains and there is a pretty little lake called Il Lai (or Heidensee) between the villages. Valbella is the quieter of the two and really little more than a collection of up-market hotels and apartments. Lenzerheide is busier and more colourful, but otherwise generally featureless in terms of its structural endowment, although a few attractive old buildings stand out on the main street. But there are good facilities here and some delightful walking terrain on over 140km of marked paths. One of the main attractions is the trip by two-stage chairlift to the 2,322m peak of Piz Scalottas, or by cable car to the 2,865m Parpaner-Rothorn. There are fine views and walking trails from both. Lenzerheide, incidentally, claims to be where skiing in Switzerland started, but many other resorts (not least Davos) could make similar claims.

Continue south for 11km (7 miles) to Tiefencastel then drive up the valley road for 36km (22miles) to the Julier pass.

Julierpass

3 The ancient mountain route, much travelled by the Romans, follows the floor of the mainly Romansch-

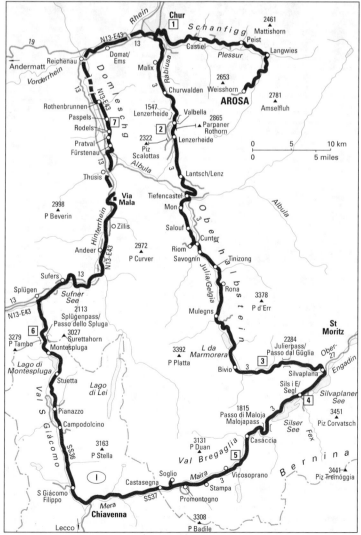

FOR CHILDREN

2 Lenzerheide/Valbella offers a special holiday programme for children which is free to guests of the resort. Supervised at all times, children between four and 16 are encouraged to 'investigate nature', witness the 'joys and problems' of local village life, and learn the 'tricks of the trade' practised by local craftsmen. If all this sounds a little too educational, sport, adventure and creative games in fact form the bulk of the programme (available between July and August – supervision and transport free, food extra).

RECOMMENDED WALKS

4 Take the cable car from Sils to Furtschellas and follow the path southwest to Marmore. From there follow the marked path to the hamlet of Curtins, via the Fex valley floor. Return via Crasta where there is a beautiful mountain chapel with ancient frescos. Continue via Platta, down the Fex river gorge, to Sils-Maria.

BACK TO NATURE

4 The Fex valley is famous for the variety of its Alpine flora. Expect to see clumps of edelweiss, enzian, gletscher-hahnenfuss (a form of daisy found in glacial regions), clematis and Alpine 'roses' (wild rhododendrons).

speaking Sursés valley (also known as the Oberhalbstein). It starts from the picturesquely sited village of Tiefencastel at the confluence of the Julia and Albula rivers. There is a surprisingly grandiose mid-17th-century baroque **church** here with a conspicuous white façade and a lavishly decorated interior. Instead of taking the main valley route, take the narrow mountain road which runs more or less parallel on the western flank via the three ancient villages of Mon, Salouf and Riom. In the first are two lovely churches: the mid-17th-century baroque **St Franciscus**, and an earlier Romanesque building below it with fine 14th-century frescos. Salouf also has a fine old Gothic church with frescos dating from the same period and, above it, the pilgrimage church of **Ziteil** marks the spot where the Virgin Mary reportedly paid a visit to a lonely shepherd in 1580. Riom is notable for its baroque **church** of 1677 and the impressive **ruins** of a 13th-century castle (restored in 1936). Back on the main Julier road you will pass through the village of Cunter before entering the main settlement of the valley, Savognin. This is a popular winter sports resort, unusual for its generous choice of three churches, all 17th-century, all baroque and all Catholic. **St Martin** is the most imposing, with an earlier Romanesque **tower** and some fine paintings of 1681. Yet another 17th-century church awaits in the village of Tinizong ahead. The road then climbs to the huge artificial lake of Marmorera, beneath which lie the drowned villages of Cresta and (the original) Marmorera. In the bleak surroundings of Bivio ahead you might be forgiven for thinking you were in a modern-day Babel. No fewer than four different languages are spoken here, including a couple of impenetrable Romansch dialects. The landscape now becomes even more unforgiving as the road climbs to the spectacular Julierpass. Lying at an altitude of 2,284m, this is one

The imposing 13th-century castle of Riom, restored in the 1930s, dominates the Oberhalbstein

of the highest passes which remain permanently open throughout the year. Note the weathered stumps of **Roman columns** by the side of the road. As you begin your descent into the Ober-Engadin (Upper Engadine) you will see dramatic views of the Bernina massif on your left. Silvaplana, a little resort at the foot of the pass, has a notable Gothic **church** with late 15th-century frescos.

Drive down to Silvaplana and turn southwest (right) to Sils (11km/7 miles).

Sils, Graubünden

4 Between 1881 and 1888 the philosopher Friedrich Nietzsche lived here (describing it as 'the loveliest corner of the Earth') and his former house, where he wrote *Thus Spoke Zarathustra*, is now a **museum**. Sils is a charming old resort attractively located between the lakes of Silvaplana and Sils (Segl). It is, in fact, two different villages, Sils-Maria and Sils-Baselgia. The former is the more popular location for visitors. It is beautifully situated on larch-covered slopes beneath the 3,451m peak of Piz Corvatsch, one of the main skiing areas of nearby St Moritz. Unlike its glamorous neighbour, Sils is a quiet little place well suited to restful contemplation, as Nietzsche clearly discovered. In summer there are horse-drawn carriage excursions up the Fex valley, generally acknowledged to be the most beautiful in the Bernina massif. At its head is the spectacular Fex glacier, rolling off the shoulder of the 3,441m Piz Tremóggia.

Continue southwest for 7km (4.5 miles) on road 3 to the Passo di Maloja which marks the beginning of the Val Bregaglia. Continue down the valley to Chiavenna.

Val Bregaglia, Graubünden

5 As beautiful in its rugged way as any valley in the Graubünden, the Bregaglia descends from the Passo di Maloja (1,815m) in a series of steps to the Italian town of Chiavenna, part of the canton until 1797. The first of many picturesque villages you will pass through is tiny Casáccia, formerly an important medieval gateway to the Septimer pass which links the Bregaglia to Bivio on the Julier pass road. The old hospice above the village dates from 1520. The next major settlement is Vicosoprano, once the chief village of the valley. Its former prosperity is reflected in the fine 16th- and 17th-century houses, some of them bearing colourful sgraffito. There are also two lovely old churches here: Santa Trinità is a mid-18th-century baroque structure, and San Cassian was built about 1003 but substantially rebuilt in the 15th and 17th centuries. Note too the tall residential Senewelenturm, a 13th-century tower with a 16th-century patrician house built on to it. Stampa, next, is scattered along the road and is home to the valley's museum, contained in the four-storey Ciäsa Granda built in 1581. Among its exhibits are paintings by members of the Giacometti family, who made the village their home. The church of San Giorgio is a late 17th-century building. A few kilometres further on, Promontogno has a 10th-century church, Nossa Donna (much altered) and the ruins of the major castle of the valley, the 12th-century Burg Castelmur. Ahead, it is worth turning off the main valley road to visit the lovely little village of Soglio, situated high on a terrace on the north flank of the Bregaglia amidst chestnut woods. The buildings are clustered tightly together by the baroque church and enjoy splendid views south. There are three elegant 'palaces' here, built by a wealthy local patrician family in the 16th and 17th centuries. Chiavenna, 10km from the little border village of Castasegna, was known by the Romans as *Clavenna* (from *clavis*, meaning key) because of its strategic location at the junction of the Splügen and Maloja passes. The 16th-century church of San Lorenzo contains a font of 1156.

*Drive up Val San Giácomo for 30km (19 miles) to Splügenpass then continue a further 9km (5.5 miles) down to the **N13** Autobahn, there following signs to Thusis and Chur.*

Splügenpass (Passo dello Spluga), Graubünden

6 Lying at an altitude of 2,113m, this ancient pass is cut dramatically into a narrow ridge between the 3,279m Piz Tambo to the west and the 3,027m Surettahorn to the east. The crossing, which now marks the border of Switzerland and Italy, was used extensively by the Romans and – more recently – by Napoleonic troops who crossed in appalling weather conditions in the winter of 1800 with considerable loss of life. The road descends in a series of switchbacks for 9km to

the busy transit village of Splügen, a popular all-year resort with a handsome collection of houses set on south-facing terraces. The baroque church was built in 1687.

*Stay on the **N13**, through the Via Mala, until the Thusis-Nord exit and then follow signs to Fürstenau and Paspels (30km/18.5 miles).*

The Domleschg, Graubünden

7 The fertile east side of the Hinterrhein valley is known as the Domleschg and the road here passes through a series of little villages distinguished by ruined feudal castles and vine-covered slopes. The castles were mostly destroyed in a peasants' revolt in the mid-16th century. Fürstenau was once a fortress town, destroyed by fire in 1742 and rebuilt

Castel Ortenstein with Piz Beverin in the distance

in less pugilistic style. Parts of its history survive – notably in the form of the 13th-century tower of the castle. Ahead there are also castles on elevated sites at Pratval and Rodels (Schloss Rietberg), and there are two more at Paspels which also has a fine old 13th-century chapel with Romanesque frescos just north of the village. Before you reach Rothenbrunnen you will also pass the extensive ruins of Ortenstein castle.

*At Rothenbrunnen, after 3km (2 miles), return to the **N13** and follow signs for Chur and Arosa for a further 45km (28 miles).*

Arosa – Chur 29 (18)
Chur – Lenzerheide/Valbella 18 (11)
Lenzerheide/Valbella – Julierpass 47 (29)
Julierpass – Sils 11 (7)
Sils – Val Bregaglia (Chiavenna) 39 (24)
Val Bregaglia (Chiavenna) –
Splügenpass 30 (18.5)
Splügenpass – The Domleschg
(Paspels) 39 (24)
the Domleschg (Paspels) – Arosa 48 (30)

SCENIC ROUTES

This circular tour is one continuous scenic drive, but there are four stretches of road of outstanding beauty. The deep wooded cleft of the Lenzerheide and, next, the Julierpass road through the Oberhalbstein valley offer a similar blend of Alpine pastures and jagged peaks, albeit with the latter on a wider scale, before traversing the wild and barren Julierpass itself. Thereafter, the scenery becomes positively friendly with a spectacular drive past the lakes of the Ober-Engadin valley, over the Passo di Maloja and into the romantic gorge of the Val Bregaglia. But a further desolate stretch of road awaits over the Splügenpass before entering the Via Mala (see Tour 19).

TICINO

This 'Italian' corner of Switzerland has been described as the 'Italian jewel in a Swiss precision watch'. Shaped like an inverted triangle, with its base abutting the broad spine of the main Alpine chain, it represents 7 per cent of the country's territory and accommodates just over 4 per cent of its population. Administratively, politically and geographically it is part of the Swiss Confederation, but culturally it is defiantly Italian.

A predominantly mountainous canton, it stretches from the southern flanks of the St Gotthard massif in the north to the Lombardy plain in the south. In between it offers a huge variety of scenery. From the eternal snows and glaciers of the north, great valleys spread southwards, their rivers discharging an icy flow into the placid waters of the palm-fringed Lago Maggiore (Lake Maggiore). In the south, lower mountains are furrowed by shallower valleys dipping into Lago Lugano (Lake Lugano). Further south still, rolling hills form the last creases of a verdant landscape before flattening out into the vast plains of Northern Italy. In the Upper Ticino, the villages are demonstrably Swiss; in the lower part of the canton Italian influences predominate, the houses stuccoed and white-washed, with roofs of rounded terracotta tiles.

Ticino's history is interwoven with that of Lombardy, of which it was a part until the 14th century. The early Swiss cantons resolved to consolidate possession of the St Gotthard pass, thereby signalling the start of a period of bloody conflict with their southern neighbours, understandably reluctant to relinquish ownership of the approach to the vital trade route. By 1512 the Swiss had conquered the entire region from the St Gotthard pass to the present Italian border, but it was not until the end of the Napoleonic occupation that Ticino became a free canton in its own right. And until the opening of the St Gotthard rail tunnel in 1882, it remained virtually cut off from the rest of the country for six months of the year. Today it is one of the most popular tourist regions in Switzerland, a fact that is hardly surprising in view of its exquisite scenery.

This is a part of Switzerland that, until relatively recently, has been one of its best-kept secrets. Its great cities and glorious lakes are well known, but its wild and remote valleys, dotted with sleepy old villages amidst a precipitous and dramatic landscape, have yet to be discovered by the majority of visitors.

Lugano

Because of its striking geographical configuration, curving around the blue waters of Lake Lugano, this ancient lakeside city has been described as the 'Rio de Janeiro of the Old Continent'. The briefest of visits will confirm that qualitative comparisons of that sort are entirely unnecessary.

Lugano is a city of rare qualities with a rich medieval inheritance, an agreeable subtropical climate, enviable lake and mountain views, and some of the finest promenades and parks in Europe. Moreover, the modern metropolis and quaint medieval town co-exist in gratifying harmony, not least perhaps because the newer architecture is imaginative and sympathetic to its surroundings. Even the lakeside hotels rank among the most elegant (and exclusive) buildings of their type in the country. The heart of the old town is the Piazza Riforma, a charming arcaded square behind which is a maze of narrow, cobbled streets. Above it is the Cathedral of San Lorenzo, an ancient structure dating from the 9th century with an impressive Renaissance façade. The city's other fine church is the late 15th-century Santa Maria degli Angioli, a surprisingly plain building housing two of the world's most famous frescos. Painted by Bernardino Luini in the early 16th century, they depict the Madonna and child with St John and, more unforgettably, the enormous Passion and the Crucifixion which faces visitors as they enter.

Locarno

This enchanting old city is a worthy rival to Lugano and even its most ardent admirers would be hard-pressed to find a sufficient range of superlatives to describe its lazy charm and delightful setting on the bank of Lake Maggiore. It too has a fine legacy of medieval buildings, and lake and mountain views to rival any in the country. Chief among its attractions is the walk along its leafy lakeside promenade, through hanging willows and brilliantly coloured gardens containing a riotous profusion of exotic flowers. But the famous 17th-century pilgrim church of Madonna del Sasso, dominating the city from its rocky bluff, is more than worth the pilgrimage alone. The views from its terrace are outstanding, and its rich collection of Gothic carvings are among the finest in the country. The 15th-century Castello Visconti is the city's other dominant structure.

Bellinzona

Capital of the canton, and a modern industrial city with an impressive cultural heritage, Bellinzona is known as the 'city of the castles'. This tag might have something to do with its remarkable triumvirate of medieval castles which dominate the town. Of these the massive Castello Grande is the oldest and most

The magnificent Castello Grande occupies the high ground in the centre of Bellinzona

imposing. Built between the 13th and 15th centuries on the site of a former Roman fortification, its huge fortified walls are visible from any point in the city. The 14th-century Castello di Montebello is located at a higher level and contains the town's museum. Higher still, with superb views, the Castello di Sasso Corbaro is another vast 15th-century structure, now containing a folk museum. At one point in their history, the three castles were linked by cavity walls (still visible in parts) spanning the valley and wide enough to accommodate a man on horseback. In the historic Piazza Collegiata, the early 16th-century church of Saints Pietro and Stefano has a magnificent baroque interior. Take time to explore this pleasant and less fashionable member of the three great population centres of Ticino. It will not be wasted.

Lugano, its lake and Monte San Salvatore seen from a restaurant terrace on Monte Brè. Lugano is the largest and most important city in Ticino

RUINS, GORGES & ROCKY PASSES

**Bellinzona • Valle Mesolcina • Andeer
Zillis • Thusis • Rhäzüns • Passo del
Lucomagno (Lukmanier pass) • Val Blénio
Biasca • Bellinzona**

This tour will take you through the some of the most striking valleys of Ticino and the Italian-speaking parts of the Graubünden. After crossing one of the most beautiful of Swiss mountain passes, the 2,065m San Bernardino, you will thread the impressive gorges of Rofla (Roflaschlucht), Via Mala and Via Medel in Romansch and German-speaking areas before returning to Ticino via the equally dramatic Passo del Lucomagno (Lukmanier pass) and down through the fertile Val Blénio back to your starting point.

One of more than 150 unique 12th-century ceiling panels in the Romanesque church of St Martin in the village of Zillis

Drive north via Arbedo, and take road 13 up the Valle Mesolcina via the villages of Lumino and San Vittore to Roveredo, a distance of 13km (8 miles). Then follow the same road to San Bernardino for 33km (21 miles).

Valle Mesolcina, Graubünden

1 Taking the old road up this pleasant valley, you will pass through a number of typically Ticino Italian-speaking villages in its southern reaches – even though all of them are in the neighbouring canton of Graubünden. The first of significance is San Vittore, just over the canton border, which has a fine 13th-century baroque church at the foot of a woody escarpment. In the 16th-century Palazzo Viscardi you will find the valley museum. In Roveredo, a short distance ahead, there is a handsome collection of 16th- and 17th-century mansions. At Grono, which has a splendidly decorated baroque church and a tall 13th-century tower (Torre Fiorenzana), take the road up the picturesque Val Calanca for Santa Maria in Calanca. This is an impressively sited village dominated by its old church and another 13th-century tower. Mesocco, the chief settlement of the valley, is worth lingering in a while. Above it lies the striking semi-restored ruin of the Castello di

FOR CHILDREN

The Museo di Castel Grande, in the largest of Bellinzona's magnificent triumvirate of medieval castles, is cleverly arranged to appeal to children of all ages. In addition to an intriguing historical and archaeological collection, there is a range of audio-visual aids which includes a highly atmospheric film, with superb effects, which convincingly evokes the various periods of human occupation of the hill on which the castle stands (about 5,000 years). The blood and thunder of the medieval period is particularly colourful. But the most tangible sense of history is gained by walking the ancient wall, which in 1487 stretched across the entire valley. Children will doubtless enjoy the underground sections of it most.

FOR HISTORY BUFFS

1 In 1583, the parish priest of the little village of Roveredo and 11 of his women parishioners were burned at the stake on the somewhat flimsy ground that they might have been dabbling in witchcraft. This was the largest mass execution of 'witches' in this region, during a period when the witch hunts were at their most relentless.

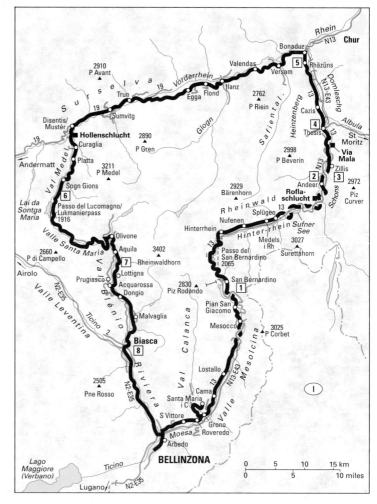

Misox, and at its foot is the early 12th-century church of Santa Maria with interesting 15th-century murals. The village of San Bernardino, below the pass of the same name, is the highest settlement in the valley and is becoming a flourishing skiing and climbing resort. There is a modest network of mountain lifts here which will transport you to below the peak of the 2,830m Piz Rodondo.

Continue up the winding pass road for 7km (4.5 miles) to Passo del San Bernardino. Drive north down the pass road, staying on the old road via the village of Hinterrhein on the north flank of the Rheinwald, and continue to descend the valley road via Medels and Splügen. Skirting the north bank of the Sufner See, continue via the scenic Rofla (Roflaschlucht) gorge to Andeer, about 30km (19 miles).

Andeer, Graubünden

2 Principal village of the Schons valley, this old spa was once an important trading post in the Middle Ages. Today it is a thriving health resort with a comprehensive range of facilities including a fine swimming pool with water drawn from the mountains. There are some pretty old houses in the village, some of them dating from the early 16th century and covered in distinctive sgraffito. Particularly notable among them is the Haus Pedrun, built about 1500. The baroque village church is late 17th-century, and incorporates an earlier tower.

*Stay on the old road for 5km (3 miles), crossing under the **N13**, to Zillis.*

Zillis, Graubünden

3 The celebrated village church here has no fewer than 153 individually painted ceiling panels dating from about 1150, acknowledged to be the finest example of their type in Europe. Even if you are a habitual avoider of churches you might make an exception and step inside for a closer look at this 12th-century interpretation of Biblical allegory. The paintings are arranged in an inner and outer section, with the outer depicting weird marine hybrids, and the inner scenes from the Apocalypse, the Last Judgement and the Life of Christ. The church itself is a mixture of Romanesque (nave and tower) and late Gothic (choir), and it was sympathetically restored just before World War II. In a nearby 16th-century peasant's dwelling is a small museum, the Tgea da Schons, which has a collection of implements and furniture common to the Schons valley through the ages.

Continue for about 7km (4.5 miles) on the old road to Thusis.

Thusis, Graubünden

4 A major junction in the Domleschg valley, this is a busy market town attractively situated at the foot of the steeper slopes of the Heinzenberg with a fine aspect east across the softer flank of the Domleschg's

Viewing platforms cut into the limestone walls of the rocky Via Mala allow visitors impressive views over the gorge

vineyards and orchards. Above it to the south, on a rocky outcrop, are the impressive ruins of the 12th-century castle of Hohen-Rhätien – and there are a number of other ruins of medieval fortresses in the near vicinity. On the north face of the same rock are the ruins of an old chapel. Although Thusis was nearly wiped out by fire in 1845, an early 16th-century late Gothic church survived largely unscathed in the older quarter, but other contemporary buildings show signs of extensive alteration. The newer part of the town has a distinctive Italian feel to it. Formerly a health resort of modest repute, the town now seems to attract more climbers than convalescents, drawn largely by the rocky pyramid of Piz Beverin to the southwest. Amidst striking scenery to the southeast is the snowy 2,972m peak of Piz Curvèr.

Stay on the old road, via Cazis, to reach Rhäzüns in 14km (8.5 miles).

Rhäzüns, Graubünden

5 A characteristic village, notable for its imposing medieval castle, Rhäzüns stands on the west bank of the Hinterrhein at the gateway to the Domleschg. As you enter there is a mountain lift on your right which traverses the valley and offers fine views from the summit of the Feldis. The castle, conspicuous on a bluff overlooking the river, is largely

SPECIAL TO...

3 Along the course of the Schons and Domleschg valleys there is a succession of ruined castles overlooking the valley floor, mostly destroyed by popular revolt. Above the little village of Donath, southwest of Zillis, stand the ruins of the feudal castle of Fardüns – formerly the seat of the governors of the Schons. According to legend, this was burned down after a local peasant took exception to the governor spitting in his soup; the peasant promptly drowned the governor in the soup.

SCENIC ROUTES

3 The old road along the Via Mala between Zillis and Thusis, now largely superseded by the N13 expressway, is a dramatic gorge cut through limestone cliffs bordering the Hinterrhein. Built in 1822, it winds sinuously through tunnels and under overhanging rock walls, in places apparently almost meeting. There are various viewing galleries (admission charges) at intervals along the route with fine views of the turbulent river and its bridges.

Scattered around the head of the Val Blénio, the village of Olivone is sheltered by the sharp peak of Sosto

15th- and 16th-century in its present appearance although it was founded in the 1200s. The village church of Saints Peter and Paul is a fine Romanesque structure of the 14th century, and contains interesting contemporary wall paintings. The catholic church of St Maria dates from the late 1600s. North of the village, just before Bonaduz, you will see high on your right the chapel of St George, another charming Romanesque structure. The remarkable 14th-century frescos depict, among other historical scenes, the suffering of St George, and (more upliftingly) his triumph over the dragon.

Continue a short distance north to Bonaduz, then take the winding road via Versam to Ilanz along the Vorderrhein valley (see Tour 15). Continue via the villages of Flond, St Martin and Egga until this minor road meets main road 19. Drive west here towards Disentis/Mustér, a total distance of about 48km (30 miles). Then follow signs to Lukmanier pass (Passo del Lucomagno) for a further 20km (12.5 miles).

Passo del Lucomagno (Lukmanier Pass)

6 South of Disentis/Mustér you enter the Val Medel via the 'Höllenschlucht' (Hell's Gorge), part of the romantically wild and woody Medel Gorges. As you climb up the valley you will pass a number of impressive waterfalls tumbling through the gorges below. The first village of interest on this old pass road is Curaglia, now a small resort with a church dating from the late 1600s (late Gothic altar) and some interesting old farmhouses (one with a colourful painted façade). The baroque church of St Martin in Platta ahead dates from 1774, and in Sogn Gions – the last village of the valley – there is an ancient chapel of 11th-century origin with a large 14th-century Gothic fresco. The scenery now becomes more desolate and before you reach the summit of the pass you will see the man-made Lai da Sontga Maria (lake of Santa Maria) below on your right. The dam was built in 1967.

At 1,916m the Lukmanier is one of the lowest of the wholly Swiss trans-Alpine passes, but is no less impressive for that. Flanked to the west by the 3,016m Piz Rondadura and to the east by the brooding black face of the 3,190m Scopi, it was one of the busiest mountain crossings in Switzerland until the building of the St Gotthard tunnel. Barbarossa crossed it twice with his armies in 1164 and 1186.

Continue down Val Blénio for 41km (25 miles).

Val Blénio, Ticino

7 The beautiful Valle Santa Maria winds its way down from the Lukmanier pass for a distance of about 20km before it reaches the

charming resort village of Olivone, lying at the head of the Val Blénio. This is one of the most scenically pleasing of Swiss valleys, characterised by enchanting small villages with lovely old Romanesque churches amidst a variety of vegetation including chestnut groves, walnut trees and vineyards. Olivone is a pretty place with some interesting 16th-century houses, and a 17th-century church with contemporary wall paintings. One of the old houses is now a local history museum. At Aquila (where there is a medieval church, rebuilt in the early 18th century) you have a choice of whether to follow the main valley road or turn right up through a series of little villages straggling its western flank before rejoining the main route at the spa village of Acquarossa or Dongio. If you have time to do the latter, aficionados of 11th-century frescos should visit the beautiful chapel of San Carlo of Negrentino, a short walk through meadows above the village of Prugiasco. This is acknowledged to be one of the most important Romanesque churches in Switzerland. On the valley floor you will pass through the village of Lottigna, another attractively sited old place, which has an interesting local museum in the 16th-century former residence of the valley's governor. It also has a 13th-century church, altered in the early 1600s. Malvaglia,

The 12th-century church of St Peter and St Paul above the town of Biasca is one of the most impressively sited in Ticino

a bit further on, is the largest place in the Val Blénio with a fine collection of old houses and another delightful old Romanesque church with a 12th-century bell tower.

Biasca, Ticino

8 Almost a microcosm of Bellinzona in its physical setting, this pleasant little town stands in a narrow basin at the fork of the Leventina and Blénio valleys. Although much of the present building verges on the ordinary, Biasca is fortunate to have one of the loveliest churches in the Ticino. Saints Pietro and Paulo's is a 12th-century Romanesque structure cut high into the mountainside, and reached by steps from the eastern edge of the town. Built out of the same granite which has been quarried here for centuries, the church blends into the rock face and is practically invisible in some lights. A series of carefully restored frescos date from the 13th century, and the building's extraordinary acoustics draw musicians and choirs from all over the world for performances. On weekdays you may need to collect a key to view the interior.

*Return to Bellinzona on the **N2**, a distance of 16km (10 miles).*

Bellinzona – Valle Mesolcina 46 (29)
Valle Mesolcina – Andeer 37 (23)
Andeer – Zillis 5 (3)
Zillis – Thusis 7 (4.5)
Thusis – Rhäzüns 14 (8.5)
Rhäzüns – Passo del Lucomagno 68 (42)
Passo del Lucomagno – Biasca 41 (25)
Biasca – Bellinzona 16 (10)

BACK TO NATURE

7 The Val Blénio illustrates both the gentle beauty of nature and the raw ferocity of its unpredictable habits. From the wild Alpine meadows of its upper reaches, the road passes through a succession of carefully tended fruit and chestnut groves, with vines, mulberries and chestnut trees gathering in increasing numbers on the southward route. But a reminder of how easily order can be disrupted comes between Malvaglia and Biasca, where the road crosses a huge mound of detritus, the result of a massive landslip nearly 500 years ago. Look up to your left to the Pizzo Magno (2,256m); there used to be more of it.

MEDITERRANEA & MOUNTAINS

Lugano • Morcote • Locarno • Ascona
Ronco • Brissago • Brig • Valle Leventina
Lugano

The lakes of Lugano and Maggiore, both part Swiss, part Italian, are among the most scenically gratifying in the country. The towns and villages which border them rarely disappoint, and it is easy to see why so many have become meccas for writers, painters and thinkers – indeed anyone whose creative energy is likely to be fortified by beautiful surroundings. The high mountain passes of Simplon and Nufenen – respectively the country's oldest and newest pass roads (1805 and 1969) – provide a remarkable illustration of how the chilling beauty of bleak mountainous terrain can be so unimaginably close to exotic environs of almost Mediterranean appeal and climate.

A pillar box-red funicular ascends a steep gradient up Monte Brè on Lugano's outskirts

[i] Riva Albertolli 5

Take the lakefront road via Paradiso and Melide for about 11km (7 miles) to Morcote.

Morcote, Ticino

1 Palms, promenades, cypresses, ornate street lamps and elegantly arcaded private villas create a colourful mosaic in this ancient fishing village on the tip of the Lugano peninsula, now bearing the dubious tag of an 'artists' colony'. But palettes, brushes and knitted brows seem to be less in evidence than ordinary passers-by enjoying a relaxing drink at pavement cafés overlooking Lago Lugano (Lake Lugano). This is unarguably one of the most picturesque of the many lakeside villages in the area. The predominant flavour of the Italianate architecture is terracotta and the shuttered façades of many of the buildings are beautifully decorated. A short climb up any one of a number of narrow cobbled alleys will bring you to Morcote's principal landmark, the 15th-century church of **Santa Maria del Sasso** (or Madonna of the Rock) with its tall, distinctive medieval campanile. Inside there are some fine 16th-century frescos. Next door is an unusual octagonal baroque **chapel**, built in the late 17th century. If you take the understandable decision to stop here for a late breakfast or early lunch, make for the charmingly arcaded 15th-century buildings on the lakefront, many of which now have cafés at street level.

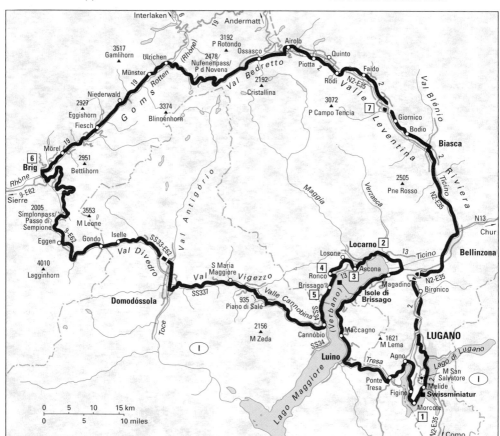

Follow the peninsula road north for 15km (9 miles), through Figino and Agno, to the frontier village of Ponte Tresa. Then take the road to the Italian resort of Luino and follow the scenic east bank of Lake Maggiore (re-entering Switzerland at Zenna) until Locarno, another 39km (25 miles).

Locarno, Ticino

2 According to popular mythology, this seductively beautiful city was chosen as the venue for the historic Locarno Pact of 1925 (signed by world statesmen in a vain bid to prevent a second world war) for one reason only. A mistress of one of the organisers recommended it on the persuasive grounds that it was an unusually romantic place to spend a week with her lover. This tranquil lakeside city is close to where Switzerland meets Italy, and the influences of both cultures conspire to create an agreeable blend of Swiss refinement and Italian flair. The city's focal point is the splendidly arcaded **Piazza Grande**, lined by fine Lombardian-style houses painted in various pastel shades. Above it, tenaciously clinging to a rocky spur, is the celebrated 17th-century pilgrim church of **Madonna del Sasso** (a popular name in the Ticino), reached by a six-minute funicular ride on the Via Ramogna, just east of the Piazza. The church terrace offers magnificent views of the city and the lake; inside, among innumerable treasures, are some fine examples of Gothic carvings, the 1520 Bramantino painting Flight into Egypt, and an intriguing full-scale figurative depiction of the Last Supper by Francesco Silva (c.1650). From the church you can either continue up to the Alpe di Cardada by cable car, and from there by chairlift to the 1,672m Cimetta (magnificent panoramas from both),

---

The graceful Italianate lines of the pilgrimage church of Madonna del Sasso above Locarno

---

or walk back down into the centre. In the **Piazza San Antonio** you will find the 17th-century **church** of the same name. Below, past the 14th-century church of **San Francesco** (which hosts Locarno's music festival), you will see the city's major historical landmark, the 15th-century **Castello Visconti**. A fortress-palace in the grand style, it has an elegant inner courtyard, and the **Museo Civico** (with a fine collection recalling the city's Roman past) is housed in its ancient halls.

ⓘ Largo Zorzi (by the station)

Take road 13 west for 3km (2 miles) to Ascona.

Ascona, Ticino

3 Notwithstanding the proximity of its larger neighbour (only 3km east) this ancient little town has managed to preserve its own distinctive identity, helped in large part by the Mággia which divide them. In common with Morcote, Ascona is a (slightly self-conscious) old fishing village which was adopted in the early part of this century by an intellectual and somewhat Bohemian community (including such unlikely bedfellows as Lenin, Jung, Isadora Duncan and Herman Hesse). High on the list of attractions in its shady labyrinth of back alleys is the **Collegio Pontificio Papio** arranged around an elegant cloistered courtyard in the Renaissance style. The church of **Santa Maria della Misericordia**, built in the late 14th century, forms part of the same building and is renowned for its cycle of medieval frescos. The **church of Saints Pietro and Paolo**, built in 1530, is a fine old basilica located nearer the waterfront. For

---

FOR CHILDREN

1 Just after the village of Melide, on the road from Lugano to Morcote, you will find the intriguing attraction known as 'Swissminiatur'. Spread over just under a hectare of landscaped park on the lakeside, this is an ambitious 1:25 scale model of the most famous sights and buildings of the country. Mountains, lakes, glaciers, bridges and buildings are all faithfully reproduced, and all the mechanical features (cable cars and trains etc) actually work.

RECOMMENDED TRIPS

1 On your way south from Lugano, a funicular leads in ten minutes from the suburb of Paradiso to the 912m peak of Monte San Salvatore which lies ahead to the right of the road. The summit offers one of the great Alpine panoramas of southern Switzerland, with the city and its lake, the Lombardy plain, and the peaks of the Bernese and Valais Alps all seen to superb advantage.

SPECIAL TO...

2 Locarno enjoys a subtropical climate and, reputedly, more hours of sunshine than anywhere else in the country. More than 60 per cent of the possible number of daylight hours receive constant sunshine. These factors help to explain the rich variety of plants and the prodigious growth-rate of the twisting vines set in orderly terraces on the slopes of Alpe di Cardada that form Locarno's backdrop.

BACK TO NATURE

4 One of the most rewarding excursions in the Ticino is by boat from Ascona to the extraordinary subtropical Isole di Brissago on Lake Maggiore. These are two tiny islands, the larger containing an exotic Botanic Garden, the smaller the ruins of an 11th-century Romanesque church. The gardens, with an elegant villa (now a restaurant) and over 1,000 rare species collected from all over the world, were laid out by a young Russian noblewoman (who married well) in the late 19th century. She died in penury in the 1920s.

an example of a striking 17th-century baroque façade, you need look no further than the tourist office housed in the **Casa Serodine** (which has to be one of the best-appointed in the country). Near by, on the waterfront, the cerise-coloured arcaded **town hall** has an equally impressive Renaissance façade. The palm-fringed lakeside is lined by numerous cafés and shops, and a variety of watersports are on offer courtesy of the clear blue waters of Lago Maggiore (Lake Maggiore). They include, for the less energetic, some gentle pedalling on a fleet of anti-quarian pedalloes complete with chrome 'headlights' (which might one day soon enrich a design museum).

[i] Casa Serodine, Via B Papio

From Ascona take the minor road north for about 8km (5 miles), up through the little villages of Losone and Arcegno, to Ronco.

Ronco, Ticino

4 One of the most beautifully positioned villages in this part of Switzerland, Ronco sits picturesquely on a terrace in an exotic Mediterranean-like setting high above the little port of the same name. In the charming 17th-century Romanesque **church of San Martino** is a splendid example of stucco decoration, and there are some beautiful frescos in the choir dating from 1492, before the church was largely rebuilt. In the graveyard is the tomb of Erich Maria Remarque, author of the famous anti-war tome All Quiet on the Western Front, who made Ronco his home when Ascona became too voguish. The view from the church terrace over the lake is lovely. In the village's piazza is a small early 18th-century baroque **chapel** of some interest.

Rejoin road 13 at Porto Ronco for Brissago (4km/2.5 miles).

Brissago, Ticino

5 A popular bathing resort, perhaps best-known for the famous slim cigars which are manufactured here, Brissago is the lowest village in Switzerland at 196m above sea

Lake Maggiore and the chestnut tree-lined promenade of Ascona

level. A stone's throw from the border with Italy, it is unremarkable in itself with a group of austere modern blocks jarring with some fine old Lombardian-style villas. But the impressive pre-Alpine background goes a long way to compensate for the less than imaginative use of a beautiful location. Sheltering under the 1,659m Pizzo Leone, it is surrounded on three sides by verdant Mediterranean gardens and serried vineyards. A fine old 16th-century **Renaissance church** is protected from the worst excesses of modern architecture by a ring of tall cypresses in the oldest part of the village. The most handsome of the private villas are situated high above the busy main road, overlooking the two exotic islands of Brissago, a short distance away in Lake Maggiore.

Re-enter Italy about 4km (2.5 miles) south on road 13, following signs to Cannóbio. Turn west here up the Valle Cannóbina following signs for Passo del Sempione and Domodóssola. Just north of Domodóssola join **E62** *for the Simplonpass (Passo del Sempione), re-entering Switzerland at Gondo. Follow the road over the pass to Brig. The total journey is about 110km (68 miles).*

Brig, Valais

6 Owing to its location at the mouth of the Simplon rail tunnel, and the foot of the Simplonpass, Brig has been traditionally thought of as a transit town with little to distinguish it. But it has a strong historical identity, developed primarily as a result of its importance as a centre of trading. Its most famous building is the **Stockalperpalast**, a flamboyantly decorated baroque palace built in the 1660s by Kaspar Jodock von Stockalper, one of the great entrepreneurs of his age. A gloriously elaborate tiered and arcaded courtyard is guarded by three great onion-domed, gilded towers, and as statements of great wealth go, this is one of the loudest. Brig has some other fine archi-tectual treasures including a mid-17th-century **Jesuit church**, and two Gothic **chapels** both pre-dating it. Throughout the town there are examples of elegant old **merchants' mansions** built on the profits of cross-border trade with Italy (not all of it legitimate).

Take road 19 up the Goms valley (see Tour 22) to Ulrichen for 39km (24 miles), then take the Nufenenpass road (Passo della Novena) down Val Bedretto (see Tour 22) to Airolo for 37km (23 miles).
*From here, take either of the old valley roads (blue signposts to Bellinzona/Biasca) which run either side of the **N2** until Faido, 17km (11 miles). The mountain road via Quinto is more scenic; the lower road via Piotta and Ambri is quicker. Stay on the old road for 18km (12 miles) to Biasca, then join the **N2** to Lugano, 49km (32 miles).*

Valle Leventina, Ticino

7 Running southeast for some 35km from Airolo to Biasca, this valley has the largest 'vertical drop' – some 974m – of any traversiable valley on the continent. In any other language, it is steep. Airolo, a well-sited town at the mouth of the St Gotthard rail and road tunnels, manages to wear a separate hat as a year-round sports resort as well as a busy transit point. The old road which you will now follow has been largely relieved by the building of the N2 autostrada, and many of the

Looking down the Val Bedretto from Switzerland's newest mountain pass, the Nufenenpass, linking the cantons of Valais and Ticino

valley's villages have recaptured some of their former tranquillity. Quinto, high on a terrace above the valley, is a sleepy illustration, and is worth a brief diversion. The church of **Saints Pietro and Paolo** in the old square has a magnificent 12th-century six-storey tower, as beautiful as any in Ticino. Between here and Faido you will weave through the Stalvedro gorge, the site of a brave defence in 1799 by a retreating French force against a much larger Russian army. After the village of Rodi there is a vertiginous drop in the valley floor, with remarkable overhead views of the autostrada on massive concrete stanchions, before you reach the charming old town of Faido. This is the major resort of the valley, a delightful spot characterised by some well-preserved 16th-century wooden houses, and a view of three spectacular cascades. The scenery softens here, helped to a large extent by chestnut forests and vineyards. About 11km south is the village of Giornico, bisected by the Ticino river and linked by a quaint medieval arched bridge. Stop here awhile for a stroll by the river. The 12th-century **church of San Nicolao** on the west bank is generally held to be one of the finest Romanesque buildings in the Ticino. Higher up on a hill, by some castle ruins, is the small 12th-century chapel of **Santa Maria di Castello**. Both churches contain fine 15th-century frescos. At Bodio, the next village along, note another fine cascade on your left.

Lugano – Morcote 11 (7)
Morcote – Locarno 54 (34)
Locarno – Ascona 3 (2)
Ascona – Ronco 8 (5)
Ronco – Brissago 4 (2.5)
Brissago – Brig 110 (68)
Brig – Valle Leventina 76 (47)
Valle Leventina – Lugano 83 (52)

SCENIC ROUTES

7 The entire tour offers mountain and lakeside scenery of considerable distinction, but one unusual feature of the drive stands out above all others. The N2 motorway which splits Ticino from Airolo to Chiasso is popularly perceived to be an architectural work of art, and it is best seen from the old road on this tour. Built late in the history of road building, Rino Tami, the architect appointed to oversee its construction, was able to avoid aesthetic and engineering mistakes that other countries had made. The result is a remarkable structure that blends into the landscape, and which, in the words of the experts, 'leaves an impression of unity and harmony'.

2 days: 260 km (161.5 miles)

RUGGED, RUSTIC & ROMANTIC

**Locarno • Valle Onsernone • Valle Mággia
Valle di Bosco/Gurin • Val Bavona
Val Lavizzara • Val Verzasca • Locarno**

The great valleys north of Locarno, spreading outwards and upwards towards the Ticino Alps, are among the most strikingly beautiful in Switzerland. Unlike the busy arteries of the Mesolcina, Leventina and Blénio, these are remote culs-de-sac for all but mules and mountain hikers. The only way out by car is the way you go in, but your time and fuel will not be wasted. Here amidst spectacular Alpine scenery are isolated mountain hamlets apparently untouched by time, ancient bridges, medieval churches, mountain grottos, stone-roofed rustici, and precipitous river gorges streaked by innumerable waterfalls. The stories of these valleys and their inhabitants are told in fascinating detail in the small local museums of the principal villages. Try to find time to visit at least one.

A waterfall in the tiny Val Bavona hamlet of Foroglio

⊡ Largo Zorzi

Drive out of Locarno on the road to Domodóssola, stopping at Intragna after 9km (5.5 miles). Then return a couple of kilometres to just before Cavigliano and take the turning left up the Valle Onsernone, a distance of 20km (12.5 miles) to its head.

Valle Onsernone

1 Characterised by steep precipices, vertiginous ravines and simple working villages, the rugged Valle Onsernone is one of the less frequented of the canton's valleys. Before you start up it, drive a little further west to the village of Intragna in the 'Centovalli' (hundred valleys) which leads eventually to the Italian border. Here, in a somewhat unexpected setting, is the tallest church tower in Ticino at well over 200ft. The church of San Gottardo which it dignifies is an early 18th-century building with rococo decor. Behind the church is the Casa Magetti which houses the museum of the Centovalli.

Loco is the first village of significance in the Onsernone, and you might want to take a look in the Casa Degiorgi at another valley museum – this one with an interesting collection of locally made furniture and a comprehensive archive of documents dealing with straw weaving, the main industry of the valley. Many of the houses in this area have wooden verandahs, specifically for drying straw. Look

FOR CHILDREN

In view of the fact that Locarno is the sunniest place in the country, with more than 60 per cent of the possible maximum number of hours enjoying sunshine, why not take the children to the marvellous Lido on the edge of the Parco della Pace. One indoor and three outdoor pools offer a variety of aquatic attractions, and there are further swimming and watersports facilities at various stages along the beautiful lakeside promenade.

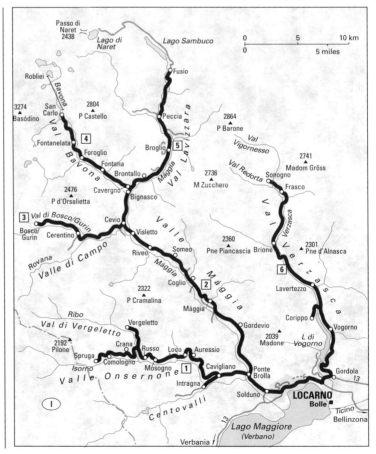

RECOMMENDED WALKS

2 The Valle Mággia is famous for its hiking trails, ranging from short strolls around the villages of the valley to 48-hour guided 'smuggler's' trails over the Basódino glacier on the Italian border. Try if you can to do at least one four- to eight-hour guided hike, particularly through the Bavona or Lavizzara valleys. For further details contact the tourist office in Mággia.

SPECIAL TO...

2 The Valle Mággia is celebrated for its rustici – low-roofed 17th-century peasants' dwellings constructed out of local gneiss laid in blocks without mortar. They are frequently distinguished by their exterior stairways and stone slab roofs, but just as easily by the Swiss-German registrations of the cars outside – the owners of which view a rustico as the ultimate in rural idylls.

FOR HISTORY BUFFS

2 The lives of the original inhabitants of the Valle Mággia were constantly at risk from the unpredictable swollen waterfalls which crashed down the mountainsides above them. Now, these torrents are largely contained and regulated by hydro-electric plants installed beneath the rocky skin of the mountains.

3 The Walser people are descended from an itinerant Germanic tribe who migrated to the southern Alpine valleys (particularly those of the eastern Valais, parts of the Graubünden, Liechtenstein and the Vorarlberg region of Austria) from the 6th century onwards. In the Ticino they settled permanently in the village of Bosco/Gurin, and there is evidence of their architecture and tradition in many other villages in the Ticino valleys.

around the village for finely crafted baskets and bags at honest prices. At Russo ahead, the ancient church of Santa Maria Assunta is a baroque structure with some interesting 15th-century wall paintings. After the little villages of Crana and Vocaglia, you will enter the larger settlement of Comologno which has an attractive collection of 18th-century houses and a 17th-century parish church. The small frontier village of Spruga marks the end of the valley road, although a bridle path leads over the mountainous border into Italy about 3km ahead. On your return to the mouth of the valley, take a detour left just before Russo for the Val di Vergeletto. The little resort of the same name is pleasantly sited among wooded slopes.

Return to the foot of the valley, and take the Locarno road for about 24km (15 miles) to Ponte Brolla. Then turn left up the Valle Mággia for about 25km (15.6 miles) to where the valley road branches at Bignasco.

Valle Mággia

2 This is probably the most famous of Switzerland's southern valleys, riven by the Mággia river which is fed by the eternal snows of the Ticino Alps. Among other things it is known for its rustici, former stone-built peasant dwellings dating from the 17th century which are now frequently let to holidaymakers seeking a taste of the simple life. There are abundant and spectacular waterfalls streaking the lower precipices, but now regulated by hydro-electric plants they no longer pose quite the same danger they once did to the people of the valley

Vines surround an ancient church in the Ticino village of Someo in the beautiful Valle Mággia

who lived with the constant fear of flash floods. The first village of note is Gordevio, set off the main valley floor on a loop road to the right, where there is a pretty little parish church of 14th-century origin with 19th-century frescos. Just before you reach the village of Mággia, next, you will pass the early 16th-century church of Santa Maria delle Grazie di Campagna. If you want to admire the medieval frescos inside, you may need to borrow the key from the Poncini restaurant in Mággia, half a kilometre up the road. The village is delightfully set amidst vineyards, and has a number of fine old arcaded houses with shady courtyards. Above, on a hill, is the baroque church of San Maurizio, the oldest in the valley. Passing the spectacular 100m Soladino waterfall on the left, beyond the village of Someo, you will shortly arrive in Cevio, the chief village of the valley and notable for its elegant collection of surprisingly patrician residences dating back to the early 17th century when this was the seat of the Milanese governors. The Museo di Valmaggia is housed in a handsomely decorated 17th-century palazzo near the 16th-century village church, and has an unusual collection of objects made from soapstone. There is an annex in the impressive semi-fortified Casa Respini in the village square. A road leads west up the Valle di Campo (see next entry) which you should follow now, returning at a later stage to the last major settlement of the Valle

SCENIC ROUTES

4 There are few roads in the southern Ticino which are visually uninspiring, but even by the unusually high standards of scenic splendour in these valleys, the Val Bavona, a tributary valley of the Valle Mággia, stands out as an area of exceptional beauty. The road passes through cool forest, rocky ravines, waterfall-streaked precipices and remote stone-built villages blending into the mountain walls.

Mággia, Bignasco – delightfully situated at the fork of the Val Bavona and the Val Lavizzara. Note the quaint old bridge over the Mággia, and the nearby 16th-century baroque chapel of San Rocco.

A road leads for 16km (10 miles) west from Cevio up the Valle di Campo to a turn-off right at the village of Cerentino to Bosco/Gurin.

Valle di Bosco/Gurin

3 Passing through Cerentino, note on a hill ahead the baroque church of Santa Maria and the clearly visible early 18th-century exterior fresco above its entrance. At the head of the valley, a few kilometres from the Italian frontier, the remote village of Bosco/Gurin, the highest in the canton at 1504m, has the unique distinction of being the only non-Italian speaking settlement in Ticino. In the 14th century an itinerant tribe of the Walser people emigrated to this secluded spot from the Valais, and their descendants still live here, keeping their language (a German dialect) and their customs alive. Much of the architecture has a distinct Valais flavour. The story of the last six centuries is fascinatingly told in the **Museo Etnostorico** in the **Walserhaus Gurin**, an unmistakable ramshackle old timber building to the west of the village. As well as ancient furniture and domestic utensils dating from the 14th century, the collection also includes an archive of books about the Walser migrations throughout Europe. Nearby is the 13th-century village church, rebuilt in the late 16th century.

Return to Cevio and turn north for Bignasco. From there take the left fork up the Val Bavona to San Carlo (30km/18.5 miles).

A cluster of stone-built rusticos in Sonlerto in the Val Bavona, arguably one of Switzerland's most scenic small valleys

Val Bavona

4 One of the most scenically impressive of Switzerland's valleys, the Bavona leads through densely wooded thickets of chestnut and walnut, opening out into boulder-strewn gorges, before reaching the remote village of San Carlo lying beneath the 3,274m peak of Basódino ahead. On the drive up note the pretty hamlets of Cavergno, Fontana and Foroglio, the latter notable for its fairy-tale setting in a river glade. The old restaurant overlooking the swiftly moving water serves a memorable bowl of gnocchi (small parcels of potato or semolina pasta). San Carlo has a cable car leading to Robièi, where there is a mountain hotel set by a cluster of small lakes.

Return 11km (7 miles) to Cavergno and take the road north to the Val Lavizzara. Continue for 17km (10.5 miles) to the village of Fusio at its head.

Val Lavizzara

5 The first village of note is Brontallo, stacked up a hillside with characteristic stone and timber grainstores and houses. On the façade of San Giorgio church is a 17th-century fresco of St Christopher, and there are even earlier examples in the adjacent chapel. At Peccia the valley divides again. Take the right fork on a narrow and frequently steep mountain road, over the gorge of the Mággia, to the picturesque village of Fusio at 1,270m. Above the village is a reservoir, Lago Sambuco, and a roughly surfaced road leads around its north bank to the dramatically sited Lago di Naret beneath the mountain pass of the same name (2,438m). The mountain walks here are very beautiful.

Return from Fusio and go back down the Valle Mággia to Locarno, a distance of 45km (28 miles). Leave Locarno on the Bellinzona road, turning off to

Tenero and Gordola. At the latter enter the Val Verzasca and drive up its length to Sonogno, about another 30km (18.5 miles).

Val Verzasca

6 This is the most inaccessible and remote of the larger Ticino valleys, a deep gouge out of the landscape which is notable for its dramatic defiles, rocky gorges and densely wooded mountain slopes. Passing the huge Verzasca dam, you will enter a series of tunnels on the east side of the reservoir before reaching the pretty village of Vogorno picturesquely sited above the water. At the end of a track around the head of the lake, set into the green mountainside like a glittering jewel, Corippo is one of the most characteristically rustic and unspoilt of the valley's villages and is worth the brief diversion. Lavertezzo, next, is famous for its quaint old medieval bridge, the **Ponte dei Salti**. This is a double-arched structure, spanning a stretch of the Verzasca river which has fast-flowing, unusually green water. Brione, after a further 8km, is the chief village of the valley and is notable for its fine 13th-century **church**, with a 14th-century fresco of St Christopher on its façade.

Ponte dei Salti in the Val Verzasca

Contemporary Gothic frescos of excellent detail are found in the interior. The little 17th-century **castello** in the village square, once owned by a patrician family from Locarno, is now a restaurant. At the end of the road, well situated at the point where the valley divides into the Val Vigornesso to the right and the Val Redorta to the left, is Sonogno, the last settlement of importance. In the Casa Genardini, in the village square, the Museo di Val Verzasca tells the story of life in the valley over the past three centuries.

Return to Locarno (30km/18.5 miles).

Locarno – Valle Onsernone (Spruga) 29 (18)
Valle Onsernone (Spruga) – Valle Mággia (Cerio) 52 (32)
Valle Mággia (Cerio) – Valle di Bosco-Gurin 16 (10)
Valle di Bosco-Gurin – Val Bavona (San Carlo) 30 (18.5)
Val Bavona (San Carlo) – Val Lavizzara (Fusio) 28 (17.5)
Val Lavizzara (Fusio) – Val Verzasca (Sonogno) 75 (47)
Val Verzasca (Sonogno) – Locarno 30 (18.5)

BACK TO NATURE

6 The estuaries of the Verzasca and Ticino rivers, on the east bank of Lago Maggiore, are now a protected and unspoilt wilderness known as the Bolle. This is home to more than 300 species of birdlife, and the area is celebrated for the rich blend of Alpine and Mediterranean flora.

VALAIS AND THE VAUD ALPS

Within the space of an hour in this southwest part of the country, travellers can find themselves juggling with the contrasting images of medieval towns surrounded by sun-baked terraced vineyards, and the awesome might of the highest peaks and longest glaciers in the country. This is the region of remote and wild valleys, mountain hamlets apparently untouched by time, scorched-wood centuries-old chalets, sun-bleached scree slopes, crystal-clear mountain lakes and stunningly beautiful Alpine scenery. It is also the region which offers the widest choice of mountain resorts, ranging from the world's most sophisticated to the pleasingly unpretentious.

But if there is one visual image that captures the essence of the Swiss Alps, it is perhaps the distinctive jagged outline of the 4,478m Matterhorn. Few mountains command the same instant recognition, or possess the same seductive mixture of stark beauty and intimidating scale, but it is by no means the highest mountain in the region which has more than 50 peaks exceeding 4,000m, including the 4,545m Dom separating the famous resorts of Zermatt and Saas-Fee. The scenery in this part of the Valaisian Alps is on a Himalayan scale.

It is no less dramatic on the north side of the Rhône valley, which slashes the canton from east to west. In the lower Vaud Alps, north and east of the Rhône, the scenery is softer with charming pastoral regions like the Pays d'Enhaut dotted with little farming hamlets, and well-sited sports resorts.

Those who prefer a different kind of high life will find it on the so-called Vaud Riviera, best exemplified by the internationally famous resort town of Montreux, one of the world's great playgrounds and festival centres. Those who prefer a more tranquil life will find it in the scores of winding tributary valleys leading off the Rhône. These are among the most beautiful and unspoilt in the Alps, ranging from the wild gorges of the Lötschental to the lush pastures of the Hérens and Anniviers valleys. In some villages, traditional dress is still worn and it is not unusual to see herdsmen and women in rough cotton garments that have changed little in style since the 17th century.

A different form of culture is found in the historic towns of the Rhône valley. In the 2,000-year-old capital town of Sion, the sense of the past is almost tangible. Here, and in delightful medieval towns like St-Maurice and Sierre, there are superb examples of Savoyard and Burgundian architecture dating from the 13th century. Encircled by the largest concentration of vineyards in the country, they are excellent places to linger and relax with a glass of local wine.

Sion
Dominated by fortified twin crags, each crowned by a spectacular castle, Sion has a powerful historical ambience. On the higher hill stand the ruins of the 13th-century castle of Tourbillon, on the lower the slightly earlier fortified church of Notre-Dame-de-Valère. The latter contains the world's oldest working organ, dating from the 14th century. In the town below, the 15th-century Gothic cathedral of Notre-Dame deserves to be visited, together with the 16th-century church of St Théodule next door. Look out also for the remarkably ornate former home of the Supersaxo family in the lower town, and the elegant old mansions in the Rue du Collège.

Zermatt
This exclusive mountain resort takes its name from the meadows ('matten') which surround it. Until the mid-19th century it was a sleepy farming community, wrenched out of pastoral seclusion by the magnetic power of the huge pyramid of the Matterhorn which dominates it. The main Bahnhofstrasse is lined with elegant boutiques, interspersed by quaint flower-decked chalets. A few steps off this colourful thoroughfare, made a little hazardous by the Lilliputian electric 'taxis' which whirr busily up and down, is a different world of narrow alleys and wooden cow sheds. Here you will find the famous English church and, near by, arguably the finest Alpine museum in the country with a fascinating collection of 19th-century mountaineering paraphernalia. Note that Zermatt is reachable only by train from Täsch, 6km north.

Saas-Fee
Terming itself the 'Pearl of the Alps', this famous old climbing resort vies with Zermatt for the most dramatic of mountain locations in the Valais. It lies at the narrow end of a ring of mountains, dominated by the 4,545m Dom, the highest peak in the beautiful Mischabel range. The village is car free, with large car parks located just outside. Electric carts trundle around, performing a shuttle service for luggage and travel-weary visitors. The centre is ringed by winding streets framed against a breathtaking glacial backdrop, and the blend of new and old timber buildings forms an attractive picture. Recreational facilities are comprehensive, and there is small local climbing museum.

Martigny
In recent years this industrial town has experienced something of a Roman renaissance. In 1976 a 1st-century Roman temple was excavated near the town centre, and two years later the impressive Gallo-Roman museum, with viewing galleries, was constructed over the foundations. Near by are the remains of an amphitheatre from the same period. Among

On the east bank of Lake Geneva, Montreux modestly describes itself as the 'pearl' of the Swiss Riviera

other historical treasures, the Château de la Bâtiaz stands out, literally, on a rocky bluff over the town. Below are two fine 17th-century churches. Any tour of the town should also include the splendid town hall with its huge stained-glass window. Martigny is also known as a convenient excursion centre, situated less than an hour from both the French and Italian borders.

Montreux

The famous lakeside town occupies a marvellous position stretching for 6km along the eastern bank of Lac Léman (Lake Geneva). There are many elegant hotels along the lakefront, not least the splendid Grand Hôtel in nearby Territet, built in 1887, but in other respects the creators of modern Montreux have perhaps been less than imaginative in the use of such an impressive site. However, in the process of its undisciplined growth, the town has developed a first-class reputation for its festivals and conference facilities, placing it as the undisputed leader among Swiss venues of its type. Diligent explorers will find an attractive old quarter tucked away at the end of the Rue du Marché, where they will find the Musée du Vieux-Montreux and a fine church of 1509. Near by, 3km southeast on a rocky islet in the lake, is the 13th-century Château de Chillon, often described as the most beautiful castle of its era in Europe. It was immortalised by Byron in the poem 'The Prisoner of Chillon'.

The twin fortified crags of Sion dominate the cantonal capital

2 days: 278km (173 miles)

PEAKS AND PASSES

**Zermatt • Visp • Ernen • Binntal • Goms Valley
Gletsch • Passo del San Gottardo
(St Gotthard Pass) • Saas-Fee**

Two of the jewels of the Swiss mountain sports industry, Zermatt and Saas-Fee, are separated by the glittering Mischabel range, of which the massive Dom (4,545m) is the highest peak entirely within Swiss borders. For the purposes of this tour, start in one resort and end in the other, but note that Zermatt is reachable only by train from Täsch (6km away). The bulk of the journey will take you through the German-speaking part of canton Valais, up the scenic Goms valley, past the formidable Rhonegletscher (Rhône glacier) and over the historic mountain passes of Furka and St Gotthard. Briefly entering Italian-speaking Switzerland, you will return via the Nufenen ('new') pass, the second highest in the country at 2,478m, with fine views of the Bernese and Valaisian Alps.

An evil looking sun motif adorns a chalet wall in the remote German-speaking village of Binn

ℹ️ Bahnhofstrasse

From Zermatt, return to Täsch by train and drive the 29km (18 miles) north down the Mattertal to Visp.

Visp, Valais

1 During its turbulent history, like many strategically sited towns in the Rhône valley, this ancient settlement was much abused by military aggressors. Today it is a busy market town with a pleasant medieval core where you will find some fine 16th- and 17th-century mansions once occupied by merchants enriched by the trade over the Simplon pass. The remains of the town's former ramparts are clearly seen in places and one of the oldest buildings is the 12th-century **Lochmatterturm**, a square tower at the end of the Treichweg. The older of the town's two Catholic churches is an elegant baroque building dating back to the 11th century. Although it underwent major rebuilding in the early 18th century, it retains a fine six-storey Romanesque belfry. Adjacent is a well-preserved mansion of 16th-century origin.

Take road 9 east to Brig (see Tour 20) and continue on road 19

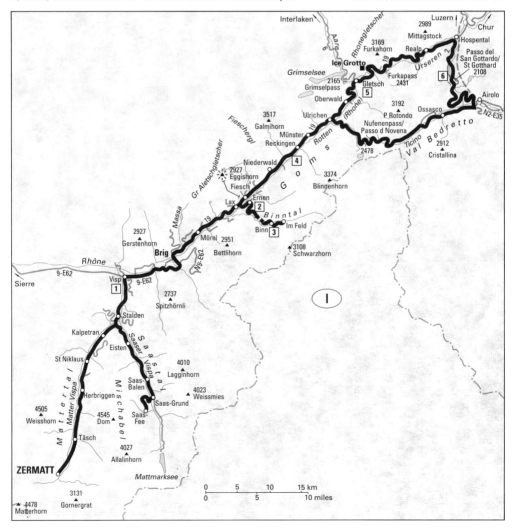

Skiers bask in the sun outside a mountain restaurant above the resort of Zermatt

---

until the turning just beyond Lax, south of the main road to Ernen (27km/17 miles).

Ernen, Valais

2 The capital of the Goms valley has a fine collection of 15th- to 18th-century houses characteristic of this German-speaking part of the Valais. The late 16th-century **Tellenhaus** in the Dorfplatz has, as its name suggests, associations with the legend of William Tell. Exterior wall paintings depict the archer's feats in slightly faded detail. Other old buildings with more contemporary frescos on their façades include the 16th-century **schoolhouse** and the stone-built 18th-century **Rathaus**, with paintings dating from the 1940s and 1950s respectively. The village's oldest structure is the Catholic **church of St George**, built after 1510 on the site of a church founded in 1214. The interior is lavishly decorated with a mixture of Gothic, baroque and rococo features and includes an unusual Gothic sculpture of the eponymous saint apparently performing complicated dental work with his lance on a recumbent dragon. Note also the famous organ dating from 1679.

Take the scenic valley road southeast for 9km (6 miles) to Binn, then continue for a further 4km (2.5 miles) to Im Feld.

Binntal, Valais

3 The valley of the river Binna is home to some of the most charming hamlets in the German-speaking part of the canton. The largest, Binn, is a particularly picturesque collection of old blackened chalets, bedecked with flowers, set on both sides of a tumbling mountain brook. Four kilometres east is the equally delightful community of Im Feld. The **chapel of St Martin** dates from the late 1600s. This whole area is very popular with hikers.

Return to the main valley road 19 and begin the gradual climb for about 43km (27 miles) to Gletsch.

Goms Valley, Valais

4 Also known as the 'Conches' (in French) and Upper Rhône valley, Goms is the preferred name given to this wide glaciated trough by its predominantly German-speaking inhabitants. On the northern flank of the valley walls between Brig and the turn-off for Ernen there is a series of magnificently sited south-facing mountain sports resorts accessed mainly by cableway. But arguably the best mountain panorama is from the summit of the 2,927m Eggishorn, reached by two-stage cable car from the pleasant little village of **Fiesch**. Here you will have a dramatic view north and west of the **Aletschgletscher** (Aletsch glacier), the largest in the Alps, which starts its 27km descent from beneath the Jungfrau massif and looks not unlike a massive tyre track. To the east, the Fieschergletscher (Fiesch glacier) appears poised to sweep away the small hamlets beneath it in the lovely Fieschertal. The village of **Niederwald**, notable for its mid-17th-century baroque **church**, is the next settlement of significance in the Goms. Another typically picturesque collection of traditional timber buildings, it also has modest fame as the birthplace of the renowned hotelier César Ritz. **Reckingen**, straddling the road some 5km ahead, also has a handsome **church**, an 18th-century baroque structure (complete with macabre glass-encased robed skeletons by the altar). The largest community of the valley is **Münster**, attractively sited at the foot of the rugged Minstigertal valley plunging steeply from the high Aargrat ridge on the Valais/Berne border. The centre is split by the main valley road and is particularly notable for its fine 15th- and 16th-century blackwood chalets and traditional storehouses raised on mushroom-shaped staddle stones to deter rodents. **St Maria's**

Looking up the Saas valley to the glittering Mischabel range above the mountain resort of Saas-Fee

church, founded in the 13th century, retains a Romanesque belfry of the same period although the main body of the church is mid-17th-century. There are some interesting interior features including an ornate Gothic altar of 1509 and several other finely carved baroque altars. In **Oberwald**, the last significant village of the Goms, there is another fine **church** with a rich baroque interior and an altar of 1716 designed by a member of the Ritz family.

Gletsch, Valais

5 The town's name means 'glacier' and its origin might have something to do with an unnerving proximity to the 10km-long Rhône glacier which hangs forbiddingly above it. The views of this source of the Rhône river are dramatic and they have had more than a little to do with the growth of an otherwise unremarkable town as a sports and tourist centre. Gletsch, a conventional Swiss mountain town with a busy main street, is the most easterly in the Valais canton and, at 1,759m, it is also one of the highest large communities in the country. The famous Ice Grotto, a huge vault hewn out of the turquoise-blue ice flow, lies above the town on the Furka road. Park at the timeless Belvedere Hotel near by, precariously located on the edge of the cataract and from where there are excellent views over the town and glacier.

Remain on road 19 east over the Furkapass via Realp until the junction with road 2 just before the turning for Hospental (29km/18 miles).

*From Hospental take the St Gotthard pass road south, staying on the new road, **N2**, which is wider and easier than the old road (and no less dramatic). Continue on it until*

just short of Airolo, about 27km (17 miles) south.

Passo del San Gottardo (St Gotthard Pass)

6 This wild mountain traverse at 2,108m was once one of the busiest Alpine crossings, but its role was rendered largely superfluous to all but summer travellers when the great railway tunnel beneath it was opened in 1882 (at a cost of 227 lives). It is a much easier journey to make since the advent of the modern road and the reward is a variety of spectacular views. There is still a **hospice** on the old road, reached a short distance after the pass, which is a successor to a much earlier 14th-century establishment. Here there is the usual mixture of hotel, bar and restaurant – and, of more interest, a fascinating **museum** with a permanent exhibition of reconstructions, vehicles and photographs which graphically tell the story of the most important mountain artery in Swiss history.

Return to the new road for the descent to Airolo (see Tour 20), then take the road signposted 'Passo della Novena' (2,478m) up the Val Bedretto for 37km (22 miles), over the pass to Ulrichen. Return via the Goms valley on the main road, turning south at Visp and following signs for Saas-Fee – a further 75km (47 miles).

Zermatt – Visp 29 (18)
Visp – Ernen 27 (17)
Ernen – Binntal 13 (8)
Binntal – Gletsch 43 (27)
Gletsch – St Gotthard Pass 39 (24)
St Gotthard Pass – Saas-Fee 127 (79)

3 days: 381km (235 miles)

The remarkable chimney-like 'Pyramids of Euseigne' stretch skywards in the Val d'Hérens

ⓘ Place de la Planta 3

From Sion drive north, via Savièse, up to the Col du Sanetsch, thence on to the reservoir beyond for about 33km (20 miles). Return down the same road, through Savièse, following the maze of winding roads through Drône and Grimisuat to the modern resort of Anzère for about 38km (23 miles). From here, drive via Ayent and Luc to Lens, then heading up to Crans, a further distance of 18km (11 miles).

Crans-Montana, Valais

1 Not so long ago the neighbouring villages of Crans and Montana were two separate entities. In some respects they still are, with the modern Crans (sur-Sierre) rather keener on designer-chic and the older Montana noticeably more scruffy. But the 'merger' which took place 20 years ago (for the soundest of Swiss commercial reasons) has made this one of the largest, most flourishing, dedicated sports resorts in the country. Although Montana's disordered sprawl is not particularly pretty, the considerable beauty of its woody, terraced setting is ample compensation. Sir Arnold Lunn, one of the pioneers of Alpine skiing, described the view south across the Rhône valley as 'one of the seven finest' in the Alps. In the summer there are extensive swimming and walking opportunities in and around the small lakes which surround Crans and the combined resort

As the moon sets, the sun rises over a sleeping glacier in the Val d'Arolla

VALLEYS & VINEYARDS

Sion • Col du Sanetsch • Crans-Montana
Venthône • Sierre • Leuk • Leukerbad
Val d'Anniviers • Zinal • Grimentz • Vercorin
Val d'Hérens • Barrage de la Grande Dixence
(La Grande Dixence Dam) • Sion

If you prefer, divide this tour into three largely self-contained parts: the sun-drenched vineyards and sports resorts of the north bank of the Rhône, the glorious tributary valley of Anniviers (Val d'Anniviers) which lies to its south, and the strikingly beautiful valleys of d'Hérens and Hérémence which run down from the Valaisian Alps, also south. The ancient fortified town of Sion is an ideal excursion base for these drives, rarely any further than 50km from the furthest points on the tour. The maze of narrow mountain roads which characterise every stage of your journey may sometimes prove to be a little difficult to navigate, but there is no such thing as a disappointing route around this part of the Valais.

SCENIC ROUTES

The road from Sion to the Col du Sanetsch starts its winding course through a number of strikingly situated villages and vineyards, then climbs through the wild and rugged ravine of the Morge before reaching the col at an altitude of 2,251m. There are marvellous views at nearly every stage of this steep and serpentine road.

RECOMMENDED WALKS

3 The 'Wine Path' is a pleasant walk through vineyards linking the two halves of the Valaisan wine museum in Sierre and Salgesch (entrance fee Sfr5). Along its course are 45 explanatory panels detailing the characteristics of the countryside, the variety of different vines and cultivation techniques. It is open all year round, and is free of charge.

BACK TO NATURE

3 The 'Bois de Finges', between Sierre and Leuk, is one of the only genuinely wild areas still left in Switzerland. It is a vast pine forest on the banks of the Rhône, with humid woods and ponds and marshes in the lower parts. Higher up are natural steppes. A nature path leads through part of the more accessible areas.

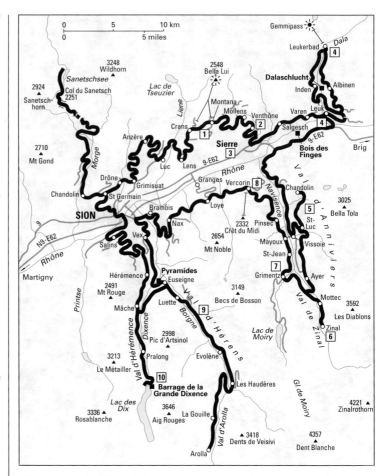

offers many facilities, including a choice of two spectacular golf courses (one of which hosts the Swiss Open). A popular skiing resort in winter, there is also summer skiing on the Plaine Morte glacier. There is a large network of mountain lifts, and the ascent by gondola and then cable car to Bella Lui (2,543m) from either of the two centres offers a panorama which manages to surpass anything at base level.

Leave Montana following signs for about 15km (9 miles) to Mollens, Venthône and Sierre.

Venthône, Valais

2 There are many small communities which you will pass through on this tour, but the ancient village of Venthône is one of the most interesting. It has a fine small **château** near by, owned by the same family since the 17th century, and a number of delightful medieval houses in the main street. The church of **St Sebastian** is a 17th-century structure with a fine baroque interior. Next to it is a 13th-century **tower**, once a church residence, later altered in the 17th century. The finest of a number of ancient towers in the village is the 13th-century **Tour Vareilli**, now the priest's house.

Sierre, Valais

3 Modestly claiming to be the sunniest settlement in the canton of Valais, this south-facing town is surrounded by vineyards on its elevated position above the Rhône valley. The Romans called it 'the town of a hundred hills'. It has an historic main street in the old

quarter, the Rue du Bourg, with numerous fine 16th- and 17th-century buildings. Near the station, the **Hôtel Château-Bellevue** (1666) has been variously employed as a mansion, an hotel and the town hall. For a brief time it was the home of the Austrian poet Rainer Maria Rilke (d.1926), and his former rooms now have a permanent **exhibition** dedicated to his memory. Further down the street is the imposing 16th-century **Château des Vidomnes**, once a bailiffs' residence and notable for its distinctive corner turrets. Note also the baroque mid-17th-century church of **St Catherine** and the earlier church of **Notre-Dame-des-Marais** with its 16th-century frescos. On the Rue du Manoir in the northwest of town, the 16th-century **Château de Villa** is home to one half of the **Valaisan Wine Museum** – the other half is in the small village of Salgesch, a few kilometres northeast. Also to the east, just on the edge of the town and surrounded by vineyards, is the 13th-century **Tour de Goubing**, the last remaining of four hilltop watchtowers which once protected the town.

From Sierre follow the minor valley road east for 11km (7 miles) via Salgesch to Leuk. Alternatively (because it is not easy to find amidst major extension works to the autoroute), join main road 9 and exit at Susten.

Leuk/Leukerbad, Valais

4 Once the summer residence of the bishops of Sion, the old market town lies on a terrace above the Rhône valley. It has two medieval **castles**, one of which is now the town hall. Founded in the 13th century and rebuilt in 1541, the **Château des Vidames** is the more imposing with its unusual stepped gables and four corner turrets. The other is of the same era and was rebuilt about the same time; the late Gothic **tower** is a conspicuous landmark. The late 15th-century **church of St Stephen** has a 12th-century Romanesque belfry, but the real ecclesiastical jewel is the **Ringacker chapel** on a natural balcony site just south of the town. Acknowledged to be one of the finest baroque buildings in the Valais, it has an extravagant stucco-decorated interior.

From Leuk drive 14km (8.5 miles) up the Dalaschlucht (Dala gorge) to Leukerbad.

This spectacularly sited ancient spa town has expanded significantly in recent years and its facilities include indoor and outdoor pools and a massive new 'Spa Temple' called the Alpentherme which is an intriguing sort of thermal theme park, unique in Switzerland. There is a cable car to the famous Gemmipass where, from an altitude of 2,346m, there are superb views of the Valais Alps and excellent altitude walks around the summit.

Return to the valley floor via the picturesque hill village of Albinen, rejoining road 9 beneath Leuk, about 20km (12.5 miles). Then return in the direction of Sierre for about 6km (4 miles) taking the left turning signposted Val d'Anniviers.

Val d'Anniviers, Valais
5 This is one of the most scenic valleys south of the Rhône, with many charming old villages which deserve exploration set at differing levels along its length. **Vissoie**, the

chief settlement, is reached after about 13km and is notable for its 14th-century square **tower** and 17th-century **chapel**. Six kilometres up a steep road east, **St-Luc** is a small but popular resort in a magnificent setting with a number of mountain lifts. After approximately the same distance again, you will come to the tiny settlement of **Chandolin**. At a height of 1,936m, this is one of the highest villages in the country and it affords superb mountain views across the valley.

Return to St-Luc and take the narrow country road for about 17km (10.5 miles), through Ayer, to Zinal.

Zinal, Valais
6 At the head of the valley of the same name, this small and traditional climbing centre was poularised by early British Alpinists in the mid-19th century who opened its first hotel. Curiously it has not developed into a sophisticated super-resort like Zermatt, just the other side of the 4,221m Zinalrothorn. It is divided into three distinct parts: the first has shops, bars and restaurants, the centre is devoted to accommodation, and at the end there is a carefully preserved mountain village which is an authentic gem. Protected by Les Amis du Vieux Zinal, it comprises some lovely old wooden chalets typical of the more rustic recesses of the Valais. On several façades are carvings of the traditional canton sport 'combat de reines' – otherwise known as a cow fight.

Return down the Zinal valley, taking the left fork just beyond

The little village of Les Haudères huddles beneath a verdant mountainside in the Val d'Hérens

FOR HISTORY BUFFS
4 Well known to the Romans who developed an existing Bronze Age settlement, the ancient spa town of Leukerbad was also frequented by 19th-century literati, including Alexandre Dumas, Guy de Maupassant and Mark Twain who described it in satirical detail in A Tramp Abroad. Throughout the Middle Ages, the town was beset by avalanches and from the late 1500s visitors were actively discouraged until an avalanche wall was built in 1829.

SPECIAL TO...
5 Some of the most colourful spectacles in the country are the pastoral festivals which celebrate the movement of cattle up to the mountain pastures when the snows melt in May. With flowers entwined around their horns and ribbons trailing from their jangling cowbells the cows, accompanied by traditionally dressed herdsmen, make a memorable sight.

BACK TO NATURE

7 Throughout the summer, Grimentz offers guided tours with a hunter and botanist to discover the flora and fauna of the Moiry valley. Rendezvous is every Thursday morning outside the tourist office at 6.30am, returning at 11am. The chasseur undertakes not to shoot anything en route.

FOR CHILDREN

8 Between Vercorin and Sion, in the village of Granges, there is a large entertainment park with different rides and attractions, including boat rides, a giant toboggan, a scenic railway, a boating lake, a monorail and a racing circuit with remote-controlled cars.

The massive concrete wall of La Grande Dixence dam dwarfs a little chapel beneath

the hamlet of Mottec and following signs for Grimentz (about 9km/5.5 miles).

Grimentz, Valais

7 This delightfully cluttered little village lies stacked up a hillside on the western flank of the Val d'Anniviers. It is a picturesque place by a mountain stream, with several traditional flower-decked old wooden chalets on stone piles, and has recently grown in popularity as an all-year resort. An interesting excursion leads south, 13km up the **Moiry valley**. Passing a number of waterfalls, and with frequent views of the Dent Blanche (4,357m) ahead, the road reaches the artificial **Lac de Moiry** then follows its eastern bank to the Glacier de Moiry (Moiry glacier). There are fine views from both the dam and the road to the end of the ice flow.

Return on the road on the west side of the valley via the hamlets of St-Jean, Mayoux and Pinsec to Vercorin (18km/11 miles).

Vercorin, Valais

8 Another lovely old high-lying village on the south side of the Rhône valley, typical of this part of the Valais, Vercorin has a fine collection of traditional timber chalets including one of wood and stone, built in 1777. Adjoining it is a **chapel** of 1784. The **church of St Boniface** was rebuilt in 1704, but is of 13th-century foundation. The village is connected by cableway to Chalais, some 800m below it to the north, and to a good vantage point for views over the Rhône valley from the 2,332m Crêt du Midi to the south.

Take the high, winding road in this part of the Rhône valley via the hamlets of Loye, Nax and

Bramois to Vex in the Val d'Hérens (30km/18.5 miles).

Val d'Hérens, Valais

9 Another beautiful tributary valley of the Rhône, the Val d'Hérens is just as accessible as the Anniviers and every bit as fascinating. About 6km after the village of **Vex** you will pass through a tunnel under the remarkable **Pyramides d'Euseigne**, great pillars of debris left by glaciers and crowned by huge boulders which have saved them from further erosion. **Evolène**, the chief village of the valley, lies about 9km ahead and its picturesque grouping of old, dark, larchwood-fronted chalets, many of them colourfully painted, is as characterful as any in the canton. If you happen to be here on a Sunday you may notice that many of the local people wear traditional costume on their way to the pleasant old church of St Jean-Baptiste (late medieval tower). Leaving the village, the view is dominated by the jagged 3,418m Dents de Veisivi at the head of the valley and, looming menacingly behind them, the huge Dent Blanche. After 4km the next village, **Les Haudères**, also has some fine examples of three- and four-storey wooden chalets arranged in ordered chaos in an equally impressive setting. The valley divides here and a winding mountain road climbs 11km to the tiny skiing and mountaineering resort of **Arolla**, another haphazard collection of timber buildings clinging tenaciously to the mountainside.

Return to Euseigne, forking left here for the Val d'Hérémence, and pass though the village of Pralong for the Grande Dixence dam, about 35km (21 miles).

Barrage de la Grande Dixence (Grande Dixence Dam), Valais

10 The Alpine setting of this artificial lake is one reason to drive up the Val d'Hérémence. Another is the exceptional beauty of the drive. But the sheer intimidating scale of the Grande Dixence, until the Aswan Dam was built in 1970 it was the world's highest hydro-electric dams at 2,365m, is perhaps the best reason of all. Not only did it break all records for altitude and concrete mass (208 million cubic feet), but it still resists the biggest force of artificially contained water in the world. The dam wall is a massive 284m high, and was completed in 1966.

Return to Sion via Hérémence, Les Agettes and Salins (about 36km/22 miles). Continue for 4km (2.5 miles) down to Sierre.

Sion – Crans 115 (71)
Crans – Venthône 11 (7)
Venthône – Sierre 4 (2.5)
Sierre – Leuk 11 (7)
Leuk – Leukerbad 14 (8.5)
Leukerbad – Val d'Anniviers 51 (32)
Val d'Anniviers – Zinal 17 (10.5)
Zinal – Grimentz 9 (5.5)
Grimentz – Vercorin 18 (11)
Vercorin – Val d'Hérens (Arolla) 60 (37)
Val d'Hérens (Arolla) – Barrage de la Grande Dixence 35 (21)
Barrage de la Grande Dixence – Sion 36 (22)

Wild bellflowers (campanulas) seek out the sunlight on the San Bernardino Pass

ℹ️ Place Centrale 9

From Martigny follow signs to Col de la Forclaz and Chamonix-Mont Blanc, following the mountain road over the col (1,526m), crossing the French border at Le Châtelard, and continuing through Argentière to Chamonix (47km/29 miles).

Chamonix-Mont Blanc, Haute-Savoie (France)

1 It was to this famous old French mountaineering town that Henry Lunn, the British inventor of the modern package holiday, brought his first British tour party in the winter of 1898. Today the core of a charming 19th-century Alpine town is still distinguishable, but the demands of maintaining its position among the leaders of world mountain resorts has led to some regrettable modern building on the outskirts and a centre choked with traffic. But Chamonix's unique character, inextricably linked to the peaks and glaciers which dominate it, is unlikely to be threatened as long as Mont Blanc stands. The massive broad-humped mountain, Europe's highest at 4,807m, looms over the town from the southeast and its presence is almost inescapable, even in the most claustrophobic of the town's narrow streets. Chamonix has all the amenities normally associated with a major ski and climbing resort, and there are many memorable excursions within easy reach. Of these, unquestionably the most impressive is the spectacular (if crushingly uncomfortable) journey by two-stage cable car to one of the most phenomenal of all Alpine panoramas from the summit of the **Aiguille du Midi**, at 3,842m the highest aerial cableway in the world. Another is to the celebrated **Mer de Glace**, a formidable glacier with chunks of ice as big as cathedrals. An hour's walk, it can also be reached by rack railway in ten minutes from close to the main station. The **Musée Alpin**, just off Avenue Michel Croz, will give you a fascinating insight into the history of the conquest of Mont Blanc.

Follow signs for Tunnel du Mont Blanc then drive through the tunnel following exit signs to Entrèves and Courmayeur (24km/15 miles).

Courmayeur, Valle d'Aosta (Italy)

2 The old Savoy town of Courmayeur is one of the leading resorts of the Val d'Aosta, formerly part of France and since 1948 an autonomous region within Italian borders. The people here are mostly French-speaking. Close to the rumble of Mont Blanc tunnel traffic, first impressions of the town are not

The 13th-century battle tower of La Batiaz Château keeps watch over Martigny and the Drance valley

2 days: 238km (148 miles)

THE GRAND ST BERNARD PASS

Martigny • Chamonix-Mont Blanc • Courmayeur
Aosta • Col du Grand St-Bernard
(Great St Bernard Pass) • Bourg-St-Pierre
Champex • Verbier • Martigny

The neighbouring countries of Italy and France have had a profound influence over the development of Switzerland as a nation, providing in different measure language, culture, and occasional uninvited military intrusion over the centuries. This tour will take you in the footsteps of warring emperors as they travelled over one of the world's most dramatic mountain crossings, the famous Grand St Bernard pass. En route you will pass beneath the chilling beauty of the Mont Blanc massif, via the mountain towns of Chamonix and Courmayeur. A glimpse of Roman history awaits in bustling Aosta, before you return over one of the highest roads in Europe, interrupting your journey at two of western Switzerland's most popular, and contrasting, resorts. Do not forget passports.

favourable. But behind its drab façade is a delightful labyrinth of twisting alleys and cobbled lanes, lined with an attractive variety of shops and buzzing cafés and bars. If you happen to find yourself here on a Wednesday, head for the market on the Verrand road near the main cable car station. Among the more intriguing locally made souvenirs are the wooden multi-spouted bowls (for the communal drinking of grappa) and the carved 'spinning' bowls with pockets, for playing a form of primitive roulette.

Take the old road (SS26) for 37km (23 miles) down the Val d'Aosta to Aosta.

Aosta (Italy)

3 Capital of the Val d'Aosta, this ancient Savoy town lies at the gateway to the Great St Bernard pass, and throughout history has been a place of considerable strategic importance. The Romans were not slow to appreciate its value, and today the former fort of Augusta Praetoria reflects much of their influence, particularly in the town centre which is still protected in part by the original **walls**, punctuated at intervals by towers. The **Roman theatre** is remarkably well preserved, with its tall façade still solidly in place. Some Roman stone blocks were used to construct the **church of St Ours**, dating from the 10th century but largely rebuilt in late Gothic style in the 15th century. Elsewhere, the 16th-century **cathedral** is notable for its Renaissance façade.

*Road directions to the Great St Bernard pass are not clear, and where they exist tend to be diminutive and well hidden. Do not confuse 'G San Bernardo' with 'P San Bernardo', the latter referring to a different pass back to the Tarentaise. Look for signs to **SS27**. Follow the pass road, via St-Rhémy, for about 33km (21 miles) to the col, re-entering Switzerland just below the hospice buildings.*

Col du Grand St-Bernard (Great St Bernard Pass)

4 This bleak, windswept mountain road is one of the oldest of the trans-alpine routes and, incidentally, is host to one of the highest permanent settlements in Europe. The famous **hospice**, founded by St Bernard of Aosta in the 11th century to provide succour for exhausted travellers, lies at a height of 2,469m and is still occupied by Augustinian monks. The hospice comprises two buildings on either side of the narrow road, one dating from the mid-16th century which replaced the original, and the other (now a modest hotel run by the monks) built in 1898. The former contains a **museum** (Celtic, Roman and Napoleonic relics) and a richly decorated **chapel** of 1676 which contains the remains of the French General Desaix, who crossed the pass with Napoleon in 1800 before subsequently losing his life in the Battle of Marengo.

Drive down the pass road for 14km (9 miles), turning left for Bourg St-Pierre.

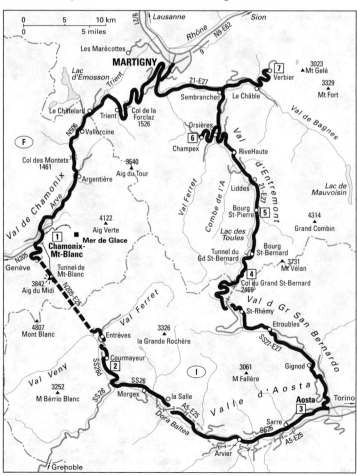

Bourg St-Pierre, Valais

5 A former staging post for the Grand St Bernard pass road, Bourg St-Pierre was developed as a small market village in the 13th century. That is much how it has remained, a picturesque cluster of russet-roofed houses grouped around an ancient church in the wider part of the Valsorey valley. At 1,634m it is one of the highest large settlements in the canton, and it now serves as a mountaineering centre, particularly for the popular, if difficult, ascent of the Grand Combin which lies east at a height of 4,314m. The **church of St Pierre** was rebuilt in 1739, but retains its 11th-century tower (with 16th-century spire). In the cemetery a 4th-century Roman milestone is embedded in the wall.

Continue down road 21 to Orsières, turning left there up the steep road for Champex (23km/14 miles).

Champex, Valais

6 Curving around the northern shore of a miniature, perfectly contoured lake, Champex is a well-sited resort of traditional charm at the mouth of the densely forested Val Ferret. It is by no means big, but it has a comprehensive selection of amenities including swimming, boating and extensive rambling. There are a good number of elegant 19th-century hotels and some colourful waterfront restaurants and bars, and across the lake stands a tiny old chapel, illuminated at night and reached by a pretty, gladed path along the shoreline. From the western end of the village a chairlift glides up the flank of La Breya from where there are many delightful walks.

The northern approach to the San Bernardino Pass

Return to Orsières, and continue down the valley road to Sembrancher, diverting off the main road here via Le Châble to Verbier (32km/20 miles).

Verbier, Valais

7 Jostling for position at the head of the superleague of European ski resorts, Verbier is much what you would expect from a modern, purpose-built village with winter sports as its raison d'être. Magnificently sited on a wide sunny plateau above the original village of the same name, the centre is a jumble of chalets of differing size and no particular appeal. What it lacks in architectural merit, however, it easily compensates for in the infectious energy of a major resort, and the excellence of its skiing and walking terrain. The views of the Grand Combin and Mont Blanc massifs are an added compensation, worth the visit alone. The central square is the hub of a complicated maze of one-way streets, often congested at weekends when members of the international community in Geneva flock here to their second homes.

Return to Sembrancher, rejoining road 21 back to Martigny for about 28km (17 miles)

Martigny – Chamonix 47 (29)
Chamonix – Courmayeur 24 (15)
Courmayeur – Aosta 37 (23)
Aosta – Col du Grand St Bernard 33 (21)
Col du Grand St Bernard – Bourg St Pierre 14 (9)
Bourg St Pierre – Champex 23 (14)
Champex – Verbier 32 (20)
Verbier – Martigny 28 (17)

RECOMMENDED WALKS

6 Take the La Breya chairlift from Champex, and from the top follow the mountain path to d'Orny and Trient. This is a precarious-looking but well-kept trail with the mountain wall to the right and a dizzy drop to the left. The views of the Grand Combin massif to the left are most impressive. You can continue up to the Cabane du Trient if you have the energy, or return at the first fork through the forest of Voutaz to Champex. Allow three hours.

BACK TO NATURE

There are botanical gardens in the villages of Bourg St-Pierre and Champex, and the rich collection of Alpine flora which both contain can be seen growing wild on the Combe de l'A between the two. Your new-found knowledge of Alpine flora and fauna can be further honed on the 'Sentier des Chamois' in Verbier, where the local tourist office organises regular guided excursions to observe wildlife and mountain vegetation on selected altitude tracks (out of a total of 400km of marked paths).

1 to 2 days: 181km (112 miles)

GLITZ AND GLACIERS

**Montreux • Aigle • Leysin • Château-d'Oex
Rougemont • Saanen • Gstaad • Lauenen
Villars-sur-Ollon • Bex • St-Maurice
Montreux**

ⓘ Grande-Rue 42

*Take the old road (no 9) south
along the lakeside via Villeneuve
for about 15km (9 miles).*

Gstaad is a name which has become universally
synonymous with glamour, an association which may
surprise you when you visit this surprisingly small and traditional resort on the fringe of the Bernese Oberland. This tour
will take you through a number of other well-known Swiss
winter sports resorts in the Alpes Vaudoises, each providing
comprehensive recreational facilities for summer visitors as
well. You will start and finish in the French-speaking medieval
towns of Aigle and St-Maurice; en route you will pass over a
number of dramatic mountain cols, drive through the beautiful
pastures of the Pays d'Enhaut, and you will briefly cross into
the western fringe of the Bernese Alps before returning to
Vaud beneath the Tsanfleuron and Les Diablerets glacier.

Aigle, Vaud

1 An important wine-making centre,
Aigle is probably best known for
its fine 13th-century **château**, surrounded by vineyards and acknowledged to be one of the most
impressive of its type in the country.
Its present appearance dates from
the time of its capture by the
Bernese in the 15th century when it
was extensively rebuilt. The former
quarters of the Bernese governors

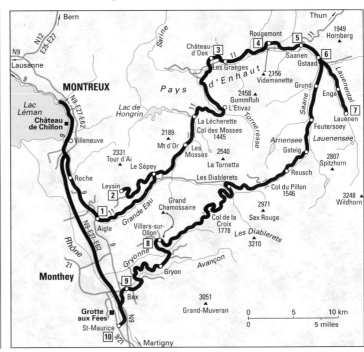

Above left: the fortress-like Imperial Palace Hotel in Gstaad
Above: A carpet of vines rolls out beneath the ancient walls of the imposing Château d'Aigle

now house two **museums** – one devoted to wine, the other to salt. A massive 17th-century barn with a distinctive half-hipped roof adjoins this charming old castle.

In Cloître, the town's oldest quarter, the church of **St Maurice** founded in the 12th century is notable for its late Gothic steeple. In the Fontaine quarter, the Rue de Jérusalem is an unexpected treasure of medieval houses connected by arcades. Other interesting sights include the old market square, the pedestrianised Rue du Bourg, and the medieval church of **St Jacques** with a tower dating from 1642.

i Avenue de la Gare 4

Take the steep mountain road 11 to Le Sépey, diverting left to Leysin (17km/10.5 miles).

Leysin, Vaud

2 The brief diversion to this rambling old health resort is worth the uphill drive if only to admire its striking south-facing balcony site. This is one of the most popular resorts in the Vaud Alps and, although it has a strong institutional flavour (the elegant Grand Hôtel is now the home of an American college), it has managed to retain much of its traditional charm and is complemented by a wide range of modern facilities. These include a revolving restaurant on the summit of the 2,048m Berneuse peak from where there are fine views of the Mont Blanc massif. In summer there is a well-signposted network of walking paths.

i Place du Marché

Return to main road 11, driving north over the Col des Mosses (1,445m), following signposts for Château-d'Oex (28km/17 miles).

Château-d'Oex, Vaud

3 Pronounced Château 'Day', the castle that gave this attractive sprawl of chalets its name has long since disappeared, destroyed by fire in 1800. Its site is now occupied by the **church of St Donat**, which incorporates part of the original building in its structure, particularly in the **tower**. The choir is 15th-century Gothic. The village is well-positioned in one of the prettiest parts of western Switzerland, in the midst of the pastoral Pays d'Enhaut, and it has increasingly become a mecca for hot-air balloonists who may frequently be seen framed against mountain backdrops whenever weather conditions are right. The surrounding Vaud Alps suit this pursuit admirably. Château-d'Oex has its own fine folk museum, the **Musée du Vieux Pays d'Enhaut**, which has an extensive collection of exhibits recalling the seven centuries during which the region was part of Gruyère. Of particular interest are the reconstructed 18th-century homes of shepherds and local craftsmen.

Continue east on road 11 for about 8km (5 miles), turning left to Rougemont.

Rougemont, Vaud

4 Lying just within the border of Vaud canton, this historic village grew up around the site of an old **Cluniac priory** founded in the mid-11th century and dissolved at the time of the Reformation. Only the

church survives of the original buildings, and you will find it on the right of the main road as you enter the village. It is a fine early Romanesque structure with a 17th-century roof and bell tower. The choir dates from 1585. Adjoining the church is a 16th-century **château**, badly damaged by fire in the 1970s but since faithfully reconstructed. The village centre lies off the busy main road, and has an attractive collection of 17th-century timber buildings with characteristic carved and painted façades. It has lately become popular with winter sports enthusiasts who prefer its quiet charm to the bright lights of Gstaad, accessible by mountain lift over the peak of the La Videmanette (2,156m). From the summit, reached by gondola lift from just outside the village, there is a splendid panorama of the Vaud and Bernese Alps.

Continue for a further 5km (3 miles) to Saanen.

Saanen, Bern (Berne)

5 A quiet, unpretentious and old-fashioned agricultural town only 3km from Gstaad, Saanen has traditionally been the also-ran in the local fashion stakes. But in many ways it has more to recommend it than its famous neighbour. The characteristic wooden chalets (the oldest of which date from the 16th century) have large overhanging eaves. The 15th-century **church of St Mauritius**, rebuilt after a fire in 1942, is Gothic in style and has a robust stone **tower** with an octagonal wooden belfry. Inside there is a carved medieval font, a pulpit of 1628 and 15th-century frescos showing scenes from the Old Testament and the legend of St Maurice. Concerts are held here during the Yehudi Menuhin Festival in Gstaad during the summer.

Turn south off road 11 and head south for 3km (2 miles) to Gstaad.

Gstaad, Berne

6 Until the railway arrived at the beginning of the century, Gstaad was little more than a church and a few farmhouses. Today this world-

Pastoral scene in the Pays d'Enhaut near the old village of Rougemont

famous ski resort has become almost a byword for fashionable winter playgrounds. It consists of a surprisingly small cluster of traditionally-styled wooden chalets, arranged around a U-bend in the railway line at the junction of four valleys. There is really only one main street, which also happens to be the busy main through-road north to south. What few genuinely old buildings there are form an attractive nucleus in the centre, but the overall impression is one of contrived tradition rather than unforced elegance. Despite its image, it is not a vibrantly exciting place. It is, however, a very exclusive place and what excitement there is clearly takes place behind the closed doors of the many privately owned chalets, empty for much of the year. Dominating the village from a wooded bluff to the east, the famous neo-baroque **Palace Hôtel** (built in 1912) is a magnet for celebrities – their privacy assured by an army of uniformed staff. Its motto is: 'Every king is a client, and every client is a king' – which says it all if your pockets are deep enough to join the clientele.

The resort has extensive sporting facilities and access to some marvellous walks via its sprawling network of mountain lifts.

ⓘ Hauptstrasse

Take the valley road, signposted Lauenen, for 7km (4.5 miles).

Lauenen, Berne

7 A sleepy hamlet set amidst peaceful Alpine pastures at the head of the Lauenental, Lauenen is a stark contrast to its sophisticated neighbour. The 16th-century late Gothic church of **St Petrus** is characteristic of its period, reflected in the geometric patterns of the choir windows and wooden ceiling. There are several attractive old houses near by, particularly one of 1765 with elaborate carvings and paintwork. Four kilometres further up the valley, reached through meadows and pine woods, is the delightful

Lauenensee, a small lake lying in a hollow at the foot of the Dungelschuss waterfalls.

Return to Gstaad (7km/4 miles), taking the mountain road south to the village resort of Gsteig for 10km (7 miles). From there take the pass road to Col du Pillon (1,546m), and continue for about 12km (8 miles) to the resort of Les Diablerets. Turn left off the main road here for the Col de la Croix (1,778m) and continue for 17km (11 miles) to Villars.

Villars-sur-Ollon, Vaud

8 An old-fashioned resort, tradition-ally popular with British winter holidaymakers since the 1920s, Villars-sur-Ollon vies with Verbier for the title of the most fashionable altitude resort in French-speaking Switzerland. Like its southern neighbour it has little of intrinsic interest to recommend it, but it does have a wealth of sports facilities and other entertainments. Moreover, it occupies an excellent site in a sunny basin at the foot of a crescent of peaks overlooking the French Alps and the Dents du Midi. The town is an agreeable mix of old and new, with some charming old chalets on its fringes. The best panorama is from the Grand Chamossaire (2,113m), reached by rack railway to Bretaye, and thence by chairlift. The Bernese Alps, the Muverans, Mont Blanc and Les Dents du Midi are all seen to good advantage.

Take the steep mountain road for 13km (8 miles) to Bex.

Bex, Vaud

9 Pronounced 'Bay', this old spa town enjoyed great popularity in the 19th and early 20th centuries when Victor Hugo and Leon Tolstoy, among others, came here to take the waters. Earlier, it was a prosperous salt-mining community, but today its predominant role is as a feeder resort to Villars, to which it is connected by rack railway. A pleasant enough place to stay, it has rather more in terms of historical interest to recommend it. In the main street the **town hall** is an elegant building of 1746, but the most imposing of the town's buildings is the **church of St Clément**, founded in the 12th century but dating mostly from the early 1800s except for the substantial **tower** of 1501. Near by is a local history museum and conspicuous on a hill south of the town is the 12th-century Tour de Duin, and the few remains of the castle of Bex of which it once formed part.

Take road 9 south to St-Maurice for about 3km (2 miles).

St-Maurice, Valais

10 Once an important Roman staging post, this old Celtic settlement is the oldest Christian site in Switzerland and it retains much of its religious heritage. An **Augustinian abbey** was founded here in the early 6th century and its **church** is an interesting hybrid of architectural influences, much rebuilt after various fires and rock falls over the centuries. The fine 11th-century Romanesque **tower** is the oldest part. The church has enormous significance in the Christian world, not least for its magnificent **treasury** assembled thanks to the generosity of wealthy pilgrims and said to be among the most valuable in Europe. Its collection includes a 9th-century golden water jug once the property of Charlemagne. Near by, beneath the rock face against which the church abuts, post-war excavations have revealed the foundations of the original abbey and a chapel of around AD360. Catacombs lead to what is believed to be the tomb of the town's illustrious patron saint. The town centre is picturesquely laid out with narrow old streets lined by a number of handsome buildings. Also of interest is the **Catholic church of St Sigismund** with its splendid baroque side altars. On the northern perimeter of the town, overlooking the Rhône, is a 13th-century **château**, rebuilt in 1523, which now houses the **Valais Military Museum**. The stone

The courtyard of the Abbey Church in St-Maurice

bridge over the river was built in 1491.

*Return to Montreux on the **N9** (taking the old road 9 for the last few kilometres from Villeneuve) for 36km (21 miles).*

FOR CHILDREN

10 Just to the north of St-Maurice, via a footpath from the old bridge over the Rhône, is the Fairies' Grotto (Grotte aux Fées) where stalactitic caves lead to an underground lake and waterfall. Near by is a restaurant which commands fine views.

FOR HISTORY BUFFS

10 The town of St-Maurice takes its name from the Roman commander of the Theban Legion, recruited in Egypt, who reportedly chose to die here in AD300 with his troops rather than fight against fellow Christians in Gaul.

INDEX

ACKNOWLEDGEMENTS

The Automobile Association would like to thank the following photographers, libraries and associations for their assistance in the preparation of this book.

ST GALLEN TOURIST OFFICE 64
SPECTRUM COLOUR LIBRARY 68/9, 76a, 105, 106
SWISS NATIONAL TOURIST OFFICE 26, 39
THUSIS TOURIST OFFICE 87
ZEFA PICTURES Cover, 1, 11

The remaining photographs are held in the Association's own library (AA PHOTO LIBRARY) and were taken by S L DAY with the exception of pages 3, 36, 38b, 40, 47, 49, 50/1, 54, 60/1, 68, 71, 75, 80, 83, 85, 89b, 94, 95, 103b which were taken by A BAKER

The author would like to thank the following organisations for their assistance during the writing of this book: P &O European Ferries, the Swiss National Tourist Office (London), Mürren Tourist Office, and the Kandahar Ski Club.

Copy editor: Rebecca Snelling